ACHI 2022

The Fifteenth International Conference on Advances in Computer-Human Interactions

June 26th – 30th, 2022

Porto, Portugal

ACHI 2022 Editors

Oky Dicky Ardiansyah Prima, Iwate Prefectural University, Japan

Weizhi Meng, Technical University of Denmark, Denmark

Hisayoshi Ito, Iwate Prefectural University, Japan

Printed from e-media with permission by:

Curran Associates, Inc.
57 Morehouse Lane
Red Hook, NY 12571

Some format issues inherent in the e-media version may also appear in this print version.

Printed with permission by Curran Associates, Inc. (2023)

International Academy, Research, and Industry Association (IARIA)
412 Derby Way
Wilmington, DE 19810

Phone: (408) 893-6407
Fax: (408) 527-6351

petre@iaria.org

Additional copies of this publication are available from:

Curran Associates, Inc.
57 Morehouse Lane
Red Hook, NY 12571 USA
Phone: 845-758-0400
Fax: 845-758-2633
Email: curran@proceedings.com
Web: www.proceedings.com

Table of Contents

ACHI 2022

Forward

The Fifteenth edition of The International Conference on Advances in Computer-Human Interactions (ACHI 2022) conference was held in Porto, Portugal, June 26 - 30, 2022.

The conference on Advances in Computer-Human Interaction, ACHI 2022, was a result of a paradigm shift in the most recent achievements and future trends in human interactions with increasingly complex systems. Adaptive and knowledge-based user interfaces, universal accessibility, human-robot interaction, agent-driven human computer interaction, and sharable mobile devices are a few of these trends. ACHI 2022 brought also a suite of specific domain applications, such as gaming, social, medicine, education and engineering.

The event was very competitive in its selection process and very well perceived by the international scientific and industrial communities. As such, it is attracting excellent contributions and active participation from all over the world. We were very pleased to receive a large amount of top quality contributions.

The accepted papers covered a wide range of human-computer interaction related topics such as graphical user interfaces, input methods, training, recognition, and applications.
We believe that the ACHI 2022 contributions offered a large panel of solutions to key problems in all areas of human-computer interaction.

We take here the opportunity to warmly thank all the members of the ACHI 2022 technical program committee as well as the numerous reviewers. The creation of such a broad and high quality conference program would not have been possible without their involvement. We also kindly thank all the authors that dedicated much of their time and efforts to contribute to the ACHI 2022. We truly believe that thanks to all these efforts, the final conference program consists of top quality contributions.

This event could also not have been a reality without the support of many individuals, organizations and sponsors. In addition, we also gratefully thank the members of the ACHI 2022 organizing committee for their help in handling the logistics and for their work that is making this professional meeting a success.

We hope the ACHI 2022 was a successful international forum for the exchange of ideas and results between academia and industry and to promote further progress in the human-computer interaction field. We also hope that Porto provided a pleasant environment during the conference and everyone saved some time for exploring this beautiful city

ACHI 2022 Chairs

ACHI Steering Committee
Flaminia Luccio, University Ca' Foscari of Venice, Italy
Marie Sjölinder, RISE, Sweden
Lasse Berntzen, University of South-Eastern Norway, Norway
Weizhi Meng, Technical University of Denmark, Denmark

ACHI 2022 Publicity Chair

Laura Garcia, Universitat Politècnica de València (UPV), Spain
José Miguel Jiménez, Universitat Politecnica de Valencia, Spain

ACHI 2022

COMMITTEE

ACHI Steering Committee

Flaminia Luccio, University Ca' Foscari of Venice, Italy
Marie Sjölinder, RISE, Sweden
Lasse Berntzen, University of South-Eastern Norway, Norway
Weizhi Meng, Technical University of Denmark, Denmark

ACHI 2022 Publicity Chair

Laura Garcia, Universitat Politècnica de València (UPV), Spain
José Miguel Jiménez, Universitat Politecnica de Valencia, Spain

ACHI 2022 Technical Program Committee

Mostafa Alani, Tuskegee University, USA
Marran Aldossari, University of North Carolina at Charlotte, USA
Obead Alhadreti, Umm Al-Qura University, Al-Qunfudah, Saudi Arabia
Asam Almohamed, University of Kerbala, Iraq
Mehdi Ammi, Univ. Paris 8, France
Prima Oky Dicky Ardiansyah, Iwate Prefectural University, Japan
Charles Averill, University of Texas at Dallas, USA
Ahmad Azadvar, Ubisoft Entertainment Sweden A.B. - Ubisoft Massive / Malmo University, Sweden
Matthias Baldauf, OST - Eastern Switzerland University of Applied Sciences, Switzerland
Catalin-Mihai Barbu, University of Duisburg-Essen, Germany
Lasse Berntzen, University of South-Eastern Norway, Norway
Ganesh D. Bhutkar, Vishwakarma Institute of Technology (VIT), Pune, India
Cezary Biele, National Information Processing Institute, Poland
Christos J. Bouras, University of Patras, Greece
Christian Bourret, UPEM - Université Paris-Est Marne-la-Vallée, France
James Braman, The Community College of Baltimore County, USA
Pradeep Buddharaju, University of Houston - Clear Lake, USA
Idoko John Bush, Near East University, Cyprus
Minghao Cai, University of Alberta, Canada
Klaudia Carcani, Østfold University College, Norway
Meghan Chandarana, NASA Ames Research Center, USA
Chen Chen, University of California San Diego, USA
Mathieu Chollet, University of Glasgow, UK
Bhavya Chopra, Indraprastha Institute of Information Technology, Delhi, India
Lara Jessica da Silva Pontes, University of Debrecen, Hungary
Andre Constantino da Silva, Federal Institute of São Paulo - IFSP, Brazil
Lea Daling, Cybernetics Lab IMA & IfU - RWTH Aachen University, Germany
Antonio Diaz Tula, University of São Paulo, Brazil
Verena Distler, University of Luxembourg, Luxembourg
Vesna G. Djokic, Institute of Language Logic & Computation (ILLC) | University of Amsterdam,

Netherlands
Krzysztof Dobosz, Silesian University of Technology - Institute of Informatics, Poland
Margaret Drouhard, University of Washington, USA
Robert Ek, Luleå University of Technology, Sweden
Ahmed Elkaseer, Karlsruhe Institute of Technology, Germany
Pardis Emami-Naeini, Carnegie Mellon University, USA
Marina Everri, University College Dublin, Ireland
Ben Falchuk, Peraton Labs, USA
Matthias Fassl, CISPA Helmholtz Center for Information Security, Germany
Stefano Federici, University of Perugia, Italy
Kenneth Feinstein, Sunway University, Malaysia
Emma Frid, IRCAM / KTH Royal Institute of Technology, Sweden
Jicheng Fu, University of Central Oklahoma, USA
Somchart Fugkeaw, Mahidol University - Nakhonpathom, Thailand
Maria Gaci, École Polytechnique Fédérale de Lausanne (EPFL), Switzerland
Pablo Gallego, Independent Researcher, Spain
Dagmawi Lemma Gobena, Addis Ababa University, Ethiopia
Benedikt Gollan, Research Studios Austria FG mbH, Austria
Denis Gracanin, Virginia Tech, USA
Andrina Granic, University of Split, Croatia
Lea Gröber, CISPA Helmholtz Center for Information Security, Saarbrücken, Germany
Celmar Guimarães da Silva, University of Campinas, Brazil
Ibrahim A. Hameed, Norwegian University of Science and Technology (NTNU), Norway
Ragnhild Halvorsrud, SINTEF Digital, Norway
Richard Harper, Lancaster University, UK
Liang He, Paul G. Allen School of Computer Science & Engineering | University of Washington, USA
Lars Erik Holmquist, Northumbria University | School of Design, UK
Haikun Huang, University of Massachusetts, Boston, USA
Yue Huang, University of British Columbia, Canada
Maria Hwang, Fashion Institute of Technology (FIT), New York City, USA
Sara Ibarra Vargas, Institución Universitaria Pascual Bravo, Colombia
Gökhan İnce, Istanbul Technical University, Turkey
Francisco Iniesto, Institute of Educational Technology - The Open University, UK
Jamshed Iqbal, University of Hull, UK
Angel Jaramillo-Alcázar, Universidad de Las Américas, Ecuador
Yue Jiang, Max Planck Institute for Informatics, Germany
Sofia Kaloterakis, Utrecht University, Netherland
Yasushi Kambayashi, Nippon Institute of Technology, Japan
Ahmed Kamel, Concordia College, USA
Suzanne Kieffer, Université catholique de Louvain, Belgium
Jeongyeon Kim, KAIST, South Korea
Si Jung "SJ" Kim, University of Nevada, Las Vegas (UNLV), USA
Susanne Koch Stigberg, Østfold University College, Norway
Uttam Kokil, Kennesaw State University Marietta, USA
Josef Krems, Chemnitz University of Technology, Germany
Wen-Hsing Lai, National Kaohsiung University of Science and Technology, Taiwan
Monica Landoni, Università della Svizzera italiana, Switzerland
Chien-Sing Lee, Sunway University, Malaysia

Maria Teresa Llano Rodriguez, Monash University, Melbourne, Australia
Tsai-Yen Li, National Chengchi University, Taiwan
Wenjuan Li, The Hong Kong Polytechnic University, Hong Kong
Fotis Liarokapis, Cyprus University of Technology, Cyprus
Richen Liu, Nanjing Normal University, China
Jun-Li Lu, University of Tsukuba, Japan
Zhicong Lu, University of Toronto, Canada
Flaminia Luccio, Universita' Ca' Foscari Venezia, Italy
Sergio Luján-Mora, University of Alicante, Spain
Yan Luximon, The Hong Kong Polytechnic University, Hong Kong
Damian Lyons, Fordham University, USA
Galina Madjaroff, University of Maryland Baltimore County, USA
Sebastian Maneth, University of Bremen, Germany
Guido Maiello, Justus Liebig University Giessen, Germany
Matthew Louis Mauriello, University of Delaware, USA
Laura Maye, School of Computer Science and Information Technology - University College Cork, Ireland
Horia Mărgărit, Stanford University, USA
Weizhi Meng, Technical University of Denmark, Denmark
Xiaojun Meng, Noah's Ark Lab | Huawei Technologies, Shenzhen, China
Daniel R. Mestre, CNRS Institute of Movement Sciences - Mediterranean Virtual Reality Center, Marseilles, France
Mariofanna Milanova, University of Arkansas at Little Rock, USA
Harald Milchrahm, Institute for Software technology - Technical University Graz, Austria
Leslie Miller, Iowa State University - Ames, USA
Alexander Mirnig, Center for Human-Computer Interaction | University of Salzburg, Austria
Arturo Moquillaza, Pontificia Universidad Católica del Perú, Peru
Nicholas H. Müller, University of Applied Sciences Würzburg-Schweinfurt, Germany
Sachith Muthukumarana, Auckland Bioengineering Institute | The University of Auckland, New Zealand
Roger Ng, The Hong Kong Polytechnic University, Hong Kong
Yoko Nishihara, College of Information Science and Engineering - Ritsumeikan University, Japan
Rikke Toft Nørgård, Aarhus University, Denmark
Nahal Norouzi, University of Central Florida, USA
Yoshimasa Ohmoto, Shizuoka University, Japan
Tom Ongwere, University of Dayton, Ohio, USA
Deepak Ranjan Padhi, IDC School of Design - IIT Bombay, India
Aditeya Pandey, Northeastern University, Boston, USA
Athina Papadopoulou, Massachusetts Institute of Technology (MIT), USA
Evangelos Papadopoulos, National Technical University of Athens, Greece
Vida Pashaei, University of Arizona, USA
Freddy Alberto Paz Espinoza, Pontificia Universidad Católica del Perú, Peru
Gerald Penn, University of Toronto, Canada
Jorge Henrique Piazentin Ono, New York University - Tandon School of Engineering, USA
Ana C. Pires, Universidade de Lisboa, Portugal
Jorge Luis Pérez Medina, Universidad de Las Américas, Ecuador
Brian Pickering, IT Innovation Centre - University of Southampton, UK
Thomas M. Prinz, Friedrich Schiller University Jena, Germany
Annu Sible Prabhakar, University of Cincinnati, USA
Marina Puyuelo Cazorla, Universitat Politècnica de València, Spain

Yuanyuan (Heather) Qian, Carleton University in Ottawa, Canada
Mariusz Rawski, Warsaw University of Technology, Poland
Radiah Rivu, Bundeswehr University Munich, Germany
Carsten Röcker, inIT - Institute Industrial IT / TH OWL University of Applied Sciences and Arts, Germany
Joni Salminen, Qatar Computing Research Institute, Qatar
Sandra Sanchez-Gordon, Escuela Politécnica Nacional, Ecuador
Antonio-José Sánchez-Salmerón, Instituto de Automática e Informática Industrial - Universidad Politécnica de Valencia, Spain
Paulus Insap Santosa, Universitas Gadjah Mada - Yogyakarta, Indonezia
Markus Santoso, University of Florida, USA
Diana Saplacan, University of Oslo, Norway
Hélène Sauzéon, Centre Inria Bordeaux, France
Trenton Schulz, Norwegian Computing Center, Norway
Kamran Sedig, Western University, Ontario, Canada
Sylvain Senecal, HEC Montreal, Canada
Fereshteh Shahmiri, Georgia Tech, USA
Yuhki Shiraishi, Tsukuba University of Technology, Japan
Marie Sjölinder, RISE, Sweden
Zdzisław Sroczyński, Silesian University of Technology, Gliwice, Poland
Ben Steichen, California State Polytechnic University, Pomona, USA
Han Su, RA - MIT, USA
Federico Tajariol, University Bourgogne Franche-Comté, France
Sheng Tan, Trinity University, Texas, USA
Jiro Tanaka, Waseda University, Japan
Cagri Tanriover, Intel Corporation (Intel Labs), USA
Ranjeet Tayi, User Experience - Informatica, San Francisco, USA
Masashi Toda, Kumamoto University, Japan
Carlos Toxtli Hernandez, West Virginia University, USA
Milka Trajkova, Indiana University, Indianapolis, USA
David Unbehaun, University of Siegen, Germany
Simona Vasilache, University of Tsukuba, Japan
KatiaVega, University of California, Davis, USA
Nishant Vishwamitra, University at Buffalo, USA
Konstantinos Votis, Information Technologies Institute | Centre for Research and Technology Hellas, Greece
Gloria Washington, Howard University, USA
Zhanwei Wu, Shanghai Jiao Tong University, China
Shuping Xiong, KAIST, South Korea
Panpan Xu, Bosch Research, Sunnyvale, USA
Sunny Xun Liu, Stanford University, USA
Ye Zhu, Cleveland State Unviersity, USA

Copyright Information

For your reference, this is the text governing the copyright release for material published by IARIA.

The copyright release is a transfer of publication rights, which allows IARIA and its partners to drive the dissemination of the published material. This allows IARIA to give articles increased visibility via distribution, inclusion in libraries, and arrangements for submission to indexes.

I, the undersigned, declare that the article is original, and that I represent the authors of this article in the copyright release matters. If this work has been done as work-for-hire, I have obtained all necessary clearances to execute a copyright release. I hereby irrevocably transfer exclusive copyright for this material to IARIA. I give IARIA permission or reproduce the work in any media format such as, but not limited to, print, digital, or electronic. I give IARIA permission to distribute the materials without restriction to any institutions or individuals. I give IARIA permission to submit the work for inclusion in article repositories as IARIA sees fit.

I, the undersigned, declare that to the best of my knowledge, the article is does not contain libelous or otherwise unlawful contents or invading the right of privacy or infringing on a proprietary right.

Following the copyright release, any circulated version of the article must bear the copyright notice and any header and footer information that IARIA applies to the published article.

IARIA grants royalty-free permission to the authors to disseminate the work, under the above provisions, for any academic, commercial, or industrial use. IARIA grants royalty-free permission to any individuals or institutions to make the article available electronically, online, or in print.

IARIA acknowledges that rights to any algorithm, process, procedure, apparatus, or articles of manufacture remain with the authors and their employers.

I, the undersigned, understand that IARIA will not be liable, in contract, tort (including, without limitation, negligence), pre-contract or other representations (other than fraudulent misrepresentations) or otherwise in connection with the publication of my work.

Exception to the above is made for work-for-hire performed while employed by the government. In that case, copyright to the material remains with the said government. The rightful owners (authors and government entity) grant unlimited and unrestricted permission to IARIA, IARIA's contractors, and IARIA's partners to further distribute the work.

Do Digital Human Facial Expressions Represent Real Humans?

Shiori Kikuchi, Oky Dicky Ardiansyah Prima, Hisayoshi Ito
Graduate School of Software and Information Science
Iwate Prefectural University
Takizawa, Iwate, Japan
e-mail: g231u017@s.iwate-pu.ac.jp, {prima, hito}@iwate-pu.ac.jp

Abstract— **The recent development of advanced digital humans has the potential to faithfully represent human nonverbal information. There are many examples of the use of digital humans for interactive communication, such as customer support and digital healthcare. There are, however, issues to be addressed as communication tools because of the lack of evidence regarding the extent to which nonverbal communication is performed by digital humans. In this study, we evaluate the quality of facial expressions by the digital human and its actors objectively using deep learning-based facial expression recognition. For the experiment, facial images of an actor expressing six basic emotions (anger, fear, disgust, happiness, surprise, and sadness) and a digital human face resembling the actor were captured, and scores of both facial expressions were measured. The results showed that the expression of "happiness" by the digital human and its actor were significantly consistent, but there were no significant differences in other facial expressions. The facial expression recognition used in this experiment was not trained on digital humans, thus there were cases in which the facial expressions of digital humans could not be judged accurately.**

Keywords-expression; digital human; facial expression; basic emotions; avatar.

I. INTRODUCTION

The spread of coronavirus (COVID-19) has changed the way people communicate to form interpersonal relationships, leading to the use of video calls for meetings and discussions. Video calls enable more effective communication by conveying visual and non-verbal information along with voice information. In Japan, the establishment of "Virtual Shibuya" [1] and the "Medical Metaverse Joint Research Chair" [2] have raised interest in virtual spaces and digital humans and are expected to promote communication using these technologies.

Facial expressions are a very important element in human communication, and in particular, human emotions play an especially important role in facial expressions. Consequently, the quality of reality of facial expressions of digital humans is also considered to be important for communication in virtual spaces. The advance computer vision has enabled facial expression recognition from facial images at a practical usage. Its application is widely available in areas, such as medicine, security, and marketing.

The representation of real buildings and people in virtual space has attracted much attention for a long time. Digital humans can be generated in high reality by capturing images of people with multiple cameras [3]. MetaHuman by Epic Games provides an elaborate representation of reading by an actor, enabling the actor's detailed changes in facial expression to be seen in the digital human [4]. These factors have led to the expectation of faithful representation of nonverbal information by sophisticated digital humans, and further research and development are currently in progress. However, it has not been fully verified to what extent the quality of facial expressions of digital humans is comparable to that of humans.

This study compares human and digital human facial expressions and examines the quality of digital human facial expressions. For this purpose, we created a system that reflects the actor's facial expressions to the digital human in real-time and automatically recognizes the six basic emotions based on their facial expressions.

The rest of this paper is organized as follows. Section II discusses the related works of facial expression analyses and digital human. Section III describes the generation of facial expression data and tools used for this purpose in this study. In Section IV, we describe our experiments to evaluate the quality of facial expressions for the digital human. Finally, Section V summarizes the results of this study and discusses future perspectives.

II. RELATED WORKS

Facial expressions are important in communication both in virtual space and face-to-face. This section describes research on facial expressions and analysis of facial expressions in face-to-face communication and research on digital human reality.

A. *Facial Expressions in Communication*

Understanding one's emotions is an important part of communication. Facial expressions in particular reveal human emotions. Ekman et al. proposed the Facial Action Coding System (FACS), which classifies the Action Units (AUs) of facial parts to identify emotions from facial expressions [5]. They pointed out that there are "display rules" based on such cultural norms thus the intensity of facial expressions differs depending on the culture. For example, Japanese people tend to suppress their facial expressions [6]. In addition to facial expression recognition using AUs, recently, facial expression recognition from facial images using deep learning has been widely used [7].

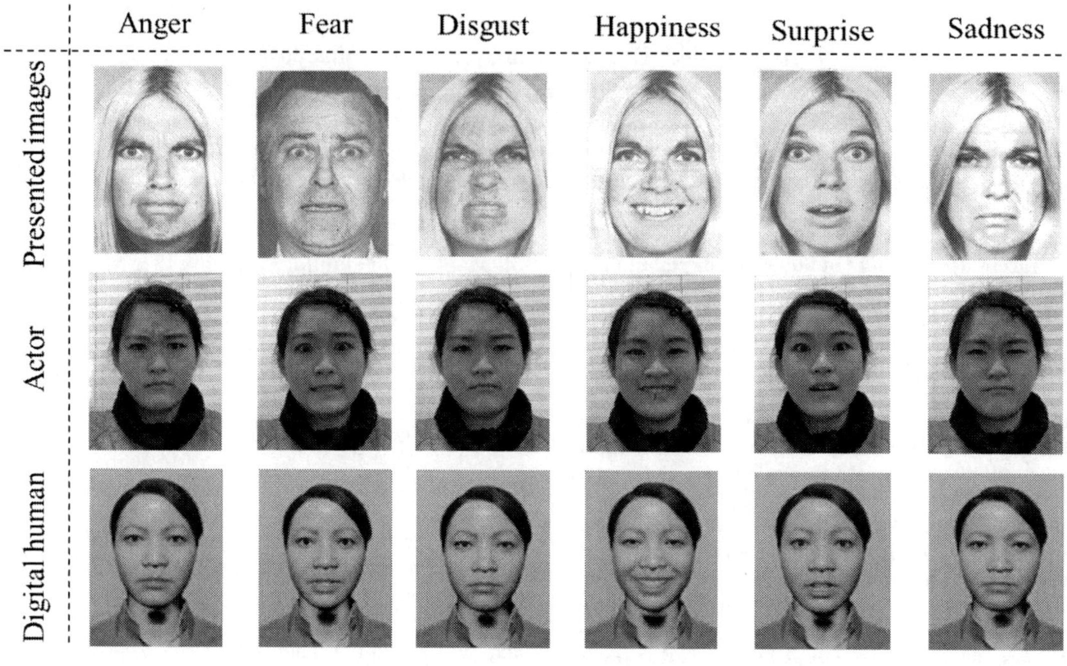

Figure 1. Expression of actors and digital humans on images of six basic emotions.

TABLE I. FACIAL EXPRESSION RECOGNITION RESULTS

Facial image	Facial images with correctly estimated emotion					
	Anger	Fear	Disgust	Happiness	Surprise	Sadness
Actor	0	28	0	80	24	29
Digital human	3	0	0	147	0	0

[frame]

B. *Reality of the Digital Human*

Recently, digital humans have been developed that resemble humans in appearance and are capable of projecting their body movements [4]. Kang et al. [8] surveyed and simplified the research on digital human reality, introducing two types of reality: visual realism, which is the similarity between the rendering of visual information of a person, and behavioral realism, which is the similarity between human behavior and the reality of a person. Visual realism is higher as the digital human looks more like a person, and behavioral realism is higher as the digital human performs natural movements. They also stated the importance of the influence of digital human reality on communication. Grewe et al. [9] compared the reality of facial expression animations created by experts with the reality of facial expression animations created statistically from a database of images and found that the statistically created animations were perceived as a more digitally human reality.

III. GENERATION OF FACIAL EXPRESSION DATA

This study compares actor and digital human facial expressions and examines the quality of digital human facial expressions. For this purpose, we create a system that reflects the actor's facial expressions to the digital human in real-time and automatically recognizes the six basic emotions based on their facial expressions. In this section, we first present the tools we used. Next, we describe the system that reflects the actor's facial expressions onto a highly realistic digital human and the collected facial images.

A. *Tools Used in This Study*

In this study, we use Epic Games' MetaHuman Creator (MHC), Unreal Engine (UE), and Live Link Face (LLF) to create a digital human and reflect the actor's facial expressions onto the digital human [10]. The MHC is a tool that facilitates the creation of photorealistic digital humans in the browser and can be used in conjunction with the 3D object rendering engine, UE. LLF, an iOS app from Epic Games, Inc. that transcribes actors' facial art to a superhuman in real-time, utilizes the device's true depth camera.

The tool for facial expression recognition used in this study is DeepFace [7], developed by Serengil and Ozpinar. It includes expression recognition trained using a convolutional neural network, which can estimate the percentages of six basic emotions from a single face image.

B. *Facial Expression Data*

For the generation of digital human facial expression data, a set of six facial images were presented in sequence to a 22-

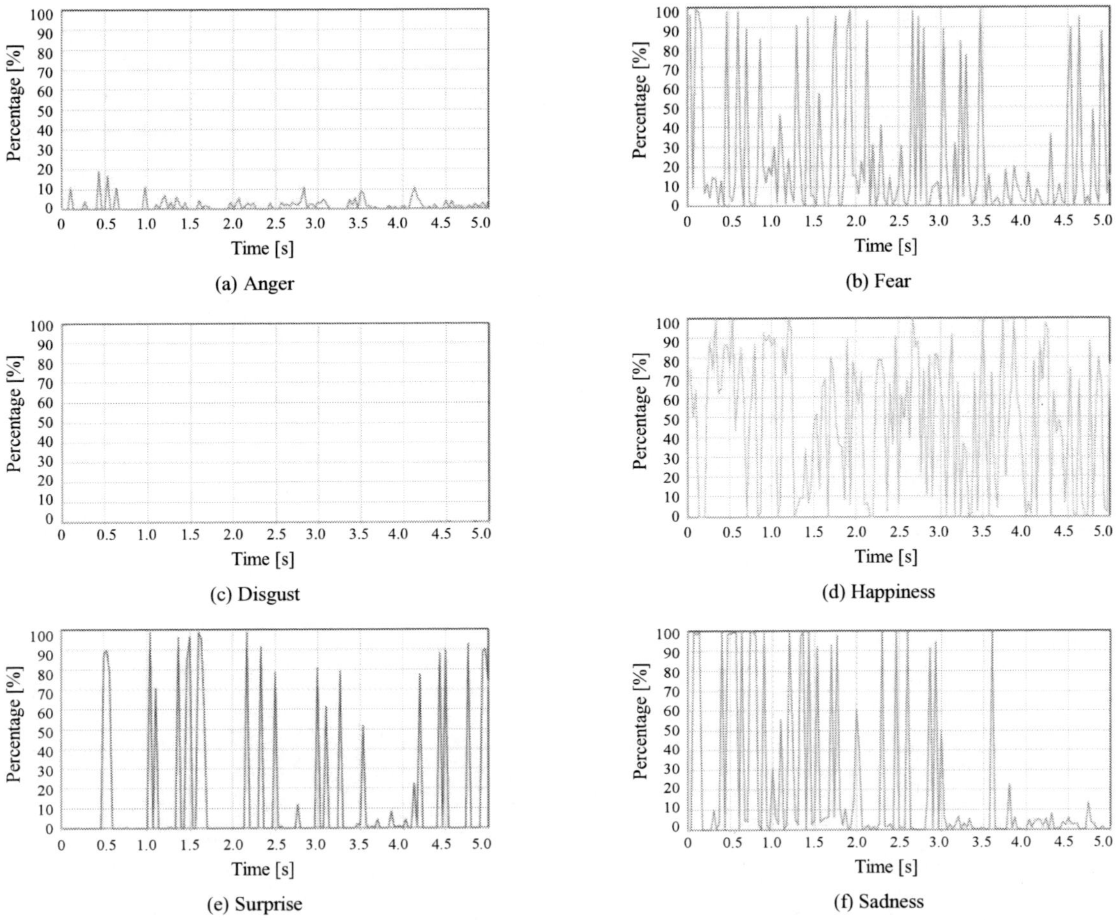

Figure 2. DeepFace estimation of the actor's emotion for each frame.

year-old Japanese female actor, who imitated each facial expression for five seconds. The facial videos were acquired, and their features were recorded using LLF. UE was used to acquire videos of the corresponding digital human facial images. Facial images and their features were recorded at 30 fps. To minimize the influence of cultural differences and the actor's experience in expressing facial expressions, a set of facial images representing Ekman's six basic emotions [5] was presented to the actor, and the facial muscles characteristic of each emotion were explained to enable the actor to imitate them properly. Finally, 150 frames of facial images were collected from each five-second video of each emotion, bringing the total number of facial images of actors and digital humans imitating the six basic emotions to 900 frames respectively.

IV. Evaluation of the Quality of Facial Expression

The actor's facial image and the facial image of the generated digital human are evaluated using DeepFace. The results of facial expression recognition for both are considered equivalent when the digital human can faithfully reproduce the actor's facial expression.

Based on the facial expression recognition results, each emotion that was estimated to be more than 50% was considered the dominant emotion expressed by the facial image. Therefore, the facial images imitated by an actor are considered similar if the percentage of emotions estimated in both the actor's and the digital human's facial images is over 50%.

The actors and the generated digital human facial images for each emotion are shown in Figure 1. The results of DeepFace of the respective facial expressions of the actor and the corresponding digital human when basic emotions were expressed in 5 seconds (150 frames of facial images) are shown in Table 1. When the actor mimicked the presented image, DeepFace correctly estimated the actor's facial expressions except for "anger" and "disgust," whereas the digital human correctly estimated only "happiness."

Figures 2 and 3 show the raw results of emotion estimation for actors and digital humans by DeepFace for each frame, respectively. As shown in the facial images in Figure 1, the actor lowered his eyebrows, glared into the eyes, and narrowed the lips to express anger. The digital human corresponding to the actor is also shown to have similar facial

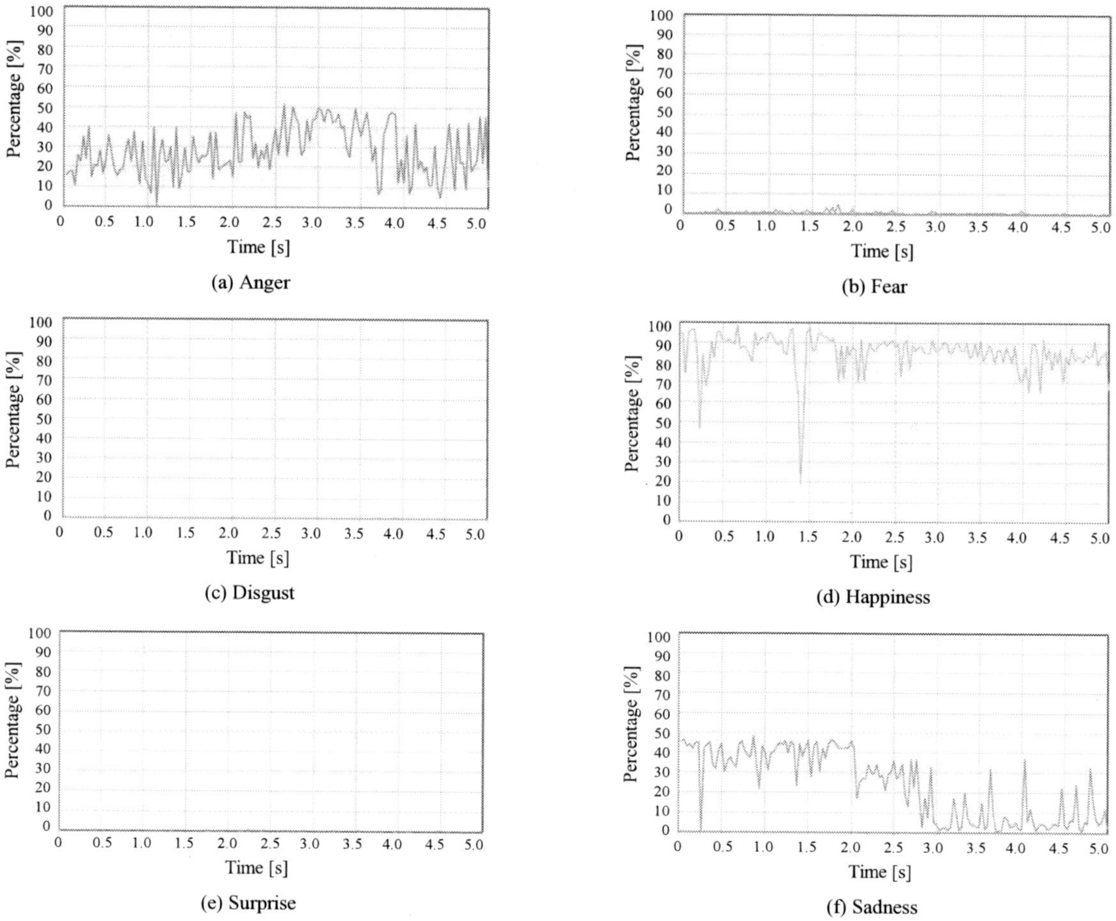

Figure 3. DeepFace estimation of the digital human's emotion for each frame.

features. However, the estimations for both emotions were low. Similarly, the results were low in disgust, despite the actor's wrinkling of the nose and raising of the upper lip. We also found that expressions of surprise and fear in digital humans were not recognized by DeepFace due to the lack of these important elements, such as pronounced raised eyebrows and widening of the eyes. The estimated emotional intensity varies from frame to frame. This suggests that the resulting emotion by DeepFace should be averaged over a certain frame length, rather than done in a single frame. Another reason why DeepFace cannot correctly estimate facial emotion in digital humans is that its neural network has not been trained on digital humans.

V. CONCLUSION

This study examined the quality of facial expressions of digital humans by objectively evaluating the facial expressions of an actor and its digital human through facial expression recognition, assuming the use of digital humans in communication. A visually realistic digital human was created to represent the actor, and facial expressions corresponding to behavioral reality were evaluated.

Facial expressions of six basic emotions were captured for five seconds by an actor and a digital human, and then facial expression recognition DeepFace was performed on each facial image for each frame. The results showed that the emotion of "happiness" was the most similar between the actor and the digital human, indicating that the quality of "happiness" by the digital human was high. However, since the emotion estimation for each frame by DeepFace varied, it seems necessary to consider multiple frames in the estimation of basic emotions.

Future work includes learning facial expression recognition using digital humans, improving facial expression estimation from continuous frames, and further validating the expression representation of digital humans.

REFERENCES

[1] Virtual Shibuya, https://new s.kddi.com/kddi/corporate/newsrelease/2020/05/15/4437.html [retrieved: May, 2022]

[2] Juntendo Virtual Hospital, https://jp.newsroom.ibm.com/2022-04-13-Juntendo-Virtual-Hospital [retrieved: May, 2022]

[3] Y. Iwayama, "Real Avatar Production - Raspberry Pi Zero W Based Low-Cost Full Body 3D Scan System Kit for VRM Format," 10th International Conference and Exhibition on 3D Body Scanning and Processing Technologies, pp. 22-23, 2019.

[4] Digital Andy Serkis, https://www.unrealengine.com/en-US/blog/epic-games-and-3lateral-introduce-digital-andy-serkis [retrieved: May, 2022]

[5] P. Ekman and W. V. Friesen, "Unmasking the Face: A Guide to Recognizing Emotions From Facial Expressions," Malor Books, 2003.

[6] T. Kudoh and D. Matsumoto, "The Emotional World of the Japanese - Uncovering the Mysteries of their Mysterious Culture," Seishinshobo, 1996.

[7] S. I. Serengil and A. Ozpinar, "LightFace: A Hybrid Deep Face Recognition Framework," 2020 Innovations in Intelligent Systems and Applications Conference (ASYU), pp. 1-5, 2020.

[8] S. H. Kang and J. H. Watt, "The impact of avatar realism and anonymity on effective communication via mobile devices," Computers in Human Behavior, 29(3), pp. 1169-1181, 2013.

[9] M. Grewe et al., "Statistical Learning of Facial Expressions Improves Realism of Animated Avatar Faces," Frontiers in Virtual Reality, 2, pp. 1-13, 2021.

[10] MetaHuman Creator, https://www.unrealengine.com/en-US/metahuman-creator [retrieved: May, 2022]

Detection of Pesticide Mist Distribution to Avoid Spray Drift

Chaitali Dutta, Oky Dicky Ardiansyah Prima,
Kanayo Ogura, and Koichi Matsuda
Graduate School of Soft. and Info. Science, Iwate Prefectural University
152-52 Sugo, Takizawa, Iwate, Japan
e-mail: g231t202@s.iwate-pu.ac.jp, {prima, ogura_k, matsuda}@iwate-pu.ac.jp

Shoichi Yuki
YAMABIKO Corporation
10-2 Sugo, Takizawa, Iwate, Japan
email: s_yukixx@yamabiko-corp.co.jp

Abstract—**Agriculture has made great progress due to technological advances. Spraying pesticides plays an important role in protecting crops from insects and pests. Large mechanical sprayers have made it easier for farmers to spray large areas in a short time. However, there is a risk of pesticides being sprayed in unintended areas, causing damage to nearby fields and bodies of water. In this study, we propose an approach to detect pesticide mist distribution using the U-Net-based semantic segmentation technique. To train the semantic segmentation model, images of mist from sprinklers and gardening mist sprayers were used as training data. Our results show that the semantic segmentation technique could infer the distribution of pesticide mist. The extracted mist areas were found to exclude areas, such as workers, gardening poles, and clouds. Furthermore, we were able to estimate the Three-Dimensional (3D) distribution of mist over the field based on the mist distribution in the continuous frame images. For the current attempt, we did not define the density of mist in the training data, however, we would like to consider estimating the density of mist in the future.**

Keywords-pesticide-mist; semantic segmentation; convolution neural network; agriculture; computer vision.

I. Introduction

Recently, agriculture has taken leaps in production due to advances in engineering technology and its application in various key areas of agriculture. Pesticides are sprayed on agricultural fields to protect the crops from pests **[1]**. There are advanced sprayers, which can cover vast agricultural fields, such as low-pressure sprayers, high-pressure sprayers, foggers, air-carrier sprayers, and hand-operated sprayers. Low-pressure sprayers are commonly mounted on a vehicle. The type of sprayer is chosen according to the size of the agricultural field. High-pressure sprayers can reach high trees and thick bushes. Foggers, also called mist blowers, convert liquid pesticides in the tank into vapor and spray them for intensive plant care. Air carrier sprayers use high-speed air to spray pesticides. Hand-operated sprayers, on the other hand, are used to spray small amounts of pesticides to affected areas and do not spray widely.

The fine mist allows for uniform spraying of plants. The spread of the spray is affected by the environment [2]. As a result, adjacent fields and water bodies can become contaminated with pesticides. This problem is known as spray drift [3]. Research has been carried out before to mitigate this problem by adjusting the nozzle strength and mechanical tuning of the machine. However, these approaches cannot optimize the spraying up to a satisfactory degree because each time a sample must be taken from a specific distance and analyzed in the lab for sedimentation of the pesticide. This process is very time and resource-consuming.

Artificial Intelligence and Computer Vision technology have been used in many fields in recent years, such as in the medical and automotive industries. Incorporating a Computer Vision approach to spray drift detection can provide highly accurate detection while saving time and resources. As video of pesticide spraying in the field is collected, tracking the position of the vehicle's movement from each of the video frames can be performed. By integrating the vehicle's position and spray distribution in all frames, the distribution of the spray in the field can be visualized in three dimensions.

This study attempts to extract the distribution of pesticide mist in the video footage to create a Three-Dimensional Mist Model (3D-MM). The extraction is done by applying semantic segmentation to the video of pesticide spraying. To train the segmentation model, we collect public mist image data and manually annotate the regions of mist in the images. Finally, we will discuss the 3D-MM created by combining mist distributions extracted from all frames of the video.

The rest of this paper is organized as follows. Section II discusses the related works of finding out an optimum method to mitigate the spray drift. Section III describes our proposed method to detect the mist distribution from an image. In Section IV, we summarize our results. Finally, Section V concludes our study and discusses future perspectives.

II. Related Works

Various studies have been conducted to prevent pesticide sprays from spreading outside the target field. The main factor in spreading is the size of the droplets. Droplet size depends on several factors, including nozzle pressure, liquid flow rate, air temperature, and humidity [1][4]. Small droplets are carried farther by the wind and thus remain suspended in the air for a longer period. Therefore, as droplet size decreases, the likelihood of spray drift increases. Most studies target spray drift for droplets less than 100 μm in diameter, while others recommend droplet thresholds of 50 μm, 150 μm, and 200 μm in diameter [5][6]. Droplets from higher nozzles are more likely to be carried further by the wind before reaching the plant [7].

Attempts were made to reduce the possibility of spray drift by improving the air induction nozzles. However, no significant differences in droplet size, spray pattern width, or

(a) Paddy field (big droplets) (b) Vegetable field (small droplets)

Figure 1. Pesticide spraying: (a) paddy and (b) vegetable fields.

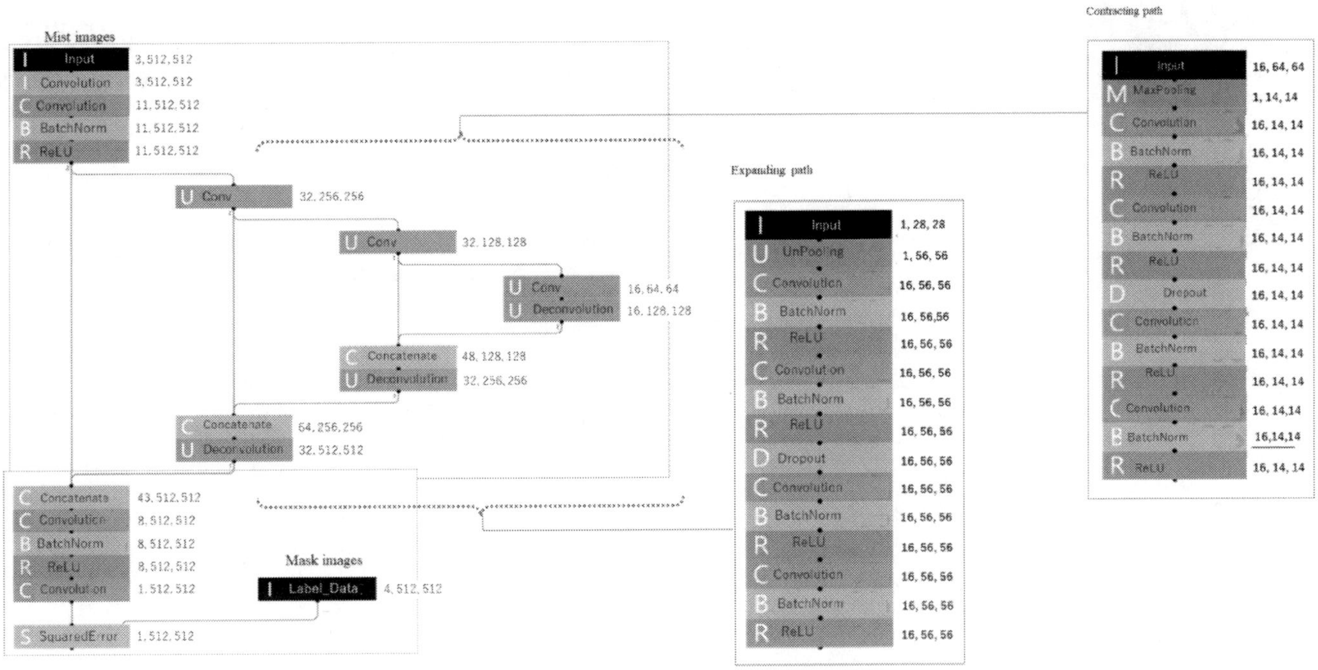

Figure 2. U-Net architecture used in this study.

spray coverage were found [8]. Nozzles installed at 0.7 m and 0.9 m with angles of 80° and 65°, respectively, would minimize spray drift. Similar results can also be obtained at 0.5 m with an angle of 100°. Installing nozzles at lower positions is preferred to avoid spray drift [9]. A single nozzle type may not give satisfactory results in all scenarios.

The combination of drift reduction methods consisting of sprayers with reflective shields and the application of coarse droplets may be an effective way to reduce spray drift [10]. Trees lined up along the wind direction in front of water bodies inside agricultural fields can significantly reduce spray drift [11].

There have been numerous advances in the field of deep neural networks for object detection and classification. Semantic segmentation based on Convolutional Neural Networks (CNNs) can classify objects at the pixel level [12] and learning an image of mist may be used to infer the distribution of pesticide mist.

III. Materials and Methods

The task of semantic segmentation is to classify image classes at the pixel level. This method inherently requires the extraction of meaningful features in the input image, but this task can now be done automatically with CNNs. This study utilized semantic segmentation to identify the distribution of sprayed pesticides. Figure 1 shows how the pesticides were applied in our fields. The mist coming out of the nozzle appears white in the image, but the low-density portions are

(a) Paddy field (b) Garden (c) Vegetable field

Figure 3. Collected mist images (top) and their corresponding masks (bottom) to train our network.

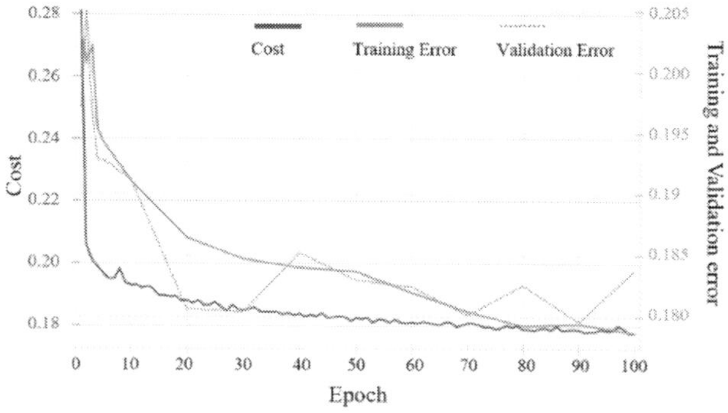

Figure 4. Training and validation learning curves of our network.

translucent. The distribution of small droplets tends to spread in more directions because they spend more time suspended in the air than larger droplets.

A. Network Architecture

Our network architecture is based on U-Net [12], as shown in Figure 2. This network was built using the Neural Network Console [13], an engineer-oriented deep learning framework developed by Sony Group Inc. It consists of two major parts: the contracting path, which is constituted by convolution layers and the expanding path by deconvolution (up-convolution) layers. Each convolution is followed by a batch normalization and a Rectified Linear Unit (ReLU). In total, the network has 11 convolutional layers. The size of the input image data and the resulting segmented image data is 512x512 pixels. The Mean Squared Error (MSE) is used as the loss function for the network optimization process.

B. Training

Approximately 500 mist images were used to train the network. All images are resized to 512 x 512 pixels. About 80% of these images were used for training, and the remaining 20% were used for validation. Figure 3 shows several of collected mist images and their corresponding masks to train our network. Despite the variation in mist concentration, a single mask was used to represent the area where the mist is distributed, rather than generating masks by concentration. LabelMe, a labeling and annotation tool, was used for annotation [14].

C. Building the 3D-MM

The 3D-MM was generated from video footage of pesticide spraying in a field by integrating the segmentation of the mist distribution in each frame image in the depth direction. These bundled image data were once converted to point cloud data to generate volumetric data. With the 3D-MM turned into volumetric data, the data can be sliced in any of the three axes allowing the distribution of mist at any point in the field to be viewed.

IV. RESULTS

Training and validation learning curves are as shown in Figure 4. The learning time required to reach 100 epochs was approximately one hour with a NVIDIA RTX3080 (8 GB) graphics accelerator. The learning and validation losses are smallest around the ninetieth epoch, and the difference between them is small. The weights of the network at this

(a) Paddy field (b) Vegetable field (c) Vegetable field

Figure 5. Extracted mist distributions from mist images in this study.

Figure 6. Visualization of 3D-MM as volumetric data. Mist distribution at any location can be visualized.

point were used as the final weights in this study, and the learned model was generated.

The resulting mist distributions extracted from each image are as shown in Figure 5. In the paddy field image, mist was successfully distinguished from clouds that were similar in color. In the vegetable field, despite the presence of people and gardening poles between the mist and the camera, we were able to successfully extract the mist area (Figure 5(b)). On the contrary, the extracted mist area will include the person behind the mist (Figure 5(c)). Overall, the results show that the network in this study was able to extract mist distributions well, although it adopted a fairly standard U-Net network.

Figure 6 shows an Open3D visualization of the mist distribution at an arbitrary location from the reconstructed 3D-MM. Our visualization method opens a new way to analyze mist distribution, whereas it has been difficult to confirm its distribution from different angles. By adding wind direction and speed data to this data, it may be possible to understand the relationship between the mist distribution and the wind.

V. CONCLUSIONS AND FUTURE WORK

In this study, we attempt to extract the distribution of pesticide mist in the video footage and create a 3D mist model. Extraction was performed by applying a U-Net based semantic segmentation to images of pesticide spraying. Despite the small number of images used to train the neural network, we were able to accurately extract the mist distribution regions in the images. The 3D mist model reconstructed in this study would provide further insight into pesticide mists and would provide an opportunity for a detailed analysis. As the present extraction of mist distribution relies on information solely from a single camera, better results could be obtained by adding multiple cameras or by considering the orientation information of the sprayer.

ACKNOWLEDGMENT

This work was done in collaboration with YAMABIKO Corporation and the Faculty of Software and Information Science, Iwate Prefectural University.

REFERENCES

[1] M. Farooq and M. Salyani, "Modeling of Spray Penetration and Deposition on Citrus Tree Canopies," Transactions of the ASAE, 47(3), pp. 619-627,2004.

[2] M. Salyani and R. P. Cromwell, "Spray Drift from Ground and Aerial Applications," Transactions of the ASAE, 35(4), pp. 1113-1120, 1992.

[3] Introduction to Pesticide Drift,

https://www.epa.gov/reducing-pesticide-drift/introduction-pesticide-drift [retrieved: Jun, 2022]

[4] K. Baetens, et al. "Predicting Drift from Field Spraying by Means of a 3D Computational Fluid Dynamics Model," Computers and Electronics in Agriculture, 56(2), pp. 161-173, 2007.

[5] M. Al Heidary, J. P. Douzals, C. Sinfort, and A. Vallet, "Influence of Spray Characteristics on Potential Spray Drift of Field Crop Sprayers: A Literature Review," Crop protection, 63, pp. 120-130, 2014.

[6] E. Hilz and A. W. Vermeer, "Spray Drift Review: The Extent to Which a Formulation Can Contribute to Spray Drift Reduction," Crop Protection, 44, pp. 75-83, 2013.

[7] P. C. H. Miller, M. B. Ellis, A. G. Lane, C. M. O'sullivan, and C. R. Tuck, "Methods for Minimising Drift and Off-target Exposure from Boom Sprayer Applications," Aspects of Applied Biology, 106, pp. 281-288, 2011.

[8] H. Guler, "Spray Characteristics and Drift Reduction Potential with Air Induction and Conventional Flat-fan Nozzles," Transactions of the ASABE, 50(3), pp. 745-754, 2007.

[9] J. Wilson, J. Nowatzki, and V. Hofman. "Selecting Drift Reducing Nozzles," FS-919 Revised, South Dakota Cooperative Extension Service and NDSU Extension Service, pp. 1- 8, 2008.

[10] M. Wenneker and J.C. van de Zande, "Drift Reduction in Orchard Spraying Using a Cross Flow Sprayer Equipped with Reflection Shields (Wanner) and Air Injection Nozzles," Agricultural Engineering International: the CIGR Ejournal, Manuscript ALNARP 08 014, X, pp.1-10,2008.

[11] C. Vischetti, et al, "Measures to Reduce Pesticide Spray Drift in a Small Aquatic Ecosystem in Vineyard Estate." Science of the Total Environment, 389(2-3), pp. 497-502, 2008.

[12] O. Ronneberger, P. Fischer, and T. Brox, "U-Net: Convolutional Networks for Biomedical Image Segmentation," MICCAI 2015. Lecture Notes in Computer Science, Springer, 9351, https://doi.org/10.1007/978-3-319-24574-4_28, pp 234–241,2015

[13] T. Narihira,et al., "Neural Network Libraries: A Deep Learning Framework Designed from Engineers' Perspectives," arXiv preprint arXiv:2102.06725, pp. 1- 12, 2021.

[14] LabelMe, https://github.com/wkentaro/labelme [retrieved: Jun ,2022.]

3D Human Pose Estimation using a Stereo Camera towards Monitoring of Drug Picking Tasks

Yuta Ono, Oky Dicky Ardiansyah Prima
Graduate School of Software and Information Science
Iwate Prefectural University
Takizawa, Iwate, Japan
email: g236s001@s.iwate-pu.ac.jp, prima@iwate-pu.ac.jp

***Abstract*—Medication dispensing errors are a critical issue that threatens the quality of health care services and patients' safety. Checks by pharmacists are effective in preventing this potential problem but increase the workload. In Japan, dispensing assistants are allowed to assist pharmacists in picking drugs to reduce their workload. However, becoming a dispensing assistant requires experiences, as drugs can easily be mistaken because of their similar names and forms. This study attempts to construct a monitoring framework using stereo camera-based Three-Dimensional (3D) human pose estimation for detecting errors and evaluating the physical workload during the drug picking task. To accurately estimate the 3D human pose, we improve the estimation of body joints and perform calibration using multiple reference points. Our results show that the proposed framework can estimate the 3D human pose with acceptable accuracy to detect errors in the drug picking task. Future work will examine the applicability of the proposed framework to the assessment of physical workload of dispensing assistants.**

Keywords-3D human pose estimation; Stereo camera; Medication dispensing error; Pharmacy.

I. INTRODUCTION

As the global elderly population grows, the proportion of patients with multimorbidity will increase [1]. Patients with multimorbidity are prescribed more medications and are therefore at higher risk for medication dispensing errors. Such errors are serious threats to the quality of health care services and a patients' safety [2].

The presence of pharmacists is essential to prevent medication dispensing errors. In addition to dispensing and supplying prescription drugs, pharmacists are expected to apply their specialized knowledge and skills to a variety of tasks, such as detecting medical side effects and providing medication guidance [3][4]. However, workload of pharmacists is increasing as their scope of work expands [5]. Previous study has shown that the high workload may lead to overlook the risk of health problems in patients [6]. High physical workload including prolonged standing, sitting and repetitive tasks may also cause musculoskeletal disorders (MSDs) of the body, such as neck and back [7].

In Japan, Pharmaceutical Safety and Environmental Health Bureau has allowed dispensing assistants to pick drugs starting April 2019 to reduce workload of pharmacists and maintain the quality of healthcare services [8]. This expects that pharmacists focus on more specialized activities. However, the task is prone to cause dispensing errors because the names and the forms of drugs are similar. In addition, pharmacists must still check the dispensed drug eventually. Various methods have been proposed to prevent the dispensing error [9][10]. However, these methods require an operator to operate the cumbersome process, such as scanning a bar-code or modifying each shelf. In addition, it is difficult for these methods to evaluate the physical workload from operator's movements during the picking task.

Three-Dimensional (3D) human pose estimation using vision cameras can measure 3D movements of human body without contact. Especially, methods using multiple vision cameras can measure the position of the body joint relative to surrounding objects. However, if there is a discrepancy between the Two-Dimensional (2D) correspondence position of the body joint estimated from each camera image, it may cause large errors in its resulting 3D position [11].

This study attempts to construct a monitoring framework based on stereo camera-based 3D human pose estimation for detecting errors in drug picking tasks and evaluating the physical workload of dispensing assistants during the tasks. We propose two methods to estimate 3D human pose more accurately. First method is a 2D body joint position correction method, which estimate plausible 2D position of a certain body joint in each camera image. Second method is a 3D calibration method using multiple reference points to refine the 3D measurement accuracy by the stereo camera. In addition, this study introduces a method to determine the correct picking task based on the estimated 3D position of the hand. Finally, we will verify accuracies of the 3D human pose estimation and of the picking task. We will also discuss whether this framework is applicable to the evaluation of the physical workload of the operator.

This paper is organized as follows. Section II describes the related work on prevention of the error during drug picking tasks and 3D human pose estimation from vision cameras. Section III describes the proposed framework to estimate accurate 3D human pose and determine the picking task. In Section IV, we clarify the 3D human pose estimation accuracy and the accuracy of the picking task. Section V consider about performance improvements and evaluation of physical workload in this study. Finally, Section VI concludes our study and describes future works.

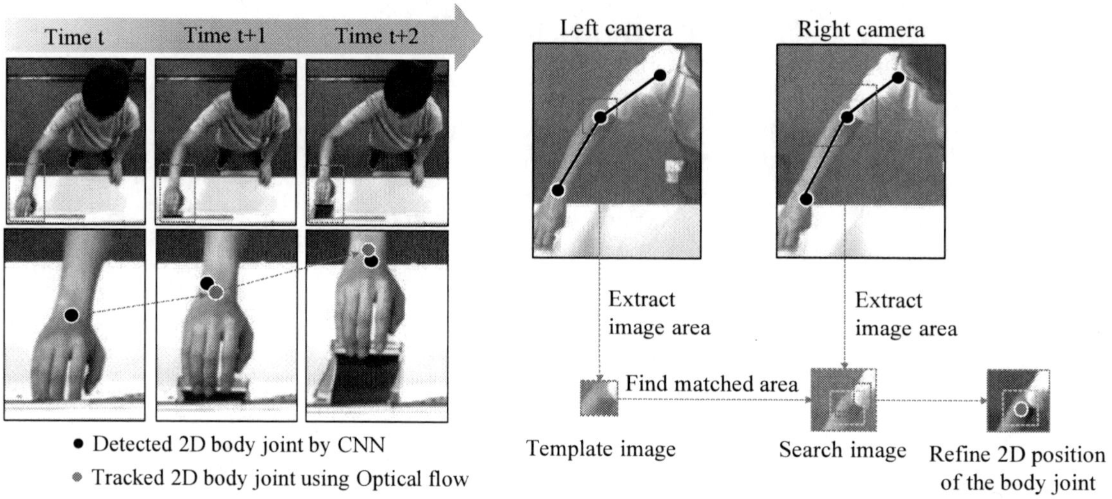

(a) Optical flow-based correction (b)Template matching-based correction

Figure 1. 2D body joint correction on a stereo image

II. Related Work

There are various methods proposed to prevent errors in drug picking tasks. Barcode-Assisted Medication Administration (BCMA) system manages drugs, prescriptions, and patient information by reading corresponding barcodes [9][12]. In addition, medical dispensing system using RFID is proposed [13]. However, these systems are complicated because they require to read barcodes or tags during the picking task. Few methods using Light Emitting Diode (LED) or Augmented Reality (AR) markers are proposed [10][14]. However, these methods are also cumbersome because we need to modify dispensing cabinets to put LEDs or AR markers.

The technology of 3D human pose estimation has made significant progress. Azure Kinect can estimate the 3D position of body joints using the Body Tracking Software Development Kit (SDK) from depth data measured by a depth sensor [15]. Ono and Prima indicated the possibility to monitor the drug picking task by utilizing 3D hand detection combining MediaPipe [16] and Azure Kinect [17]. However, this method can only measure the picking task within the range that can be measured by the Azure Kinect.

There are also methods using visible light cameras to estimate the 3D position of body joints. These methods can be roughly classified into methods using single camera and methods using multiple cameras. Methods using single camera utilize deep neural network to estimate 3D human pose from a camera view [18][19]. However, it is difficult for these methods to measure the accurate 3D position of the body joint and other objects in real space due to the direction of the body and self-occlusion and so on. Methods using multiple cameras have advantageous that these can calculate 3D position of objects using triangulation. Nakano et al. used the Convolutional Neural Network (CNN) [20] to estimate the 2D position of body joints and estimated the 3D position of the body joint by triangulation. However, this method needs accurate the 2D position of body joints for accurate estimation of the 3D position of body joints with multiple cameras [11]. Sayo et al. proposed a refinement network that estimates the difference between the 2D position of body joints estimated using a CNN and the 2D projection of the actual 3D position of body joints [20]. This method can estimate the accurate the 2D position of body joints by subtracting the difference the network estimated. However, this method doesn't consider the temporal consistency of the 2D position of body joints or the discrepancy of the 2D correspondence position of body joints estimated on multiple camera images.

III. Proposed Framework

We installed a stereo camera on the top of the dispensing cabinet to capture drug picking tasks. Our framework detects the 2D position of body joints on each camera image using CNN [21]. The resulting 2D body joints are corrected to identify plausible 2D position for the same body joint on each camera image. The 3D position of body joints is estimated based on triangulation method and optimized by a 3D calibration method using multiple reference points. Finally, our framework determines the picking task of the operator using the estimated 3D hand position.

A. 2D Body Joints Position Tracking Using Optical Flow

In this study, we utilize optical flow to track the 2D position of body joints consistently in time. Figure 1(a) shows correction of 2D position of body joints using optical flow. Because the tracking using only optical flow may fail due to occlusion, we set multiple tolerance levels on the distance between the 2D position of body joints tracked by the optical flow and the 2D position of body joints detected by the CNN. We then define new 2D position of body joints according to the tolerance levels. Our body joint tracking is as follow. The 2D position of the body joint $p_t(x_j, y_j)$ detected by the CNN at time t is defined as an initial position of the body joint. Next, we track the 2D position of the body joint $p'_{t+1}(x'_j, y'_j)$ on the image at time $t + 1$ using optical flow based on the Lucas-Kanade method [22]. We calculate the distance between the

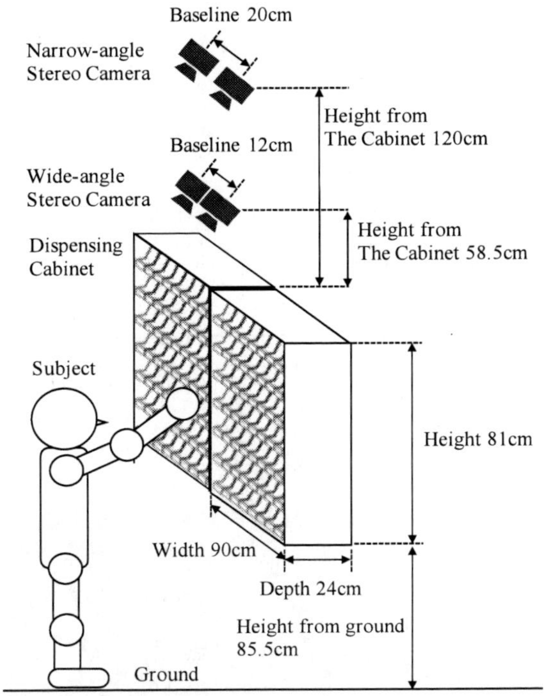

Figure 2. Setup of stereo cameras and dispensing cabinets

2D position of the body joint $p_{t+1}(x_j, y_j)$ detected by CNN and the 2D position of the body joint $p'_{t+1}(x'_j, y'_j)$ tracked using optical flow. Finally, new 2D position of the body joint is determined according to the distance. In this study, $p'_{t+1}(x'_j, y'_j)$ is adopted if the distance is less than 5px. If the distance is greater than 5 pixels and less 10 pixels, the midpoint of both points is adopted. If the distance is greater than 10 pixels, $p_{t+1}(x_j, y_j)$ is adopted.

B. 2D Body Joint Correction on a Stereo Image Using Template Matching

To identify plausible 2D position for same body joint across stereo images, this study corrects the 2D position of the body joint between two images by finding plausible the position using template matching. Figure 1(b) shows illustration of method for correction of the 2D position of the body joint. At first, we generate a template image and a search image. These images are within a certain range from the body joint detected in each image. Next, we find the plausible 2D position of the body joint by searching for the area of highest similarity to the template images. Finally, the center of the area is defined as the corrected 2D position of the body joint. In this study, the size of the template image is 16×16 pixels, and the search range is 33×33 pixels.

C. 3D Calibration Using Multiple 3D Reference Points

The 3D position of body joints cannot be accurately estimated due to camera lens distortion. To solve this problem, we propose a 3D calibration method using multiple reference points. The reference points are placed entirely in the field of view of a stereo camera. Next, the 3D position of them is estimated based on triangulation. The actual measured position of the reference point $P_i = (X_i, Y_i, Z_i)$ and the estimated position $P'_i = (X'_i, Y'_i, Z'_i)$ is equal to

$$P_i = A \cdot P'_i + \zeta. \tag{1}$$

where A is $m \times n$ refinement matrix, ζ is residuals. The matrix A is calculated by least squares method.

$$\mathrm{argmin} \sum_{i=1}^{N} \|A \cdot P'_i - P_i\|. \tag{2}$$

The final 3D position of the body joint $J'_j = (X'_j, Y'_j, Z'_j)$ is defined by

$$J'_j = A \cdot J_j. \tag{3}$$

where J_j is 3D position of the jth body joint before the application of the 3D calibration method.

D. Picking Task Evaluation Based on 3D Hand Position

The method for evaluating drug picking tasks based on the 3D position of the operator's hand is as follows. First, the 3D position of the hand is calculated as the center position of 3D hand landmarks estimated by our framework. Next, the distance between the hand position and each shelf position is calculated to determine the closest shelf. Finally, when the shelf and hand positions overlap for more than 0.5 seconds, the operator is considered to have operated the shelf.

IV. EXPERIMENTS AND RESULTS

We verify the performance of the proposed framework towards monitoring of the drug picking task. First, we calculate the measurement error of the 3D position of multiple reference points placed in the field of view of the stereo camera to clarify the 3D measurement accuracy. Next, we capture the picking task by subjects installed few markers to verify the estimation accuracy of the 3D human pose. Finally, we also verify whether the proposed framework can determine the correct picking task based on the 3D hand position.

A. Experimental Environment

Figure 2 shows the setup of stereo cameras and dispensing cabinets. The experimental room is 300cm high from the floor to the ceiling. In this experiment, we use the dispensing cabinet that can store 63 shelves. The size of a shelf is 9.4cm×10.6cm×13.3cm. Two dispensing cabinets are placed side by side. Two types of stereo cameras are used in this experiment: the MD-SUA133GC-T and the CaliCam, manufactured by Shenzhen MindVision Technology Co. Ltd. and Astar.ai Inc., respectively. Each camera in the MD-SUA133GC-T has a 48.5° x 36.9° field of view and captures images at 60 Frames Per Second (FPS). The baseline length between cameras is 20cm. The CaliCam stereo camera has a field of view of 120° x 100° at 30 FPS and the baseline length is 12 cm. Hereinafter, MD-SUA133GC-T is referred to as a narrow-angle stereo camera and CaliCam as a wide-angle stereo camera.

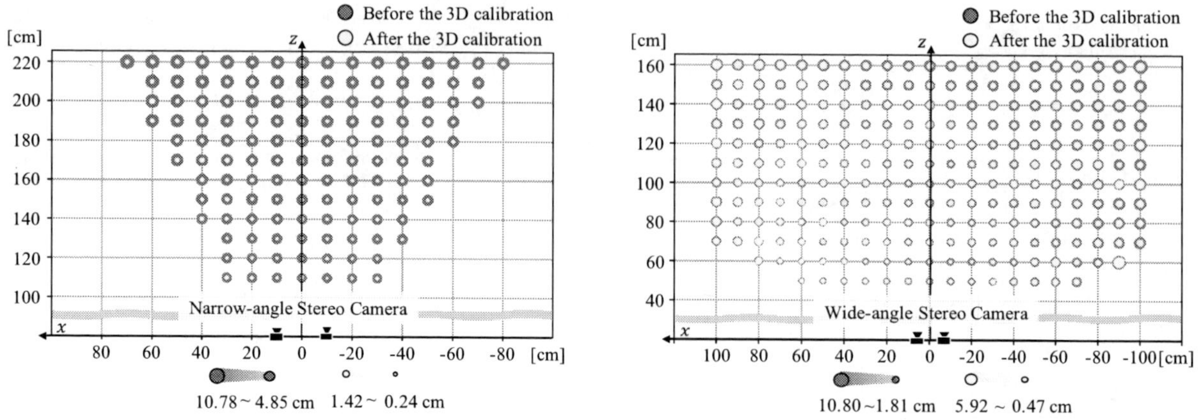

(a) Narrow-angle Stereo Camera

(b) Wide-angle Stereo Camera

Figure 3. Measurement error of 3D reference points

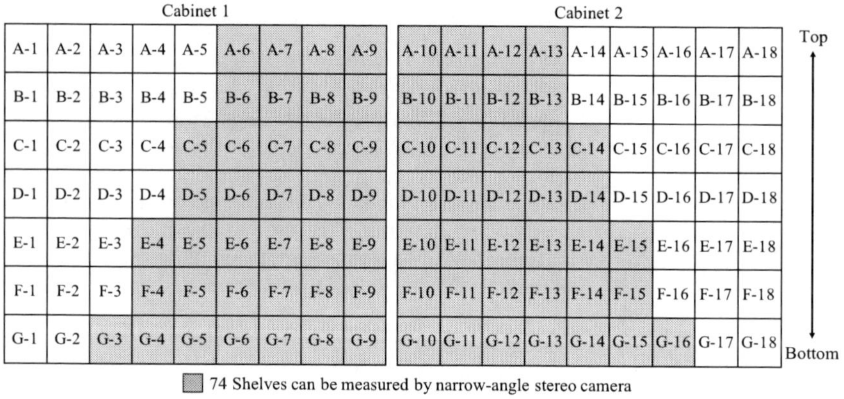

Figure 4. Location of shelves used in this study

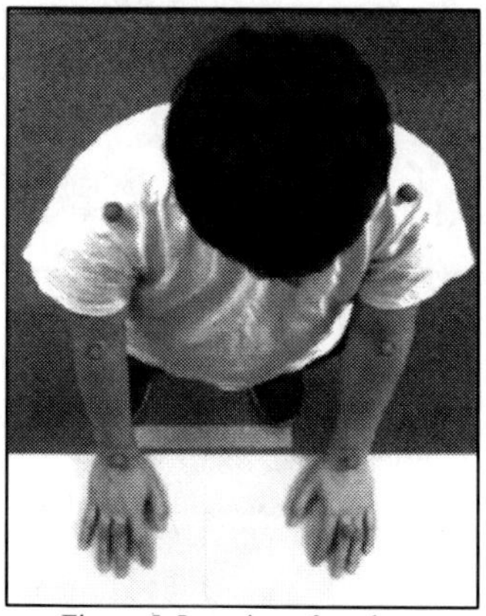

Figure 5. Location of markers

B. *3D Point Measurement Accuracy by a Stereo Camera*

First, reference points were placed in the field of view of each stereo camera. These points for correction were regularly placed at 10 cm intervals. Next, these 2D positions were obtained from each camera image and the corresponding 3D positions were measured. Finally, the difference between the estimated and actual 3D positions was calculated in Root Mean Square Error (RMSE).

Figure 3 shows the measurement error of the reference points. By using the narrow-angle stereo camera, the RMSE of all reference points was 7.8 cm before and 0.8 cm after the application of the 3D calibration. Whereas, the RMSE of all reference points was 5.0 cm before and 1.8 cm after the application of the 3D calibration when a wide-angle stereo camera was used. As a result, we found that the 3D calibration method can improve the 3D measurement accuracy regardless of the angle of view of the stereo camera.

C. *The Accuracy of 3D Human Pose Estimation*

To verify the accuracy of the 3D human pose estimation, markers were attached to the body of the operator doing the picking task, and the difference between the position of markers and the position of body joints estimated by the proposed framework was calculated. Six shelves near the center of the two cabinets (A-6, D-6, G-6, A-13, D-13, G-13) and four shelves on either side of the cabinet (A-1, A-18, G-1, G-18) were used for the picking task. Figure 4 shows the location of shelves used in this study. The wide-angle stereo camera can measure all shelves, whereas the narrow-angle stereo camera can measure only 74 shelves. Four subjects participated in this experiment.

The procedure for the evaluation of the 3D pose estimated by our framework is as follows. Figure 5 shows the location of markers. We put markers on subject's shoulders, elbows, wrists, and hands. The marker is a blue sphere with a diameter of 1.8cm. First, the subject stands in the center of the two cabinets and performs the picking task. Next, the 2D position of each marker is extracted by using HSV color extraction and blob detection. Then, the 3D position of each marker is calculated by triangulation and refine the position by the 3D calibration method. Finally, the error between the 3D position of body joints estimated by our framework and the position of the corresponding markers is calculated as RMSE and Standard Deviation (SD). We calculate the hand position as the center position of the detected 3D hand landmark by our framework.

Tables I and II show the accuracy of the 3D human pose estimation during the picking task for shelves that can be measured both stereo cameras. Table III shows the accuracy of the 3D human pose estimation during the picking task for

TABLE I. ACCURACY OF 3D HUMAN POSE ESTIMATION USING THE NARROW-ANGLE STEREO CAMERA DURING DRUG PICKING TASK [CM]

Body Joint		Methods			
		None	Optical Flow	Template Matching	Optical Flow and Template Matching
		RMSE (SD)	RMSE (SD)	RMSE (SD)	RMSE (SD)
Right	Shoulder	4.8 (2.1)	4.8 (2.1)	2.5 (1.0)	2.4 (0.9)
	Elbow	5.6 (2.7)	5.5 (2.5)	2.8 (1.6)	2.8 (1.6)
	Wrist	4.8 (2.1)	4.5 (2.0)	1.6 (0.7)	1.6 (0.7)
	Hand	3.1 (0.9)	3.0 (0.9)	2.1 (0.8)	2.2 (0.8)
Left	Shoulder	4.3 (2.1)	4.2 (2.1)	2.0 (0.9)	1.9 (0.8)
	Elbow	4.9 (2.4)	5.1 (2.4)	1.9 (0.7)	1.8 (0.7)
	Wrist	4.4 (2.1)	4.1 (1.9)	2.0 (0.8)	2.0 (0.8)
	Hand	3.0 (1.1)	3.0 (1.1)	2.1 (0.8)	2.1 (0.8)
Mean of RMSE		4.36	4.28	2.13	2.10

TABLE II. ACCURACY OF 3D HUMAN POSE ESTIMATION USING THE WIDE-ANGLE STEREO CAMERA DURING DRUG PICKING TASK [CM]

Body Joint		Methods			
		None	Optical Flow	Template Matching	Optical Flow and Template Matching
		RMSE (SD)	RMSE (SD)	RMSE (SD)	RMSE (SD)
Right	Shoulder	8.3 (3.6)	7.6 (3.4)	3.7 (1.3)	3.5 (1.2)
	Elbow	6.5 (3.1)	5.9 (2.8)	3.6 (1.7)	3.6 (1.7)
	Wrist	8.1 (4.5)	8.4 (4.9)	2.8 (1.3)	2.9 (1.3)
	Hand	3.8 (1.5)	3.8 (1.5)	2.6 (1.1)	2.6 (1.1)
Left	Shoulder	7.4 (3.7)	6.3 (3.3)	2.5 (1.1)	2.4 (1.0)
	Elbow	6.5 (3.6)	6.2 (3.5)	2.8 (1.1)	2.8 (1.1)
	Wrist	6.6 (3.4)	7.0 (3.9)	2.8 (1.1)	2.9 (1.2)
	Hand	4.2 (1.8)	4.2 (1.8)	2.6 (0.9)	2.6 (0.9)
Mean of RMSE		6.43	6.18	2.93	2.91

TABLE III. ACCURACY OF 3D HUMAN POSE ESTIMATION USING THE WIDE-ANGLE STEREO CAMERA DURING WIDE-AREA DRUG PICKING TASK [CM]

Body Joint		Methods			
		None	Optical Flow	Template Matching	Optical Flow and Template Matching
		RMSE (SD)	RMSE (SD)	RMSE (SD)	RMSE (SD)
Right	Shoulder	8.6 (4.1)	7.5 (3.6)	3.9 (1.7)	3.8 (1.7)
	Elbow	7.6 (4.0)	6.9 (3.9)	3.6 (1.5)	3.5 (1.5)
	Wrist	8.1 (4.2)	7.8 (4.2)	3.3 (1.4)	2.9 (1.2)
	Hand	4.8 (2.2)	5.0 (2.4)	3.2 (1.5)	3.0 (1.4)
Left	Shoulder	6.9 (3.5)	5.7 (3.2)	3.2 (1.5)	3.0 (1.5)
	Elbow	7.0 (3.7)	6.6 (3.5)	3.4 (1.2)	3.4 (1.1)
	Wrist	7.5 (3.9)	7.8 (4.2)	3.1 (1.3)	3.0 (1.2)
	Hand	5.3 (2.4)	5.6 (2.6)	3.5 (1.5)	3.3 (1.5)
Mean of RMSE		6.98	6.61	3.40	3.24

shelves that can be measured only the wide-angle stereo camera. These results show the accuracy of 3D human pose estimation from a wide-angle stereo camera is equivalent to that from a narrow-angle stereo camera. Table IV shows the result of Tukey-Kramer multiple comparison test on the mean of RMSE of 3D human pose estimation improved using optical flow and template matching. A significant difference was found in mean score of RMSE of the 3D human pose estimated using template matching and not. However, there was not a statistically significant difference in mean score of RMSE of the 3D human pose estimated using optical flow.

D. The Determination Accuracy of Picking Task

This experiment confirms whether the proposed framework can determine the correct picking task based on the estimated 3D position of the hand. Subjects are randomly instructed which shelf to operate. Pulling a shelf and returning it to its original position is defined as a picking task. The left-hand shelf is operated by the left hand whereas the right-hand shelf is operated by the right hand. In addition, when the subject operates the shelf, the back of the hand should face upward. In this experiment, we first captured the picking task for 74 shelves that could be measured from both stereo cameras to compare the determination accuracy of the picking task. Then, we also captured the picking task for all shelves using only the wide-angle stereo camera. Four subjects participated in this experiment.

Table V shows the determination accuracy of the picking task in this experiment. The results show that the proposed framework enabled an accurate assessment of the picking task. Measurements with the wide-angle stereo camera were more accurate. The narrow-angle stereo camera is mounted higher than the wide-angle stereo camera. This results in measuring the subject from a more extreme angle, and if the subject is leaning forward, the camera may not be able to detect the subject in the image.

TABLE IV. TUKEY-KRAMER MULTIPLE COMPARISONS TEST FOR THE ACCURACY OF 3D HUMAN POSE ESTIMATION

Group 1	Group 2	Experiment Setting		
		Using the NA stereo camera	Using the WA stereo camera	
		Drug Picking Task p-value	Drug Picking Task p-value	Wide-area Drug Picking Task p-value
None	Optical Flow	.994	.974	.840
None	Template Matching	< .001	< .001	< .001
None	Optical Flow and Template Matching	< .001	< .001	< .001
Optical Flow	Template Matching	< .001	< .001	< .001
Optical Flow	Optical Flow and Template Matching	< .001	< .001	< .001
Template Matching	Optical Flow and Template Matching	.999	.999	.982

NA:"Narrow-angle", WA:"Wide-angle"

TABLE V. DETERMINATION ACCURACY OF DRUG PICKING TASK

Subject	Stereo Camera		
	Narrow-angle	Wide-angle	
	74 shelves	74 shelves	All shelves
A	91.9 %	95.9 %	92.9 %
B	93.2 %	100.0 %	93.7 %
C	100.0 %	100.0 %	95.2 %
D	95.9 %	100.0 %	96.0 %
All	95.3 %	99.0 %	94.4 %

V. DISCUSSION

In this study, we attempted to determine which shelf was operated by the operator using the proposed framework. The result shows the proposed framework can accurately determine which shelf was operated during the picking task. Although the proposed framework can measure a wider area than the Azure Kinect, the determination accuracy of picking task is lower than that of Ono et al. [17]. For more accurate determination, it would be possible to use the 3D position of the pulled-out shelf in addition to the 3D position of the operator's hand. This would allow detection of errors during picking tasks where the 3D human pose could not be estimated by the stereo camera. In future, we plan to improve the determination method of picking tasks and clarify the accuracy on experiments with more subjects.

The proposed framework allows to measure not only the picking task but also other tasks, such as storing drugs into the cabinet, packings of drugs or syrups. Since our framework can calculate the angle of body joints or the body movement based on the estimated 3D human pose, it might be possible to visualize and evaluate the physical workload from this data. This attempt will be useful to improve the working environment or the workflow in pharmacies.

VI. CONCLUSION

This study attempted to construct a monitoring framework based on 3D human pose estimation using a stereo camera for detecting errors in drug picking tasks and evaluating the physical workload during the picking task. Our framework utilized optical flow and template matching to accurately estimate the 2D body joints. A 3D calibration method using multiple 3D reference points was also introduced for more accurate estimation of 3D positions. Our results show that accuracy of the 3D human pose estimated by the framework was acceptable to determine whether the operator performed the picking task properly or not. Furthermore, the framework can be applied to the evaluation of the physical workload on the operator. Future work will include extending the framework to monitor the actual drug picking tasks.

REFERENCES

[1] A. H. Lavan, P. F. Gallagher, and D. O'Mahony, "Methods to reduce prescribing errors in elderly patients with multimorbidity," Clinical Interventions in Aging, vol. 11, pp. 857-866, Jun. 2016, doi:10.2147/CIA.S80280

[2] G. P. Velo and P. Minuz, "Medication errors: prescribing faults and prescription errors," British Journal of Clinical Pharmacology, vol. 67, No. 6, pp. 624-628, Jun. 2009, doi: 10.1111/j.1365-2125.2009.03425.x

[3] J. L. Schnipper et al, "Role of pharmacist counseling in preventing adverse drug events after hospitalization," Archives of Internal Medicine, vol. 166, No. 5, pp. 565-71, Mar. 2006, doi: 10.1001/archinte.166.5.565

[4] M. D. Murray, M. E. Ritchey, J. Wu, and W. Tu, "Effect of a pharmacist on adverse drug events and medication errors in outpatients with cardiovascular disease," Archives of Internal Medicine, vol 169, No. 8, pp. 757-63, Apr. 2009, doi:10.1001/archinternmed.2009.59

[5] S. Shao et al, "Workload of pharmacists and the performance of pharmacy services," PLoS ONE, vol. 15, No. 4, pp. 1-12, Apr. 2020, doi:10.1371/journal.pone.0231482

[6] D. C. Malone et al, "Pharmacist workload and pharmacy characteristics associated with the dispensing of potentially clinically important drug-drug interactions," Medical Care, vol. 45, No. 5, pp. 456-462, May. 2007, doi:10.1097/01.mlr.0000257839.83765.07

[7] A. D. Nasution and E. L. Mahyuni, "The impact of work method on musculoskeletal disorders complaints in pharmacy unit," Disease Prevention and Public Health Journal, vol. 14, No. 2, pp. 81-89, Sept. 2020, doi:10.12928/dpphj.v14i2.2478

[8] Pharmaceutical Safety and Environmental Health Bureau, "The state of dispensing operations", https://www.mhlw.go.jp/content/000498352.pdf [retrieved: June, 2022] (in Japanese)

[9] E. G. Poon et al., "Effect of bar-code technology on the safety of medication administration,", The New England Journal of Medicine, Vol 362, pp. 1698-1707, May. 2010, doi: 10.1056/NEJMsa0907115

[10] AIOI SYSTEMS CO., LTD, "Projection Picking System," https://www.hello-aioi.com/en/solution/digital_picking/projection/pps/ [retrieved: June, 2022]

[11] N. Nakano et al., "Evaluation of 3D markerless motion capture accuracy using OpenPose with multiple video cameras," Front. Sports Act. Living, vol 2, pp. 1-9, May. 2020, doi:10.3389/fspor.2020.00050

[12] J. Bonkowski et al., "Effect of barcode-assisted medication administration on emergency department medication errors," Academic Emergency Medicine, vol. 20, pp. 801-806, Aug. 2013, doi: 10.1111/acem.12189

[13] S. C. Shieh, C. C. Lin, T. F. Yang, and G. H. Tu, "Using RFID technology on clinic's pharmacy operation management and development of intelligent medicine dispensing cabinet," 2008 IEEE International Conference on Industrial Engineering and Engineering Management, pp. 2006-2009, Dec. 2008, doi: 10.1109/IEEM.2008.4738223

[14] C. Han et al., "The assistance for drug dispensing using LED notification and IR sensor-based monitoring methods," 2018 9th International Conference on Awareness Science and Technology (iCAST), pp. 264-267, Sept. 2018, doi:10.1109/ICAwST.2018.8517168

[15] Microsoft Azure, "Azure Kinect DK," https://azure.microsoft.com/en-us/services/kinect-dk/ [retrieved: June, 2022]

[16] F. Zhang et al., "MediaPipe hands: on-device real-time hand tracking," pp. 1-5, Jun. 2020, arXiv:2006.10214

[17] Y. Ono and O. D. A. Prima, "Assessment of drug picking activity using RGB-D camera," The Fourteenth International Conference on Advances in Computer-Human Interactions, ACHI2021, pp. 6-11, 2021

[18] J. Martinez, R. Hossain, J. Romero, and J. J. Little, "A simple yet effective baseline for 3d human pose estimation," Proceedings of the IEEE International Conference on Computer Vision (ICCV), pp. 2640-2649, Oct. 2017

[19] G. Moon, J. Y. Chang, and K. M. Lee, "Camera distance-aware top-down approach for 3d multi-person pose estimation from a single RGB-image," Proceeding of the IEEE/CVF International Conference on Computer Vision (ICCV), pp. 10133-10142, Oct. 2019

[20] A. Sayo, D. Thomas, H. Kawasaki, Y. Nakashima, and K. Ikeuchi, "PoseRN: A 2D Pose Refinement Network For Bias-Free Multi-View 3D Human Pose Estimation," 2021 IEEE International Conference on Image Processing (ICIP), pp. 3233-3237, Sept. 2021, doi:10.1109/ICIP42928.2021.9506022

[21] Z. Cao, G. Hidalgo, T. Simon, S. Wei, and Y. Shikh, "OpenPose: realtime multi-person 2D pose estimation using Part Affinity Fields," arXiv preprint, pp. 1-14, 2018, arXiv:1812.08008v2

[22] B. D. Lucas and T. Kanade, "An interative image registration technique with an application to stereo vision," Proc. the 7th international joint conference on Artificial intelligence, vol. 2, pp. 674-679, Aug. 1981, doi:10.5555/1623264.1623280

Assessment of Differences in Human Depth Understanding Between Stereo and Motion Parallax Cues in Light-Field Displays

Raymond Swannack, Oky Dicky Ardiansyah Prima
Graduate School of Software and Information Science
Iwate Prefectural University
152-52 Takizawa, Iwate, Japan
e-mail: g231s501@s.iwate-pu.ac.jp, prima@iwate-pu.ac.jp

***Abstract*—As Three-Dimensional (3D) digital content has become widely recognized, virtual and augmented realities have received a lot of attention. The Light-Field display (LFD), which allows users to view stereoscopic images from multiple viewpoints at the same time, provides a new 3D experience. LFDs are complicated to set up, but this display has been made available for personal use. This study aims to evaluate the differences in task accomplishment between stereo versus motion-parallax cues for users performing 3D interactions on a multi-view display. Our task scenario involves user tests for 3D alignment accuracy and questionnaires about the experience during the test. For each task, 3D contents are presented in stereo and motion parallax cue presentation, respectively, using the LFD "Lume Pad" developed by Leia Inc. Results on six subjects showed that task alignment could be achieved with greater accuracy when stereo cues were available. Questionnaires showed that depth perception appeared to be easier with stereo cues. Future work will include observing whether LFDs provide better 3D perception than current Virtual Reality (VR) devices.**

Keywords-3D, Light-Field Display; 3D human perception; motion-parallax; stereoscopic vision.

I. Introduction

The human ability to view and understand three dimensions allows us to interact with the world in detail. Translating this to the digital field has not been an easy task. A Two-Dimensional (2D) screen does not have true depth to it, so the human eye does not interact with objects on a screen the same as it would with an object in the real world [1].

There are nine widely agreed upon sources of information that the brain uses for perceiving depth. They are as follows, binocular disparity, convergence, occlusion, relative size, height in the visual field, relative density, aerial perspective, accommodation, and motion parallax [2]. To a greater or lesser extent, they are used in conveying depth in a 2D screen, and it is the manipulation of these sources that forms the basis of 3D displays. There are many different types of 3D displays, each being varied to suit different tasks.

VR headsets are Head Mounted Displays (HMDs) that have had the most exposure in popular culture. Popularity of products such as the HTC VIVE and Facebook's Oculus are seeing use both in entertainment as well as scientific research. Augmented Reality (AR) headsets, such as HoloLens by Microsoft, are becoming more well-known as well. VR and head-mounted AR displays use similar concepts where they display slightly different images to each eye. Both rely heavily on binocular disparity to create stereopsis, as well as motion parallax.

Hand-held displays are largely composed of smartphones and tablets. Some are specifically designed as AR devices while others have apps, such as Pokémon Go and IKEA Place, that use the inbuilt camera to give the appearance of projecting their scenes into the real world. These rely largely on height in the visual field for the user to believe that what they are looking at is real.

Another form of 3D display is LFDs. An LFD uses lenticular lenses to bend the light coming out of the screen of the display, giving a different view to each eye. In this way, they work similarly to head mounted displays but perform this job without the need for a headset.

The rest of the paper is structured as follows. In Section II, we present the details of the LFD hardware used in the experiment. Section III details the experiment methodology, such as the design concept as well as the software and hardware used. The results for the experiment and the questionnaire are given in Section IV. Finally, we conclude our work in Section V, with our conclusion and future work.

II. Lume Pad

This research was performed on the Lume Pad, the LFD tablet by Leia Inc. This allows users to see the illusion of depth inside of a 2D screen by showing each eye a different image, creating stereopsis. The tablet boasts a 10.1-inch screen with a resolution of 2560x1600 pixels. To create the light field effect, the tablet displays four views at a time and uses the lenticular lenses to allow the user to see two of these images at a time. This gives the user the best of both the HMD-typed VR set up, as well as the tablet-typed AR device. The Lume Pad displays what looks like a real 3D image to multiple users at one time.

To generate the different views, the Lume Pad generates four views in 2x2 grids. Each image has a resolution of 640x400 pixels but is displayed in such a way as to be perceived as having a higher resolution [3].

The device dissects the images and displays them under lenticular lenses so that the user sees different images with each eye. This achieves stereoscopy and gives the user the perception of depth within the 2D screen.

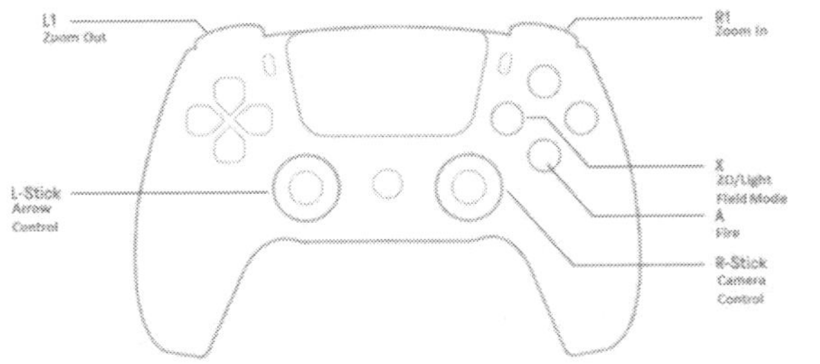

Figure 1. Sony Dual Sense Controller - Button layout.

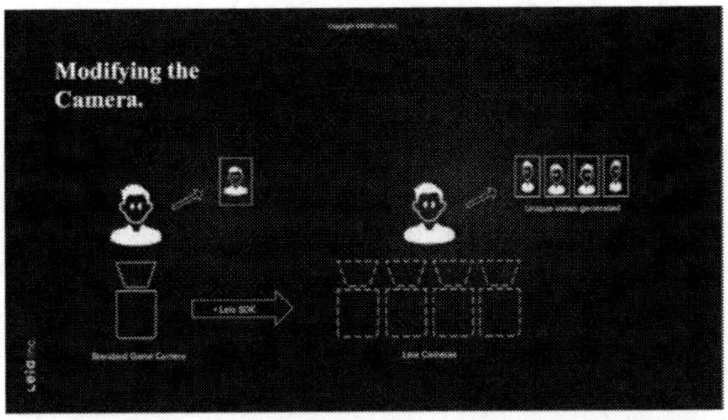

Figure 2. Scene-Camera layout for optimal Lume Pad experience [3].

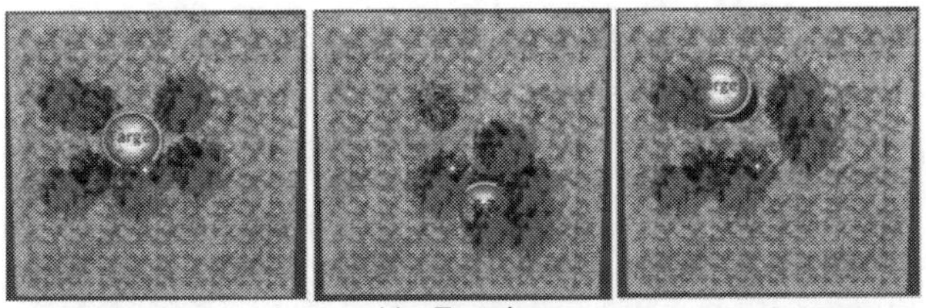

(a) Top view.

(b) Side view.

Figure 3. Scenes from different angles used in the experiment.

III. Experiment

In this study, the test was conducted using the Lume Pad for the display and a Sony Dual Sense controller for user input. Subjects were given control of an arrow and needed to aim it at a target that appears at a point above the arrow. This target is at a set y position and is offset by some distance in the x and z directions. The right control stick controls the arrow, allowing the user to rotate it to be facing the target to the best of their ability. The left stick controls the scene rotation, but it can only rotate the scene-camera around the center point on the horizontal axis. The right shoulder button zooms the camera in while the left zooms the camera out. The southern button is used to fire the arrow while the western button changes the display from stereo to motion parallax mode and back again. The button layout can be seen in Figure 1.

Subjects were forced to focus on horizontal angles because the scene could only be rotated horizontally. Since the Lume Pad has four horizontal and two vertical views, the decision was made to put more focus on the horizontal axis. To further increase the difficulty of the test, a large rock is placed behind the arrow so that the subject must view the scene from different angles to understand the direction that the arrow is facing. There are five trees that are placed within the scene, so that some sight lines will be blocked. In addition, the target starts relatively close to the center of the scene, near the arrow's starting point, and gets further away with each attempt.

Our experiment was designed using the Leia Unity Software Development Kit (SDK) [4]. The SDK allows to utilize the Lume Pad's features, such as the special lenticular camera, as seen in Figure 2. Moreover, the screen can be switched from stereo to motion parallax mode with a press of a button.

The experiment was carried out as follows. First, the subject is presented with a scene where the target is in random positions x and z and the trees are all in random positions. This allows the subject to learn the controls of the experiment and familiarize themselves with how to look around the scene. The results of this first attempt are ignored so the subject was encouraged to take their time and ask questions. After this practice, the subject was asked to perform three more attempts. These attempts will be the same for every user, with no random elements. The layouts for these attempts can be seen in Figure 3.

Each subject was seated at a desk, positioned between 45-50 cm from the tablet. This is the distance that Leia Inc states is the best viewing distance for the Lume Pad tablet. The tablet was then angled towards the subject's face to maximize the light-field effect.

For the experiment, there were 12 subjects (three females and nine males). They ranged in age from 22 to 31 with an average age of 25. All had normal or corrected-to-normal vision. They were split into two groups, one group would see the scene in motion parallax first, followed by the scene in stereo. This group did their practice attempt on the motion parallax version and then after their three actual attempts, the display was switched to stereo mode for the final three attempts. The second group was shown the stereo version for their practice attempt and first three actual attempts, followed by the motion parallax version for the final three attempts.

Accuracy is measured based on Euclidean distance, with a lower score being desirable.

$$Distance = \sqrt{(x_1 - x_2)^2 + (z_1 - z_2)^2} \qquad (1)$$

Here, x_1 and z_1 correspond to the position of the target while x_2 and z_2 to the final location of the arrow. The unit of measure for the experiment is Unity units (m).

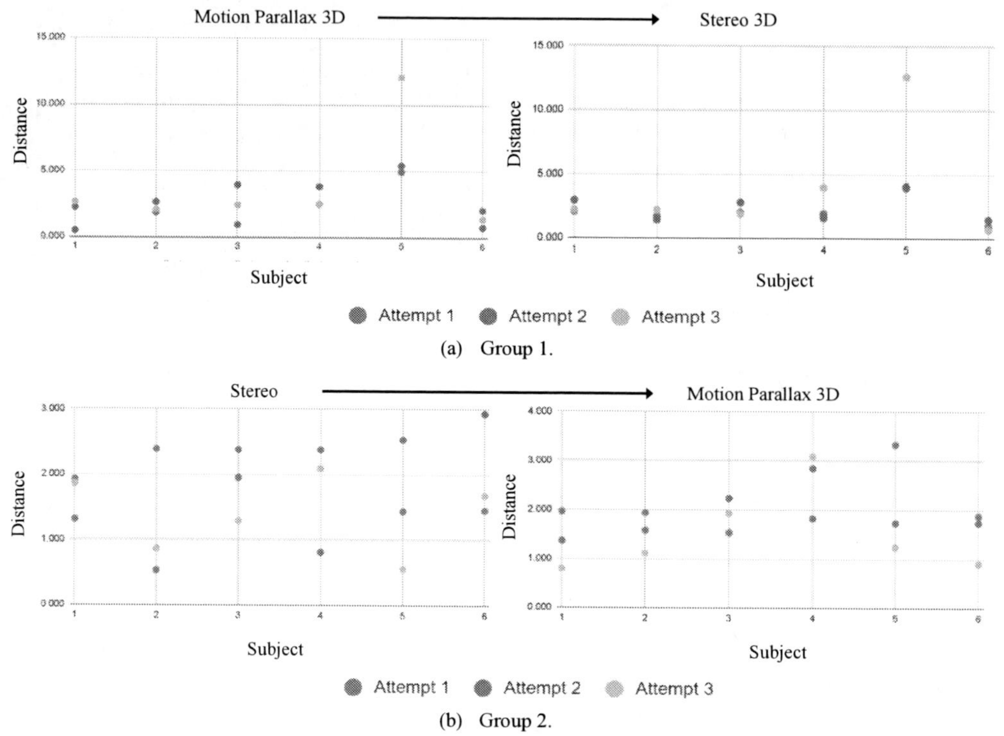

Figure 4. Experiment results.

IV. RESULTS

Figure 4 shows the results of the experiments. Each subject is displayed on their own line, where attempts 1, 2, and 3 are in blue, red, and yellow, respectively. The direction of the arrows in the figure indicates the order of the experiment performed by the subject. Group 1 shows the results for the motion parallax attempts followed by the stereo attempts, while Group 2 shows the results for the stereo attempts followed by the motion parallax attempts. Group 1 was more accurate than Group 2. There is an argument to be made that Group 1 learned the test during the motion parallax attempts so it made sense that they would do better at the second round of attempts, the stereo portion of the test. The fact that Group two was more accurate during the stereo attempts as well, even though it is marginal, disproves this at least to some level.

Subjects were also given a questionnaire to ascertain how well they believed they had understood the test as well as how the test made them feel. The questions were as follows:

a. How well do you feel that you understood the scene? Did you know where everything was?
b. How confident were you in your aim? Did you think you would be close to the target?
c. How much discomfort did you feel? Did your eyes hurt? Did you feel sick?
d. Could you see the 3D effect? Do you feel a 3D sensation?

Subjects were given the same questions to answer after both the stereo and motion parallax tests. They were asked to give an answer on a Likert-typed scale from 1 to 5, where 1 was not at all or no and 5 was completely. On average subjects felt like they understood the scene more in the stereo mode as well as feeling more confident in their accuracy. Some users felt discomfort or sickness from the test, specifically in the stereo mode. More subjects from Group 1 felt discomfort than in Group 2. One subject stated that they felt dizzy after switching from motion parallax to stereo mode. Another subject said they could not see the 3D effect, though they had very high accuracy and moved the camera around frequently in the tests to make sure they were as accurate as possible.

V. CONCLUSION AND FUTURE WORK

In this study, we examined how accurate a user could be, given some constraints, in a stereo and a motion parallax environment. While the subjects were more accurate with the stereo attempts, it is not conclusive that the human brain understands distance in the light field display more so than on a motion parallax display.

To improve on this test, the next step will be to add eye tracking. We did not measure eye movement and eye vergence in this test. Both would give us a better understanding of how well individuals understood the scene they were interacting with [5].

Another concept which we plan to investigate is a multiscreen display. The pCubee [6] display is a cube shaped display, created by the University of British Colombia, that utilizes trackers to alter the display for a single user's perspective. Combining this with the light field effect should make for a very believable 3D display.

A point to be weary of is how much this technology relies on stereoscopic vision. There is an overabundance of depth cues that can confuse the human brain [7]. It is unclear if this affected the subjects in this test.

REFERENCES

[1] K. Kato and O. D. A. Prima, "3D Gaze Characteristics in Mixed-Reality Environment," eTELEMED 2021 : The Thirteenth International Conference on EHealth, Telemedicine, and Social Medicine, IARIA, pp.11-15, 2021.

[2] J. E. Cutting and P. M. Vishton, "Perceiving Layout and Knowing Distances : The Integration, Relative Potecney, and Contextual Use of Different Information about Depth," Percept. Sp. Motion, 22(5), pp. 69-117, 1995.

[3] 3D Lightfield Experience Platform, https://www.leiainc.com/ [Retrieved at May 2022]

[4] SDK and Developer Resources, www.leiainc.com/sdk. [Retrieved at 10 June 2022]

[5] E. Mlot, H. Bahmani, S. Wahl, and E. Kasneci, "3D Gaze Estimation Using Eye Vergence," Proceedings of the 9th International Joint Conference on Biomedical Engineering Systems and Technologies (BIOSTEC 2016), 5, pp. 125-131, 2016.

[6] Stavness, I., Lam, B., & Fels, S. (2010, April). pCubee: a perspective-corrected handheld cubic display. In Proceedings of the SIGCHI Conference on Human Factors in Computing Systems (pp. 1381-1390).

[7] T. S. Murdison, G. Leclercq, P. Lefèvre, and G. Blohm, "Misperception of Motion in Depth Originates from an Incomplete Transformation of Retinal Signals," Journal of vision 19(12), pp. 21-21, 2019.

Detection of Pinbones in Japanese Shime-saba

Hisayoshi Ito Oky Dicky Ardiansyah Prima Takehiro Sasaki
Graduate School of Software and Information Science
Iwate Prefectural University
152-52, Sugo, Takizawa, Iwate, Japan
e-mail: {hito, prima}@iwate-pu.ac.jp, g231t201@s.iwate-pu.ac.jp

***Abstract*—Shime-saba is a Japanese seafood marinated in salt and rice vinegar, which makes it last longer and gives it a sashimi-like flavor. The vinegar softens most bones, but pinbones remain hard and need to be removed. The food processing industry manually removes these bones. However, this process needs to be automated to cope with the shortage of human resources. This study attempts to detect the location of the tips of pinbones by using infrared imaging techniques to highlight bone features and quantifying these features based on image geometry. The shape of the response image obtained by correlating the gaussian template image to the infrared-irradiated shime-saba image revealed that the tip of the remaining bone resembled convex-up shapes. These shapes were detected by applying a quadratic surface equation to the resulting image after pre-processed, allowing the location of the tips of pinbones to be determined by picking their maxima. Future work will include a deep learning solution to improve the detection accuracy of pinbones.**

Keywords-fishbone; infrared imaging; bone detection; image geometry; template matching; computer vision.

I. Introduction

Improvements in quality inspection and food supply chain visualization have become necessary to guarantee the safety and quality of food products as well as their traceability. Methods have been developed to automate these tasks to accomplish these tasks more efficiently and cost-effectively [1]. Robotics can play an important role as a solution. However, the food industry has been slow to adopt robotics relative to others. The use of robots instead of people in food processing is expected to have many tangible, intangible, social, and economic benefits [2][3]. Hygiene and safety risks, as well as high labor and social costs, will drive the adoption of robots in the food industry.

Fish and fishery products have long been a large part of the Japanese diet. Traditional Japanese seafood preparations include the shime-saba (mackerel marinated with sugar, salt and rice vinegar) and dried or salted fish for preservation. Raw foods such as sashimi and sushi, as well as deep-fried foods such as tempura, have also enriched Japanese food culture [4]. Hachinohe City, Aomori Prefecture is the center of production of shime-saba. It was the first city in Japan to begin producing shime-saba in 1968. Although the number of mackerel landings is decreasing, the production of shime-saba is on the uptrend.

The food industry in Japan is suffering from a chronic shortage of labor. While there are efforts to actively introduce robots, it is difficult for small and medium-sized companies to consider introducing robots by themselves. The processing of shime-saba requires human intervention to remove the bones remaining in the fish body. Vinegar can soften most bones, but the middle bone remains hard and must be removed manually, as shown in Figure 1. This work is physically demanding because of the long hours spent standing. In addition, more workers are needed to ensure production capacity.

The objective of this study is to develop an image sensing system that detects the pinbone tips of shime-saba to assist the deboning robot. Our system identifies the tip of the bone by analyzing features from fillet image of shime-saba taken by a camera that can capture images in both visible and near-infrared light. The shape geometry of the fillet image is analyzed from its features, and the geometry representing the tip of the bone is automatically identified. Finally, we will discuss the implementation of this system and consider further improvements in detection accuracy.

The rest of this paper is organized as follows. Section II describes related works on fish bone detection using image sensing techniques. Section III describes our proposed method for detecting pinbone tips from near-infrared transmitted images. Section IV summarizes our results. Finally, Section V concludes our work.

II. Related Works

Traditionally, tweezers or needle nose pliers have been used to remove bones from fish fillets. Today, hand-held pin bones have been made available, allowing for easier manual deboning. To use these machines to remove bone, the tip of the bone must first be located. Therefore, an important step in the automation of bone removal is to find the bone tip.

Image sensing techniques such as X-ray, Ultraviolet (UV), and infrared spectroscopy have been proposed for detecting fish bones. Mery et al. (2011) developed an X-ray machine vision approach to detect fish bones in fish fillets [5]. Their device is a digital radiography system consisting of an X-ray source and a flat panel detector. Filter banks including Discrete Fourier Transform (DFT), Discrete Cosine Transform (DCT), and Gabor were used to extract features from the resulting X-ray images. The results showed that by photographing the fish bones, which are arranged in strips and range from 14 mm to 47 mm in length, these bones can be detected with a high accuracy. Wang et al. (2015) investigated the fluorescent properties of cod bone under UV irradiation and found that the optimum wavelengths of excitation and

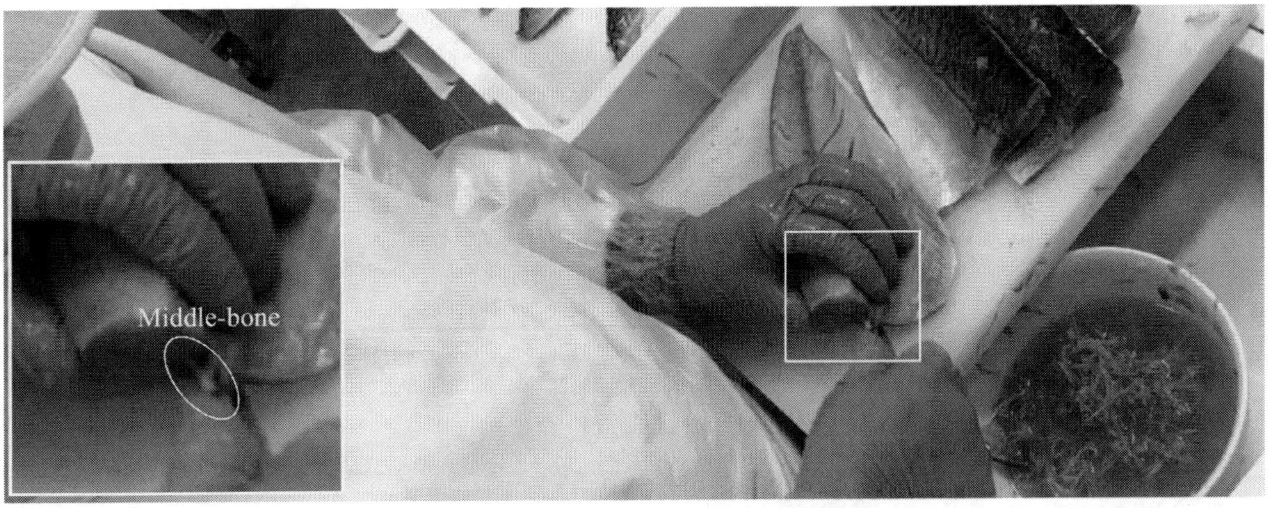

Figure 1. Removal of the remaining middle-bone from the shime-saba manually.

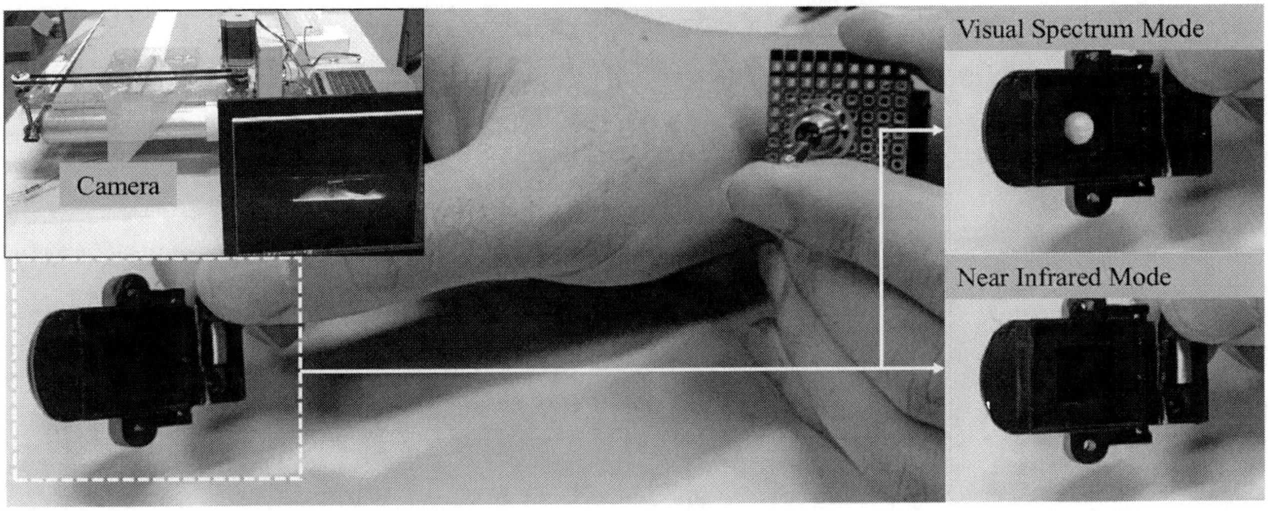

Figure 2. The device for NIR imaging in this study.

emission were 320 nm and 515 nm. They were the first to develop UV fluorescence-assisted candling for detecting fish bones, but the detection accuracy was lower than that of X-ray-based techniques [6]. Wei et al. (2018) used infrared spectroscopy to identify fish bone contents in surimi. The absorption peak in the infrared spectrum at around 9,890 nm wavelength was observed from fish bones. Song et al. (2019) proposed a fish bone detection based on Raman hyperspectral imaging technique to improve detection rate and achieve automatic detection [7]. This technique was found to effectively detect fish bones down to a depth of 2.5 mm.

The above optical sensing at various wavelengths has been used to bring up the feature values of fish bones in an attempt to locate the position of the bones in the body of the fish. However, putting these technologies to practical use in food processing facilities is problematic due to their high cost. Furthermore, while it can detect bones of a certain length, it is not capable of detecting objects where only the tip of the bone can be seen.

III. METHODS

In this study, we focus on the broad application of near-infrared light to food analysis, based on various sample presentation techniques [8]. In addition to reflection, Near Infrared Ray (NIR) absorbed and transmitted from the sample may be used to detect the presence or absence of pinbones in the fish body. Here, we attempt to detect the tips of pinbones by photographing the NIR transmitted through the fish body.

A. Image Acquisition

The device for NIR imaging in this study is shown in Figure 2. The camera can capture images in the wavelength

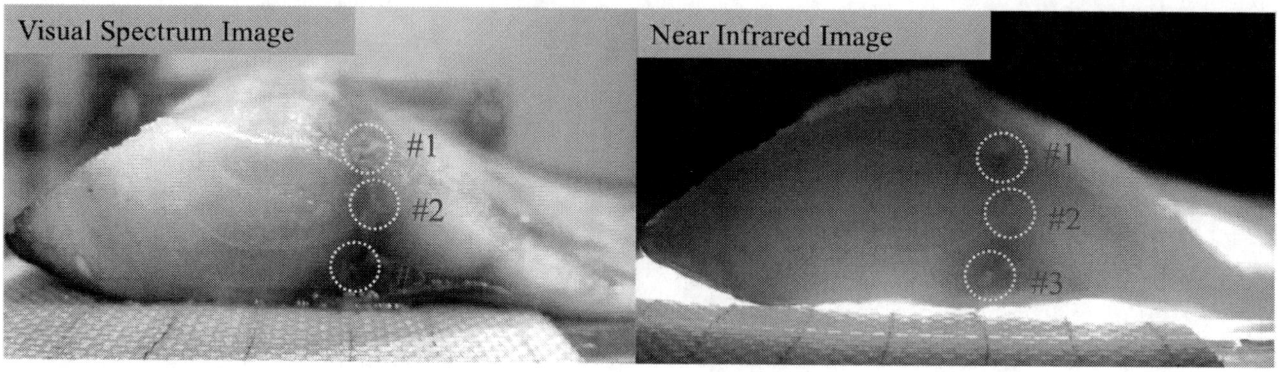

Figure 3. Three bones in the shime-saba to be deboned.

Figure 4. The response image obtained by pre-processing.

range from visible spectrum to near-infrared spectrum. To obtain images in each band, an infrared filter is attached to the camera lens. By switching these filters electronically, both visible and near-infrared images of the fish body can be captured. For the NIR source, 840-nm near-infrared LEDs were used.

As shown in Figure 3, there are three pinbones in the shime-saba mackerel to be deboned. The presence of these bones is not clear in the visible spectrum image, so boning staff must touch the fillet to check for their presence. In contrast, the NIR image reveals features at the tip of the pinbone.

B. Pre-processing

To enhance the features of the bone tips in the NIR images, these images were correlated with a Gaussian template image. This template image produces a response image with the region of image maxima as the convex-up region of the image. As shown in Figure 4, the obtained response image shows that the region at the tip of the bone is clear as a convex-up image. The extent of the convex structure can be adjusted by changing the size of the Gaussian template image.

C. Detection of Bone Tips Using Qudratic Surface

Given the above observation, we developed a morphometric characterization algorithm to determine geomorphometric features (e.g., peaks, pits, ravines, or ridges) from the derived response images. The quadratic surface is fitted to the image within a moving local analysis window using least-squares [9], with the general equation being

$$z = f(x, y) = Ax^2 + Bxy + Cy^2 + Dx + Ey + F \quad (1)$$

where (x, y) is the location's coordinate, z is the pixel value calculated by the quadratic function, and A to F are the coefficients of the quadratic function. By analyzing the second-order coefficients A to C, the shape of the quadratic surface can be characterized as follows.

$$\text{Elliptic paraboloid:} \quad B^2 - 4AC < 0 \quad (2)$$

$$\text{Hyperbolic paraboloid:} \quad B^2 - 4AC > 0 \quad (3)$$

$$\text{Parabolic paraboloid:} \quad B^2 - 4AC = 0 \quad (4)$$

Here, if A=B=C=0 then the quadratic is a plane. Equation (2) divides the quadratic surface into convex-up and concave-up. If the center of the convex-up surface is within the analysis window, this surface can be determined as the peak. Hence, this property can be used to determine the location of the pinbone tips from the response image.

IV. Experiments and Results

Experiments were conducted to detect pin bones in non-processed shime-saba using the equipment shown in Figure 2. Since the pinbones are in the center of the fillet, this region was preprocessed as a Region-of-Interest (ROI) and used to approximate the quadratic surfaces. Figure 5 shows the candidate pinbones detected in the fillet. There are several convex-up regions in the ROI, but the five candidates with the largest difference in convexity were displayed. Among these candidates, the presence of the pinbones were confirmed. Thus, the five convex-up candidates from the sample of fillets used in this study can be used to narrow down the candidates for the correct pinbone locations. At this point, we will continue to work on how to select the correct pinbone from among the candidates.

V. Conclusion

In this study, an image sensing system for detecting the pinbone tips of shime-saba was developed. By analyzing the surface geometry of a fillet transmitted by near-infrared ray,

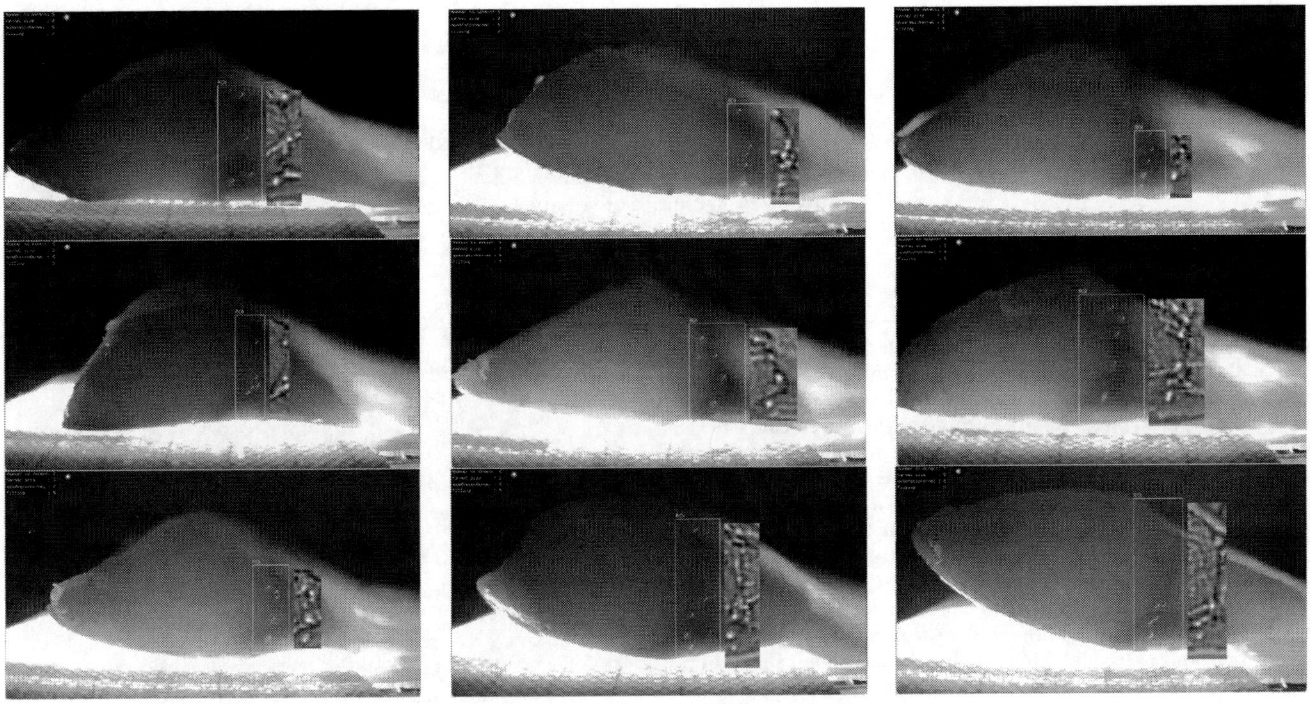

Figure 5. Candidates for the pinbones in shime-saba.

we were able to identify convex-up shapes that represent the tips of the bones. At this point, we were able to narrow down the convex shapes in the center of the fish body to five in order of size. The future focus will be on identifying tips of the bones from the candidates identified by the current system, including deep learning solutions.

ACKNOWLEDGMENT

This work was supported by the IoT Human Resource Development Support Project of Iwate Prefecture, Japan.

REFERENCES

[1] C. Alejandro, "Food Analysis: Present, Future, and Foodomics," International Scholarly Research Network (ISRN) Analytical Chemistry, pp. 1-16, 2012.

[2] P . Graham, "Robotic Equipment in the Meat Industry," Meat Science, 49(1), pp. 297-307, 1998.

[3] H. Einarsdottir, B. Guoundsson, and V. Omarsson, "Automation in the fish industry," Animal Frontiers, 12(2), pp. 32–39, 2022.

[4] Fish-Loving Food Culture Refreshed, https://www.gov-online.go.jp/eng/publicity/book/hlj/html/201804/201804_07_en.html [retrieved at May 2022]

[5] D. Mery, et al., "Automated fish bone detection using X-ray imaging," Journal of Food Engineering, 105(3), pp. 485–492, 2011, https://doi.org/10.1016/j.jfoodeng.2011.03.007

[6] S. Wang, R. Nian, L. Cao, J. Sui, and H. Lin, "Detection of fish bones in cod fillets by UV illumination," Journal of Food Protection, 78(7), pp. 1414–1419, 2015. https://doi.org/10.4315/0362-028X.JFP-14-358

[7] S. Song, et al., "Detection of fish bones in fillets by Raman hyperspectral imaging technology," Journal of Food Engineering, 272, pp. 1-10, 2019. https://doi.org/10.1016/j.jfoodeng.2019.109808

[8] B. G. Osborne, "Near-Infrared Spectroscopy in Food Analysis," Encyclopedia of Analytical Chemistry, pp. 1–14, 2006. https://doi.org/10.1002/9780470027318.a1018

[9] D. Wang, S. W. Laffan, Y. Liu, and L. Wu, "Morphometric characterisation of landform from DEMs," International Journal of Geographical Information Science, 24(2), pp. 305–326, 2010. https://doi.org/10.1080/13658810802467969.

Egg Surface Inspection Using Infrared Transmitted Light Images

Hisayoshi Ito Oky Dicky Ardiansyah Prima
Faculty of Software and Information Science
Iwate Prefectural University
Takizawa, Iwate, Japan
e-mail: {hito, prima}@iwate-pu.ac.jp

Abstract—**Factories that mass-produce boiled eggs do not use eggs with minute surface irregularities as out-of-spec eggs in order to reduce the risk of damage during transportation. The inspection is performed visually by human workers to check for abnormalities, but this is a heavy burden on the workers because of the number of eggs they handle. In this study, a method to detect minute irregularities in eggshells using transmitted infrared light was attempted. By using an infrared camera to capture images of infrared light transmitted into the egg, we were able to detect areas where the shell was locally thicker. In the future, we plan to try deep learning to detect irregularities distributed on the sides near parallel to the optical axis of the camera by matching the three-dimensional shape of the shell measured by a 3D scanner with the transmitted infrared light image.**

Keywords-boiled eggs; surface inspection; infrared light; protrusions; image processing.

I. INTRODUCTION

Currently, boiled eggs are produced and shipped in large quantities daily as a food product. In addition to preventing eggs from being damaged during transportation, the surface of boiled eggs as a product must be free of blemishes and stains to maintain their good appearance as a product. For example, if the surface of the shell has a different color than the rest of the shell, it is out-of-spec as having stains. Similarly, any unevenness on the surface of the shell that exceeds the standard is called "Zara" (which means roughness) and is considered out-of-spec. Figure 1 shows the uneven surface of an egg, which has many protrusions. These out-of-spec eggs are removed before boiling and used as raw materials for other egg products. Thus, the quality inspection of eggs for the production of boiled eggs requires a more detailed inspection of the surface texture, unlike the inspection for cracks and stains on the shell, which is conducted to guarantee food safety.

Thus, in producing boiled eggs, it is necessary to remove off-spec eggs before processing them according to the established standards. Currently, workers visually inspect the eggs to remove out-of-spec. However, in a certain boiled egg production plant, the process is not as thorough as it should be. A certain boiled egg factory produces 150,000 boiled eggs per day, and a larger number of them must be inspected in advance. This is a heavy burden for even the most experienced workers. In addition, the temperature and humidity inside the boiling egg factory are high due to the handling of boiling water, and the workers are fatigued when they work in clean clothing. As described above, the high workload, including environmental aspects, may affect the accuracy of the inspection. In response to the above issues, we believe that if the detecting and removing process could be automated, it would not only improve the efficiency of boiled egg production but also solve the problems caused by the shortage of human resources.

Figure 1. Protrusions on the egg surface.

This study focuses on the inspection of egg surface irregularities and aims to develop a method to automate the process of removing out-of-spec. Specifically, we propose a method to inspect the surface of the shell from an image of the egg taken by infrared transmitted light and to detect out-of-spec eggs when the number of irregularities exceeds a standard.

The rest of this study is organized as follows: Section II describes the existing methods for egg quality inspection; Section III describes the egg surface inspection method used in this study; Section IV describes the relationship between the image features obtained by the proposed method and the egg surface features. Section V summarizes this study and discusses prospects.

II. RELATED WORKS

Visual inspection has been used in the egg inspection process. The main purpose of this method is to assure the quality of food products by checking whether there are any abnormalities on the surface or inside. However, the accuracy of this method, which relies on human skill, depends on the skill and fatigue of the inspector and the environment of the inspection site. Therefore, attempts have been made to automate the inspection process and sort out eggs that do not meet a certain level of quality.

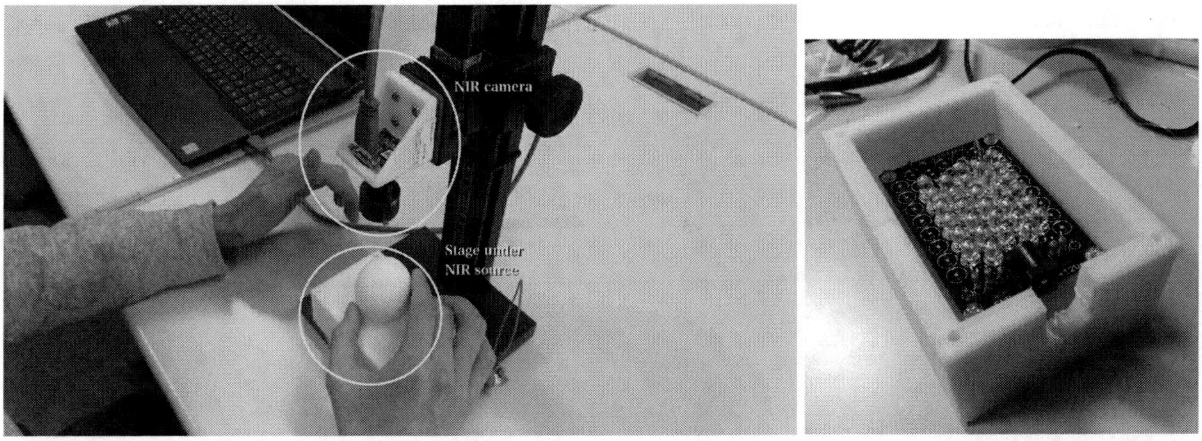

Figure 2. The device for NIR imaging.

A typical inspection method is candling. The method of checking freshness by shining light on eggs and using the color of the yolk inside as a guide [1] has been used for many years. Liu *et al.* [2] developed a method to inspect freshness by measuring the spectrum of light transmitted through the interior of the egg. They used the ultraviolet and visible (UV/VIS 200–800 nm) spectrum as the light source. On the other hand, De Katelaere *et al.* [3] proposed a method for detecting cracks on the surface using the analysis of frequency response by acoustic measurement when the shell is subjected to mechanical impact. For inspecting surface conditions, Wang *et al.* [4] used the surface image of the eggshell to detect black spots, and Wang *et al.* [5] examined a neural network to detect contamination.

These previous studies aimed to ensure the safety of eggs as food by detecting blood or meat spots inside or by inspecting relatively large cracks or stains on the surface. On the other hand, eggs that have passed these inspections are received at the plant where boiled eggs are produced, and it is required to detect even finer irregularities. This is because the protrusions on the surface of the shell are easily affected by vibration during transportation, and there is a high risk of cracking. To reduce the risk of product breakage, only eggs with smooth surfaces should be used as material. Furthermore, eggs with even a slight lack of smoothness in appearance will be shunned by consumers because of their poor appearance. There are no existing studies aimed at detecting the fine texture of eggs that meet these conditions.

III. Methods

In this study, we focus on the wide application of near-infrared light to food analysis, based on various sample presentation techniques [6]. In addition to reflection, Near-Infrared Ray (NIR) absorbed and transmitted from the sample may be used to detect the internal state of the eggshell. Here, we attempt to analyze the surface shape of the shell by photographing the NIR transmitted through the egg.

A. Image Acquisition

The device for NIR imaging in this study is shown in Figure 2. As shown on the right side of the figure, the NIR light source is under the stage where the eggs are placed, and the NIR light transmitted from the light source through the eggs is captured by a camera mounted directly above the stage. Near-infrared LEDs with a wavelength of 840 nm were used as light sources. The eggs were photographed in two ways: face up or face down. Therefore, the image acquired in this case was always centered directly above or below the egg, with the sides of the egg at the periphery.

Figure 3 and Figure 4 show examples of images captured by this device. The brightness of each pixel is determined by the thickness of the eggshell, not by the egg's internal structure. High brightness areas indicate that the shell is relatively thin, while low brightness areas indicate that the shell is thicker than the surrounding area.

Figure 3 shows an image of a good surface quality egg with an even texture. Although there are differences in brightness and darkness, the brightness is within a certain range. On the other hand, Figure 4 is an image of the surface of a substandard egg with deep irregularities. There are some darker areas in the image, as indicated by circles. Those areas are where the shell is thicker, indicating the appearance of protrusions on the surface.

B. Thresholding

Areas with large changes in shell thickness are deeply uneven and have a coarse texture. Using this feature, the size of the area occupied by areas with large changes in brightness can be used as a criterion for judging whether an egg is out-of-spec or not.

The acquired NIR image is binarized with predefined threshold L, and then shrunk and expanded to remove noise, leaving blobs. Figure 5 shows the resulting blobs superimposed on the original image. In this figure, the blobs are drawn as yellow areas.

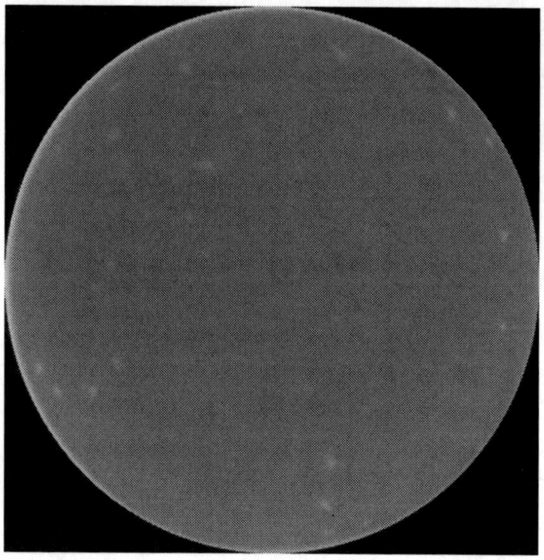

Figure 3. Captured NIR Image of an egg with a good shell.

C. Blob Detection

As shown in Figure 5, the blobs remained in the low-lightness areas annotated in Figure 4, indicating that this process correctly detects out-of-spec eggs. On the other hand, a large blob remains on the left side. This is because the amount of transmitted light was low when the image was taken and the overall image was dark, which resulted in the blob being below the threshold value L. To judge out-of-spec eggs, we define a blob whose area is between S_{min} and S_{max} as a protrusive blob and judge an egg to be out-of-spec when the number of protrusive blobs exceeds the reference value.

IV. Experiments and Results

In this study, 10 eggs with good shells and 30 out-of-spec eggs were prepared, and NIR images were taken from above and below for each. As a result, 20 images were obtained for eggs suitable for producing boiled eggs, and 40 images were obtained for eggs unsuitable for producing boiled eggs. The processing of these images with the proposed method did not stably extract protrusive blobs for all images under the same threshold value L. This may be because the thickness of the shell differs from egg to egg and the amount of transmitted light varied. On the other hand, false positives of protrusive blobs were rarely observed for good eggs.

Figure 6 shows the change in the distribution of blobs as the threshold is varied. The same NIR image is used as the source for binarization in each column, and in each row, images are binarized with thresholds L=0.333, L=0.352, and L=0.376, respectively. These threshold values represent relative amounts when the highest brightness is set to 1. All of these eggs are out-of-spec, and the NIR images contain local dark spots. This figure shows that the percentage of shadow remaining as blobs varies greatly from egg to egg, and that

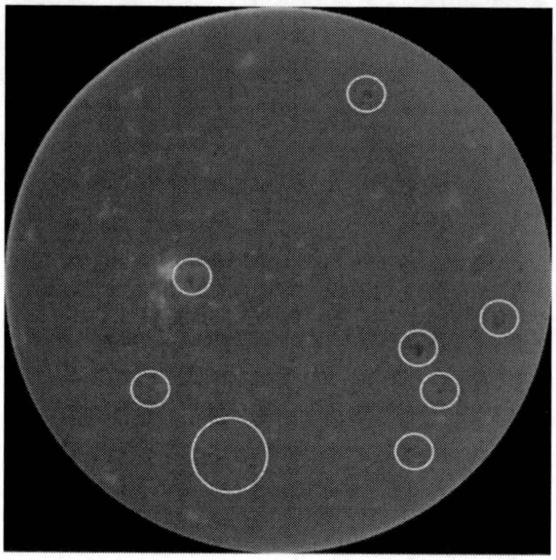

Figure 4. Captured NIR image of a substandard egg.

defining the threshold as a constant does not give good overall results.

As a general trend, blobs distributed in the center of the image were more appropriately detected. This may be because the sides of the shell are inclined to the image plane and occupy a small area in the image, making it difficult to detect their characteristics.

V. Conclusion

In this study, we developed a method for detecting

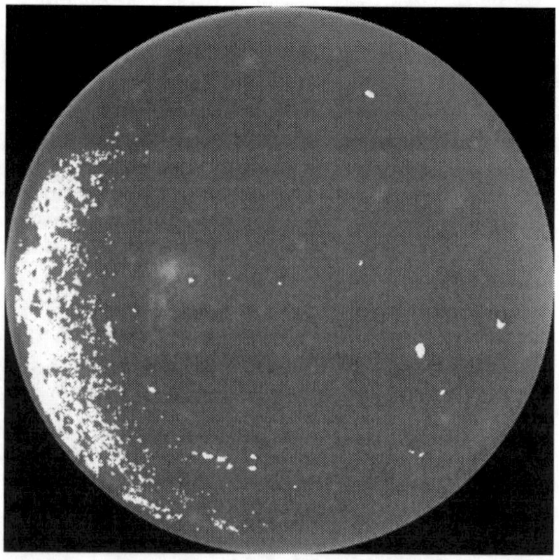

Figure 5. The result after image processing imposes the original.

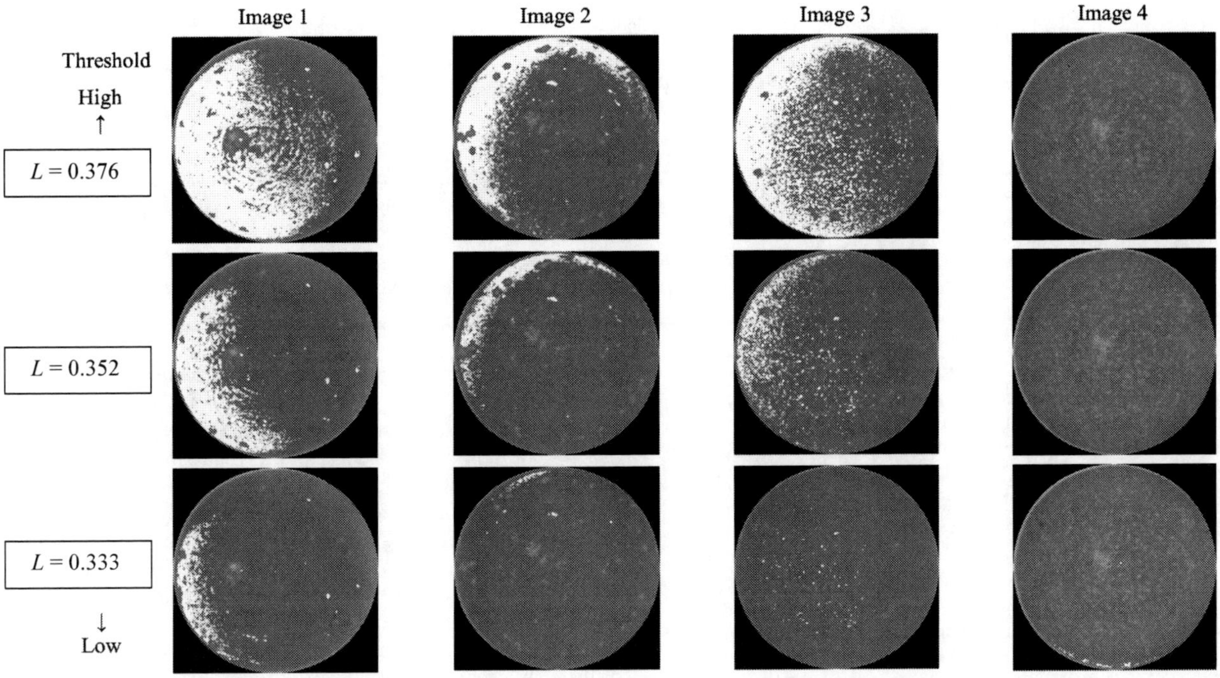

Figure 6. Distribution of blobs with different thresholds in processed NIR images of out-of-spec eggs.

irregularities on the surface of eggshells using transmitted infrared light. By analyzing the shape of the eggshell transmitted by near-infrared light, we were able to detect local thickness variations. In the future, we will try to match the NIR image with the three-dimensional shape of the shell acquired by a 3D scanner to deal with variations in the thickness of the entire shell and to detect protrusions near the sides of the shell. In addition, we will investigate more stable detection methods, including a solution that uses deep learning to estimate the three-dimensional shape of the shell from the infrared transmitted light images.

ACKNOWLEDGMENT

This work was done in collaboration with Iwate Eggdelica Co., Ltd. and the Faculty of Software and Information Science, Iwate Prefectural University.

REFERENCES

[1] S. L. Parker, S. S. Gossman, and W. A. Lippincott, "Studies on egg quality: I: Introductory note on variations in yolk color," Poultry Science, vol. 5, no.3, pp. 131-145., February 1926.

[2] Y. Liu, Y. Ying, A. Ouyang, and Y. Li, "Measurement of internal quality in chicken eggs using visible transmittance spectroscopy technology," Food Control, vol. 18, no. 1, pp. 18-22, January 2007., doi: 10.1016/j.foodcont.2005.07.011.

[3] B. De Ketelaere, P. Coucke, and J. De Baerdemaeker, "Eggshell Crack Detection based on Acoustic Resonance Frequency Analysis," Journal of Agricultural Engineering Research, vol. 76, no. 2, pp. 157-163, June 2000, doi: 10.1006/jaer.2000.0542.

[4] C. Wang, J. Zhou, H. Wu, J. Li, Z. Chunjiang and R. Liu, "Research on the Evaluation Method of Eggshell Dark Spots Based on Machine Vision," IEEE Access, vol. 8, pp. 160116-160125, 2020, DOI: 10.1109/ACCESS.2020.3020260.

[5] X. Wang, X. Yue, H. Li, and L. Meng, "A high-efficiency dirty-egg detection system based on YOLOv4 and TensorRT," 2021 International Conference on Advanced Mechatronic Systems (ICAMechS), pp. 75-80, 2021, doi: 10.1109/ICAMechS54019.2021.9661509.

[6] B. G. Osborne, "Near-Infrared Spectroscopy in Food Analysis," Encyclopedia of Analytical Chemistry: applications, theory and instrumentation, pp. 1-14, 2006, doi: 10.1002/9780470027318.a1018.

Relationship between 3D Eye-Gaze and the TrueDepth Measured by Vive Pro Eye

Kenta Kato and Oky Dicky Ardiansyah Prima
Graduate School of Software and Information Science
Iwate Prefectural University
152-52, Sugo, Takizawa, Iwate, Japan
e-mail: g236s002@s.iwate-pu.ac.jp, prima@iwate-pu.ac.jp

***Abstract*—The widespread availability of eye tracking devices has led to the active application of eye-gaze information, such as input interfaces, eye-gaze-based interaction with computers, and understanding of human visual information. More recently, various Head-Mounted Displays (HMDs) for Virtual Reality (VR) with built-in eye trackers have become commercially available. The Vive Pro Eye has been used for in-depth analysis of saccadic eye movements and in clinical ophthalmology. Unlike any other HMD-type eye tracker, the advanced slippage compensation in this device allows to maintain gaze accuracy and provides stable gaze measurement over a long period. We believe that this advantage may help in estimating accurate Three-Dimensional (3D) eye-gaze, and therefore it is necessary to investigate the accuracy of 3D gaze with the Vive Pro Eye. This study attempts to evaluate the accuracy of eye-gaze in two- and three-dimensions by measuring 3D eye-gaze when gazing at targets placed at different spatial positions with the Vive Pro Eye. Results showed that the relative position of the 3D eye-gaze to the 3D targets placed radially in 40-cm increments from 40 to 200 cm was confirmed. The accuracy of 2D eye-gaze measurements tends to decrease as the viewing angle increases, and consequently the accuracy of the corresponding 3D eye-gaze measurements also decreases. The 3D eye-gaze to the centrally located visual targets increases linearly, while the rest of the eye-gaze increases logarithmically.**

Keywords-3D eye-gaze; eye vergence; eye tracking; 3D perception; computer vision.

I. INTRODUCTION

Two-Dimensional (2D) and Three-Dimensional (3D) contents are now accessible to consumers as Head-Mounted Display (HMD)-type Virtual Reality (VR) devices become available to the general consumers. Since these contents can be easily and cost-effectively created using VR, HMD-type VR is being used for applications that are difficult to reproduce in a real environment, such as product design and new training methods for sports [1]-[3]. Users can manipulate 3D contents in VR mostly by using controllers or hand gestures. Recently, HMDs with an eye-tracking function has been introduced as an alternative method to control the contents. Since then, interactions based on eye tracking in VR have been actively developed [4]-[6]. In addition, with the commercialization of HMD-type eye trackers, the use of eye-gaze information in VR environments is being explored in brain science, psychology, disease assessment, and behavioral analysis [7]-[9]. These eye trackers are expected to provide more accurate eye-gaze measurements because they block out ambient light.

Stein et al. [10] evaluated several HMDs with built-in eye trackers, including Fove-0, Varjo VR-1, and the Vive Pro Eye. Their results showed that the Vive Pro Eye had the highest latency, even though it was the best in terms of field of view and tracking sampling rate. However, the results also indicated possibly due to data filtering within the Software Development Kit (SDK). To our knowledge, Vive Pro Eye is the only HMD with advanced slip compensation that handles headset motion to maintain accuracy and calibration. This solution allows users to move naturally throughout the experience without losing eye tracking performance. The Vive Pro Eye has been reported to be effective in performing saccadic eye movement assessment [11] and clinical ophthalmology [12].

The Vive Pro Eye outputs eye-gaze information in 3D coordinates, which could enable 3D eye-gaze estimation by crossing both extensions of the left and right eye-gaze raycasts without triangulation. This will allow for a simpler calculation for obtaining 3D eye-gaze than that based on vergence eye movements and is expected to lead to the analysis of various types of visual information using 3D eye-gaze. However, there is currently a lack of rigorous research investigating the accuracy of 3D eye-gaze with the Vive Pro Eye and the impact of gazing distance and direction on the accuracy.

In this study, we use the Vive Pro Eye to collect eye-gaze information while gazing at targets placed at different spatial locations and analyze their distribution in two 2D and 3D. To characterize the eye-gaze at any given direction and distance, we place the visual targets radially on a plane at a given distance. Here, three seconds of fixation was performed to analyze the representative eye-gaze information during the fixation task, since small involuntary eye movements continuously change the eye-gaze position during the fixation. At the end, we will compare the characteristics of 3D eye-gaze measured with the Vive Pro Eye with those obtained with our previous experiments based on vergence eye movements to explore new insights.

The rest of this paper is organized as follows. Section II describes related works on 3D eye-gaze measurements. Section III describes our experiments to characterize the 3D eye-gaze derived by Vive Pro Eye. Section IV summarizes our results. Finally, Section V concludes our study and discusses prospects.

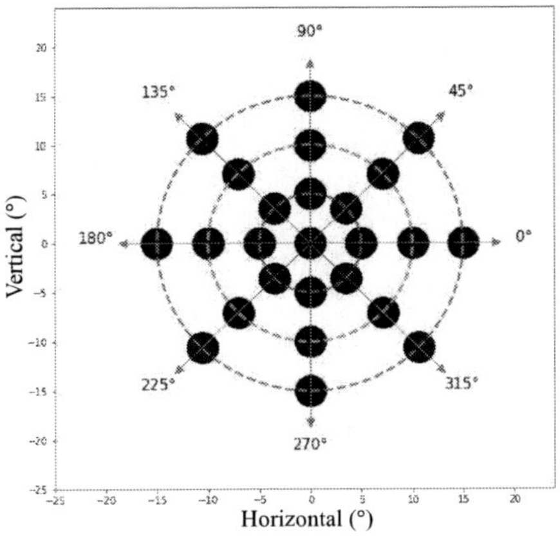

(a) Visual targets placed radially in eight directions.

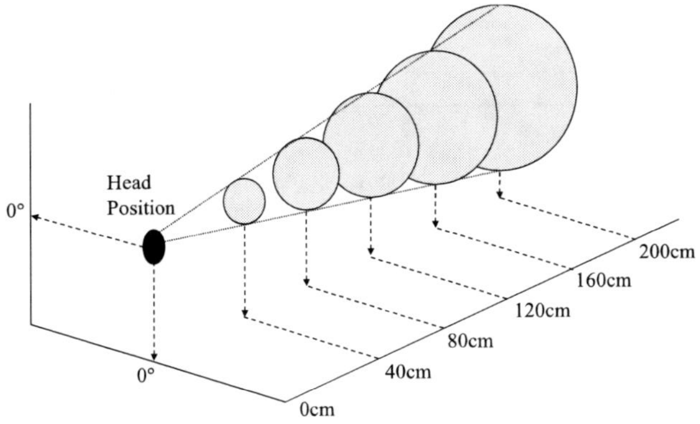

(b) Arrangement of planes containing the visual targets.

Figure 1. Visual targets and their arrangement in this study.

II. RELATED WORKS

The 3D eye-gaze measurement relies on the relative position of the two eyes with respect to a given visual target. Vergence angle (the angle in the direction of the line of sight of both eyes) changes when the visual target moves to a certain distance from the viewer. Since our eyes never remain completely still as we try to align our eye-gaze with the object [13], 3D eye-gaze measurement is less stable than that of 2D eye-gaze. Small eye movements can cause changes in the position of both eyes, reducing the measurement accuracy. Kato & Prima [14] performed 3D eye-gaze measurements in an MR environment and confirmed that the relative size of the 3D visual target and the surrounding physical environment do not affect the accuracy of 3D eye-gaze.

Some studies have attempted to measure 3D eye-gaze without calibration in order to make such measurement easier. Palmero et al. [15] used recurrent Convolutional Neural Network (CNN) to automatically estimate 3D eye-gaze from still images using information from faces, eye regions, and facial landmarks. Liu et al. [16] proposed automatic 3D eye-gaze estimation using an automatic calibration method that combines 3D salient pixels from RGB-D images and eye-gaze vectors. These attempts yielded plausible results, but their accuracies were not sufficient for the analysis of eye-gaze characteristics.

Vive Pro Eye enables 3D eye-gaze estimation without the need for 3D calibration. It can record 3D eye-gaze origin and eye-gaze direction data estimated by constructing cones passing through the camera's focal point and pupil ellipses on the image plane and finding the circular intersection of these cones at a given distance.

III. 3D EYE-GAZE MEASUREMENT USING VIVE PRO EYE

In this study, we evaluate 3D eye-gaze measured with the Vive Pro Eye, which is currently the most popular eye tracking system for VR HMDs. Because the effect of vergence eye movements is not significant beyond 2m, many studies on vergence eye movements have conducted experiments on visual targets up to 2m [17][18]. For these reasons, our evaluation will be conducted by measuring eye-gaze up to 2m from the subject. The eye tracking accuracy of the Vive Pro Eye is 0.5° to 1.1° within a 20° Field of View (FoV). To evaluate the quality of 3D eye-gaze within and outside this FoV, we will measure the eye-gaze at broader FoV.

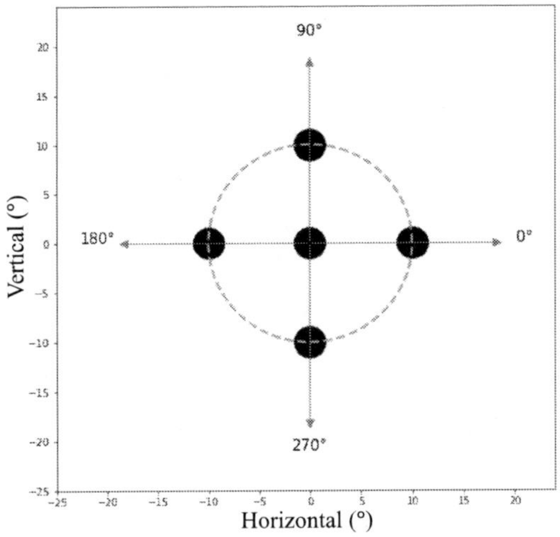

Figure 2. Visual targets for the eye-gaze validation.

A. Equipments

Our experiment will be performed using Unity3D 2019.4.31f1 and SteamVR 1.21.12 software to drive the Vive Pro Eye. Eye-gaze data will be acquired using SRanipal Runtime 1.3.2.0. The computer for the experiment features a Ryzen 9 3900 3.1Ghz, DDR4 64GB RAM, and a NVIDIA GeForce RTX 2060 Super graphics card.

B. Visual Targets

Visual targets are placed radially from 40 cm to 200 cm to the subject in 40 cm increments. Visual targets and their arrangement are illustrated in Figure 1.

TABLE I. 2D EYE-GAZE ACCURACIES (PRECISIONS) AT VARIOUS DISTANCES.

UNITS: °

Subject	40cm	80cm	120cm	160cm	200cm
1	1.34 (0.09)	**0.84 (0.10)**	**0.91 (0.10)**	**0.95 (0.10)**	**0.83 (0.10)**
2	**0.63 (0.08)**	**0.55 (0.08)**	**0.56 (0.08)**	**0.61 (0.09)**	**0.53 (0.08)**
3	**0.47 (0.06)**	**0.48 (0.06)**	**0.45 (0.05)**	**0.49 (0.06)**	**0.74 (0.82)**
4	**0.49 (0.05)**	**0.48 (0.05)**	**0.57 (0.06)**	**0.59 (0.04)**	**0.60 (0.06)**
5	**0.78 (0.06)**	**0.56 (0.06)**	**0.85 (0.08)**	**0.68 (0.09)**	**0.75 (0.82)**
6	1.25 (0.09)	**1.00 (0.10)**	1.20 (0.10)	1.06 (0.09)	**0.90 (0.09)**
7	1.61 (0.09)	1.09 (0.07)	1.04 (0.06)	1.08 (0.08)	1.11 (0.07)
8	1.60 (1.04)	1.64 (0.83)	1.05 (0.16)	1.08 (0.08)	1.00 (0.13)
Mean	1.02 (0.20)	0.83 (0.18)	0.83 (0.09)	0.82 (0.10)	0.81 (0.18)
Std. Dev.	0.451 (0.321)	0.380 (0.270)	0.254 (0.031)	0.231 (0.054)	0.182 (0.244)

TABLE II. 2D EYE-GAZE ACCURACIES (PRECISIONS) AT VARIOUS ANGLES.

UNITS: °

Subject	0°	10°	20°	30°
1	1.17 (0.11)	**0.95 (0.12)**	**0.99 (0.09)**	1.01 (0.08)
2	**0.51 (0.06)**	**0.51 (0.10)**	**0.63 (0.08)**	**0.60 (0.07)**
3	**0.28 (0.06)**	**0.36 (0.06)**	**0.52 (0.06)**	**0.70 (0.65)**
4	**0.46 (0.03)**	**0.45 (0.04)**	**0.54 (0.07)**	**0.65 (0.05)**
5	**0.40 (0.06)**	**0.67 (0.10)**	**0.62 (0.06)**	**0.91 (0.05)**
6	**0.55 (0.07)**	**0.65 (0.08)**	**0.95 (0.11)**	1.53 (0.09)
7	**0.83 (0.09)**	**0.79 (0.07)**	1.06 (0.08)	1.65 (0.07)
8	**0.92 (0.13)**	**1.03 (0.15)**	**0.81 (0.12)**	1.87 (1.10)
Mean	0.64 (0.08)	0.68 (0.09)	0.76 (0.08)	1.11 (0.27)
Std. Dev.	0.283 (0.030)	0.222 (0.031)	0.201 (0.021)	0.467 (0.367)

C. Procedure

Subjects are provided with information about the experiment and then are asked to give informed consent to participate in the experiment. The subjects are then asked to answer an eye health questionnaire, and their visual acuity is measured using a Landolt ring placed three meters away from them. In addition, we give training on how to operate the Vive Pro Eye to ensure that the subject does not make any mistakes during the experiment. The subject is seated on a chair, wearing the Vive Pro Eye and its controller. The camera pose in the virtual space is fixed so that changes in the subject's head pose do not affect the measurement. Our experiment is performed according to the following procedure.

Step 1: Perform the Vive Pro Eye 5-point eye-gaze calibration.

Step 2: Validate the eye-gaze accuracy using the 5-point validation target created for this experiment. If binocular eye-gaze accuracy is greater than 1°, return to Step 1.

Step 3: Trigger the controller to perform eye-gaze measurements on each target for 3s. The experiment is terminated after 125 trials.

The Step 2 is performed because the Vive Pro Eye's eye-gaze calibration does not provide the accuracy with numerical values. Figure 2 shows the placement of the visual targets to be used for the validation. Targets are placed 1m away from the subject and at 20° FoV in four directions.

IV. EXPERIMENTS AND RESULTS

Eight subjects (seven males, a female, mean age 23.4) participated in the experiment. They were tested for visual acuity using a Landolt ring to confirm that their vision achieved 1.0 or better. They were also asked to fill out a questionnaire to confirm that they had no health concerns.

A. Pre-processing

The Vive Pro Eye detects the opening and closing of the eyes, and the degree of eye opening is defined as 0 (closed) to 1 (open). In this study, to obtain accurate eye-gaze data, we extracted only data in which the degree of eye opening was greater than 0.9 for both eyes of the subject. Eye opening at 0.9 or less may result in false detection as the eyelid falls to hide some portion of the pupil.

B. Eye-Gaze Accuracies and Precisions

The accuracy and precision of the 3D eye-gaze depends on that of the 2D eye-gaze. The following equation was used in the calculations.

$$Accuracy_{2D} = \sqrt{\frac{1}{n}\sum_{i=1}^{n}(T_{xi} - G_{xi})^2 + (T_{yi} - G_{yi})^2} \tag{1}$$

$$Precision_{2D} = \sqrt{\frac{1}{n}\sum_{i=1}^{n}(G_{xi+1} - G_{xi})^2 + (G_{yi+1} - G_{yi})^2} \tag{2}$$

Here, n is the number of targets used for the measurement, T_{xi}, T_{yi}, and G_{xi}, G_{yi} are the coordinates of the i-th target and the associated eye-gaze points.

Table I shows the results of the 2D eye-gaze accuracies and precisions for visual targets placed at various distances, as shown in Figure 1. The numbers in bold indicate an accuracy

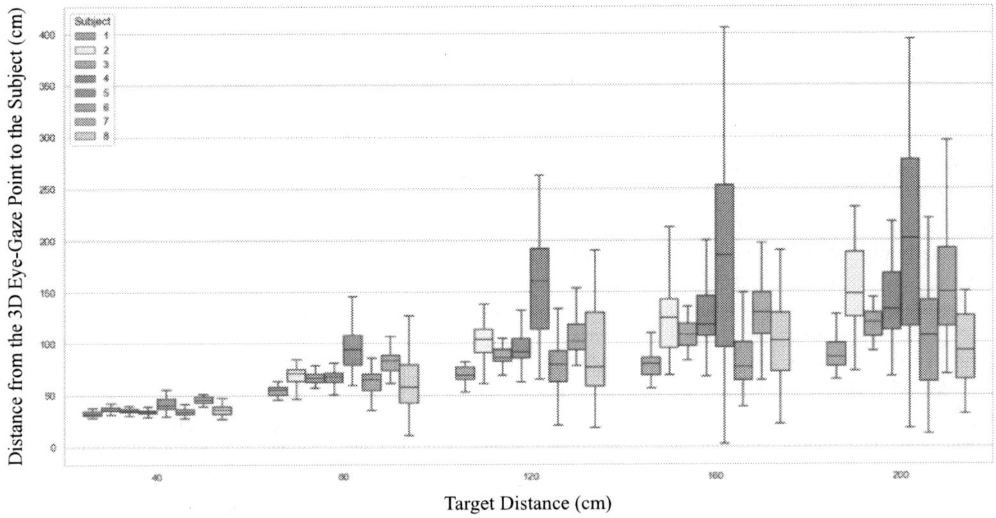

Figure 3. Distribution of distance from 3D eye-gaze point to subject.

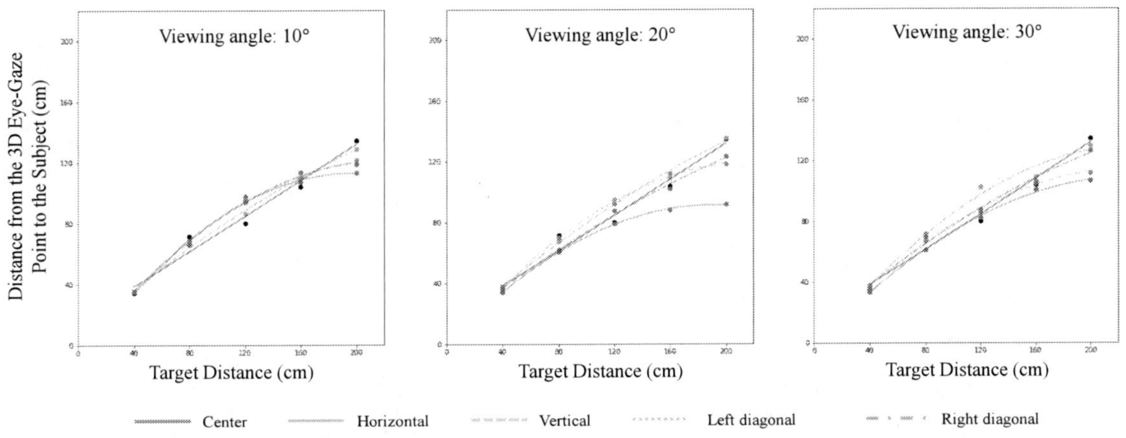

Figure 4. Distribution of distance from 3D eye-gaze point to subject at each viewing angle.

of 1 degree or less, which accounts for 62.5% in total. A one-way Analysis of Variance (ANOVA) revealed that there was not a statistically significant difference in mean accuracy score between at least five groups in distances ($F(4, 35) = 0.572, p = 0.685$). The results for accuracies and precisions by angles are shown in Table II. The accuracy of the eye-gaze measurement tends to decrease as the viewing angle increases. ANOVA revealed that there was a statistically significant difference in mean accuracy score between at least four groups in angles ($F(3, 28) = 3.379, p = 0.0321$).

C. 3D Eye-Gaze versus TrueDepth

The TrueDepth of 3D eye-gaze is defined by the actual distance from the viewing point to the observer. As shown in Figure 3, the distribution of each subject's 3D eye-gaze increases with gazing distance. This trend was not observed from the accuracy of the 2D eye-gaze in Table I. However, this result is acceptable because, as mentioned earlier, 3D eye-gaze measurement is less stable than 2D eye-gaze measurement because the eye-gaze is not completely still as we attempt to align our eye-gaze with the object. To further investigate the behavior of 3D eye-gaze in detail, we took the median values of all subjects' 3D eye-gaze for each viewing angle, as shown in Figure 4. The 3D eye-gaze to the centrally located visual targets increases linearly, whereas the rest of the eye-gaze shows logarithmic growth. Since the Vive Pro Eye uses a Fresnel lens, the estimated 3D eye-gaze results may be closer to the gazing subject as the viewing angle increases. However, since the scanpaths of the 3D eye-gaze obtained from dynamic visual cues measured in Kato & Prima (2021) also show such a curved trajectory [14], this phenomenon is still open for further study.

V. Conclusions

This study evaluated the eye-gaze measurement capability of the Vive Pro Eye in terms of 3D eye-gaze measurement. Although this measurement was performed without triangulation and only by crossing the two extensions of the left and right eye-gaze raycasts, the resulting 3D eye-gaze point was found to be acceptable. The estimated distance from the 3D eye-gaze measurement point to the subject tends to be closer than the actual distance (TrueDepth). However, this can be corrected by using methods such as linear regression analysis.

Small involuntary eye movements were found to affect the stability of the 3D eye-gaze measurement. The distribution of eye-gaze points was found to increase with gazing distance. We also found that 3D eye-gaze to a centrally located visual target increased linearly, while the rest of the eye-gaze increased logarithmically.

From these findings, we can conclude that the Vive Pro Eye is capable of measuring 3D eye-gaze. However, users will need to construct their own measurement methods in order to reveal the accuracy and precision of the eye-gaze, although this type of library is commonly available in commercially available scientific eye trackers.

References

[1] S. C. Mallam, S. Nazir, and S. K. Renganayagalu, "Rethinking maritime education, training, and operations in the digital era: Applications for emerging immersive technologies," Journal of Marine Science and Engineering, 7(12), pp. 1–9, 2019.

[2] F. Bellalouna, "New approach for industrial training using virtual reality technology," Procedia CIRP, 93, pp. 262–267, 2020

[3] H. Ujiie et al., "Developing a virtual reality simulation system for preoperative planning of thoracoscopic thoracic surgery," Journal of Thoracic Disease, 13(2), pp. 778–783, 2021.

[4] P.Mohan, W. B. Goh, C. W . Fu, and S. K. Yeung, "DualGaze: Addressing the Midas Touch Problem in Gaze Mediated VR Interaction," IEEE International Symposium on Mixed and Augmented Reality Adjunct (ISMAR-Adjunct 2018) , pp. 79–84, 2018.

[5] F. L. Luro and V. Sundstedt, "A comparative study of eye tracking and hand controller for aiming tasks in virtual reality," Proceedings of the 11th ACM Symposium on Eye Tracking Research & Applications (ETRA '19), pp. 1–9, 2019.

[6] L. Sidenmark, C. Clarke, X. Zhang, J. Phu, and H. Gellersen, "Outline Pursuits: Gaze-assisted Selection of Occluded Objects in Virtual Reality," Conference on Human Factors in Computing Systems - Proceedings, pp. 1–13, 2020.

[7] Y. Imaoka, A. Flury, and E. D. de Bruin , "Assessing Saccadic Eye Movements With Head-Mounted Display Virtual Reality Technology," Frontiers in Psychiatry, 11(September), pp. 1–19, 2020.

[8] P. H. Yeh, C. H. Liu, M. H. Sun, S. C. Chi, and Y. S. Hwang, "To measure the amount of ocular deviation in strabismus patients with an eye-tracking virtual reality headset," BMC Ophthalmology, 21(1), pp. 1–8, 2021.

[9] M. Meißner, J. Pfeiffer, T. Pfeiffer, and H. Oppewal, "Combining virtual reality and mobile eye tracking to provide a naturalistic experimental environment for shopper research," Journal of Business Research, 100(September), pp. 445–458, 2019.

[10] N. Stein et al., "A Comparison of Eye Tracking Latencies Among Several Commercial Head-Mounted Displays," i-Perception, 12(1), pp. 1–16, 2021.

[11] Y. Imaoka, A.Flury, and E. D. de Bruin, "Assessing Saccadic Eye Movements With Head-Mounted Display Virtual Reality Technology," Frontiers in Psychiatry, 11:572938, pp. 1–19, 2020.

[12] A. Sipatchin, S. Wahl, and K. Rifai, "Eye-Tracking for Clinical Ophthalmology with Virtual Reality (VR): A Case Study of the HTC Vive Pro Eye's Usability," Healhcare, 9, pp. 1-15, 2021.

[13] J. Otero-Millan, S. L. Macknik, and S. Martinez-Conde, "Fixational Eye Movements Binocular Vision," Frontiers in Integrative Neuroscience, 8(52), pp. 1-10, 2014.

[14] K. Kato and O. D. A. Prima, "3D Gaze on Stationary and Moving Visual Targets in Mixed Reality Environments," International Journal on Advances in Life Sciences, 13(1&2), pp. 104-113, 2021.

[15] C. Palmero, J. Selva, M. A. Bagheri, and S. Escalera, "Recurrent CNN for 3D Gaze Estimation Using Appearance and Shape Cues," ArXiv, pp. 1-13, 2018.

[16] M. Liu, Y. Li, and H. A. I. Liu, "3D Gaze Estimation for Head-Mounted Eye Tracking System With Auto-Calibration Method," in IEEE Access, 8, pp. 104207-104215, 2020. https://doi.org/10.1109/ACCESS.2020.2999633

[17] A. Gibaldi and M. S. Banks, "Binocular eye movements are adapted to the natural environment," Journal of Neuroscience, 39(15), pp. 2877–2888, 2019.

[18] C. Mestre, H. E. Bedell, F. Díaz-Doutón, J. Pujol, and J. Gautier, "Characteristics of saccades during the near point of convergence test," Vision Research, 187, pp. 27–40, 2021.

RIDES: Realistic and Immersive Dental Education Simulation Using Virtual Reality and Haptic Device Implementation

Casey Melrose, Daniel Briz, Charlotte Atwill, Hao Huang, Andrew Marlow, Markus Santoso
Digital Worlds Institute
University of Florida
Gainesville, FL. US
markus.santoso@ufl.edu

Cortino Sukotjo
Restorative Dentistry Department
University of Illinois at Chicago
Chicago, Illinois. United States
csukotjo@uic.edu

***Abstract*— Virtual reality (VR) is an emerging technology for simulation and training experiences in a variety of fields. It is becoming widely available and increasingly accessible in cost. The field of dentistry can greatly benefit from the use of this technology as it presents breakthroughs that augment the education process. In this paper, the authors developed RIDES: Realistic and Immersive Dental Education Simulation. In this project, the authors implemented VR technology and a haptic device to allow dental students to train their psychomotor skill virtually, all while maintaining a realistic experience and an easy to navigate interface. This simulation can be experienced from anywhere, given a sufficiently powerful computer, and does not require the professor to be physically present. This distinction was vital to the continued education of students after the Covid-19 global pandemic. The social distancing restrictions that were implemented for public safety severely limited in-person education, which prompted the exploration of digital methods. It allows for a digital approximation of a task that gives the user freedom to explore the subject without fear of damaging expensive equipment before given the proper training to handle it. By utilizing the immersive virtual reality capabilities of the VR headset and the realistic tactile feedback of the haptic pen, the authors developed a unique and realistic simulation for dental education.**

Keywords-virtual reality; haptic device; dental simulation.

I. Introduction

At the end of 2019, the world was alerted to a high number of pneumonia-like disease cases in Wuhan, China. This disease was identified to be caused by a novel coronavirus, named by the International Committee for Taxonomy of Viruses as Severe Acute Respiratory Syndrome Coronavirus 2 (SARS-CoV-2). The World Health Organization (WHO) later announced this disease as the Coronavirus Disease 2019 (COVID-19). COVID-19 was known to be an airborne transmission disease because the virus efficiently spread from person to person through respiratory droplets by sneezing, coughing and direct contact. This infection affected 222 countries and territories around the world, prompting WHO to declare COVID-19 as a pandemic in March 2020. As the situation worsened, many countries implemented restrictive mass quarantines and lockdowns to decelerate and break the chain of infection. The COVID-19 pandemic led to a sudden shutdown of institutions in 2020, including the United States of America. The US government implemented a lock down order to encourage the public to stay at home and practice social distancing. This condition forced all educational institutions to be closed, halting all face to face education. For dental students, all clinical and lab practice sessions were halted. As a consequence of this pandemic, all universities in the US were strongly affected and were forced to face the new challenge of implementing "distance/online learning".

In restorative dentistry, cavity preparation concepts have evolved towards a tissue-sparing approach, requiring a high level of skill and precision when preparing cavities. Traditionally, preclinical dental instruction was accomplished in a bench-type laboratory environment where students learned psychomotor skills using hand-held dentiform or mannequin heads mounted on metal rods. Recently, computer-assisted training systems such as *Simodont* are developed and used for the practical training of dental students. However, this technology showed some limitations. The cost, both hardware and learning modules, is expensive. The product's size and dimension also pretty big therefore it is site-dependent. Student needs to come to the college to operate the machine.

Virtual simulation such as VR could potentially provide efficient educational pathway to achieving a high level of practice. The use of haptic simulators coupled with virtual reality is expected to address the limitations of native VR controller regarding tactile feedback. The objective of RIDES project is to develop a VR simulator coupled with haptic device as an educational tool for tooth cavities preparation. While an integration of VR and haptic has been explored in several directions previously, the application of these technologies for dental education specifically cavities preparation teaching session is a novel direction.

In section 2, it covers several related previous works that we observed as references. Section 3 discusses about our project, RIDES. In this section, authors describes technical aspects including VR headset and haptic device that we used. Authors also explain about the VR experience related with this project. Finally, in section 4 authors will close it with summary and potential future development.

II. Previous Works

Related with VR applications for implant surgery, Matsuo et al developed a virtual reality head-mounted display for endoscopically-assisted implant surgery [1]. Several VR haptic projects were explored. The group of researchers published a paper regarding haptic interaction for needle insertion training in medical applications. In this project, the authors developed a virtual needle insertion training simulation based on haptic interaction [2].

Our project is inspired by the work done by a previous research group [4]. In that project, authors implemented VR for implant surgery simulation as shown in Figure 1.

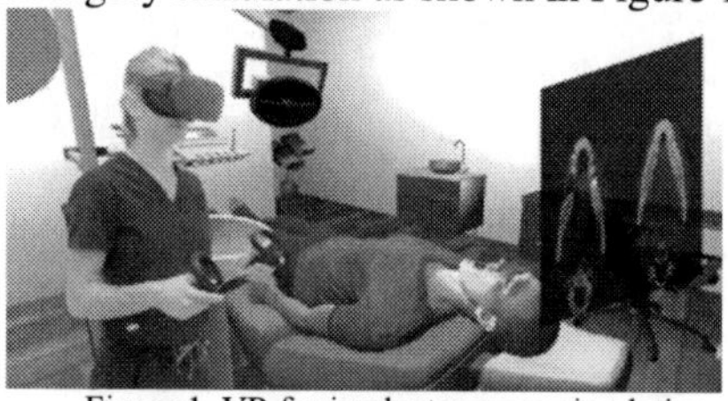

Figure 1. VR for implant surgery simulation

Based on the conducted study, it was concluded that the application of VR technology in dental education was promising and offered positive learning enhancement. However, several study participants suggested the lack of haptic sensation including feeling the tissue density when using rotary and surgical instruments.

III. RIDES Project

To tackle the tactile/haptic limitations from previous study, our current research team explored the implementation of haptic device into VR learning module, specifically cavities preparation training. In the beginning, the authors tried to integrate haptic gloves as shown in Figure 2. Since the primary goal in the cavity preparation simulation is to drill into a tooth, the authors observed that the haptic gloves were not an appropriate input device for an accurate simulation because it has no resistance feel. The glove also proved to be unintuitive for new users, as well as generally unrealistic for the purposes of the simulation.

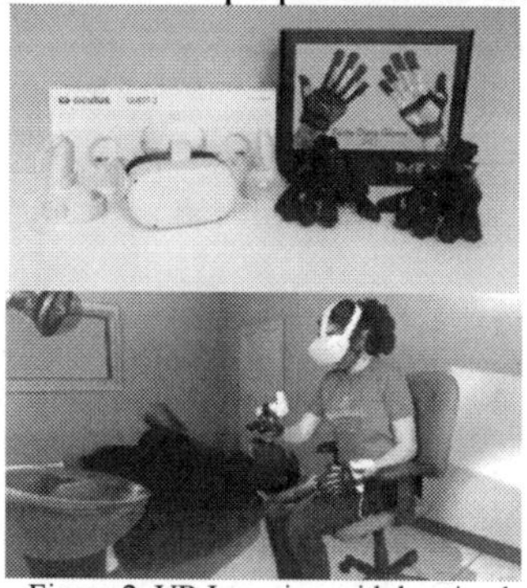

Figure 2. VR Learning with haptic glove

Due to this issue, the authors decided to switch over to a 3D Systems Touch Haptic Pen (see Figure 3). It is a desktop stylus that hangs on rotating motors that can lock on any axis to simulate the stylus coming into contact with an object in the virtual world. The haptic pen provides a more realistic approximation of using a handheld drill, while making it easier for the user to interact with the dentistry experience. The combination of rumble motors and locking arms could simulate tooth drilling, largely because the user is holding an object in the physical world that they are also using in the virtual realm to manipulate the tooth.

Figure 3. 3D Systems touch haptic pen

The purpose of this project was to simulate dental training, specifically tooth cavities preparation, with virtual reality and haptic feedback as shown in Figure 4. This would enable dental schools to provide their students with the real life experience that they require without spending the usual amount of time and resources needed to teach them in person. When students are given training in a virtual environment we expect it can help them to become more confident when working and practicing in the real world, potentially reducing or eliminating mistakes. This also gives students more time and accessibility to practice skills they've learned in classes. Techniques that need many hours of practice to master are more easily rehearsed with a virtual reality program that can be used anytime outside of the classroom.

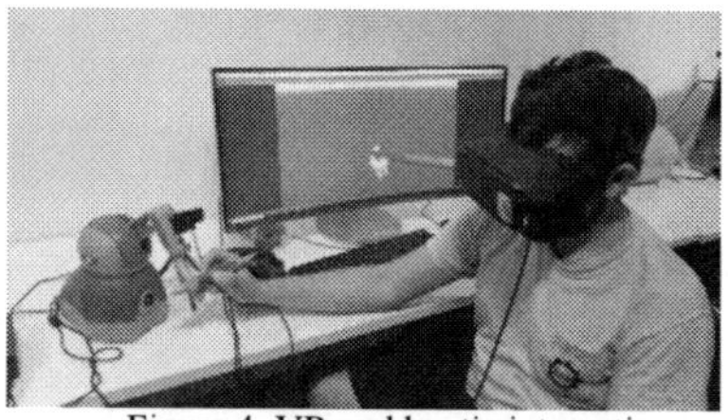

Figure 4. VR and haptic integration

A. Cavities Preparation VR Training Session

One of the essential activities for cavity preparation is drilling. The haptics pen allows us to replicate the drilling experience inside computer-generated environment. Furthermore, the haptic pen could also provide a resistance sensation that is important to achieve the learning goal.

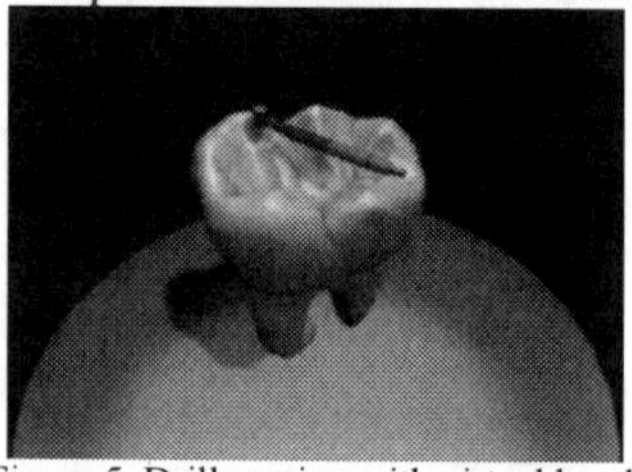

Figure 5. Drill session with virtual handpiece

As shown in Figure 5, the virtual hand piece controlled by the haptic pen is able to deform the mesh of the tooth and mimic the conventional cavities preparation training session. The authors also arranged the drill to vibrate at different frequencies to emulate the different layers of the tooth by tracking the depth of the pen in the tooth's mesh.

To complement the training session, the authors offered a "pop-through" feature that enables users to pop through the drilled tooth and analyze their result as shown in Figure 6. When user in this state, they also have an option to change the transparency of the dentin layer. This will allow them to compare their drill result with the overall tooth anatomy structure, including nerves (see Figure 7)

Figure 6. 'Pop-through' feature to analyze drill result

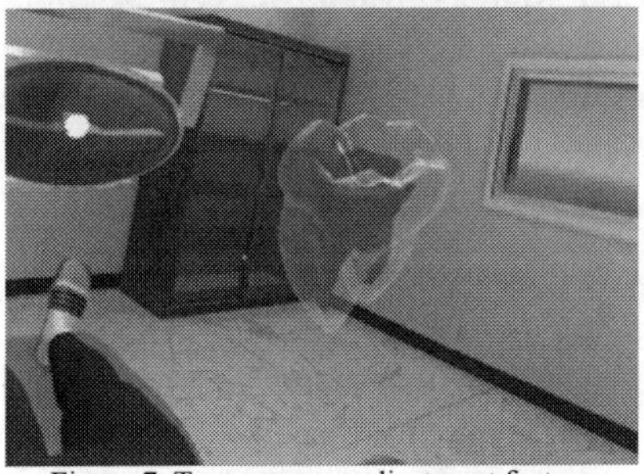

Figure 7. Transparency adjustment feature

IV. CONCLUSION

The COVID 19 pandemic surged the urgency to utilize distance learning for all education levels including higher education. However, it is quite challenging to deliver psychomotor skill-related training using conventional online learning modalities. Immersive learning using VR technology is one of the emerging solutions and in this project, the authors also integrated a haptic device to provide a more realistic immersive learning experience in the dentistry direction.

For this project, the authors developed a haptic VR learning simulation for cavities preparation entitled RIDES: Realistic and Immersive Dental Education Simulation. When this project started the authors explored BeBop haptic gloves, however this device lacked the resistance feel that is essential for the cavity preparation learning process. Therefore, authors switched to the haptic pen which offered a more realistic learning experience and the possibility to mimic a conventional training session. The implementation of the haptic pen is expected to answer limitations from previous study, namely the lack of a resistance sensation.

In the future, the authors plan to extend this project so it could accommodate multiple VR users interacting with each other at the same time. Therefore, the instructor or professor could meet with their student and run the training session inside the VR environment. This multiplayer feature will also open an opportunity to run a test session where the professor or instructor could examine their student's progress from distance. The authors also plan to conduct several user studies including measuring the effectiveness of this project, the user perception, and others.

REFERENCES

[1] A. Matsuo, H. Hamada, H. Oba, K. Shibata, Virtual reality head-mounted display for endoscopically-assisted implant surgery, British Journal of Oral and Maxillofacial Surgery, Volume 56, Issue 7, 2018, Pages 636-637, ISSN 0266-4356.

[2] Chen, X., Sun, P., & Liao, D. (2018). A patient-specific haptic drilling simulator based on virtual reality for dental implant surgery. International journal of computer assisted radiology and surgery, 13(11), 1861-1870.

[3] Correa C, Nunes F, Ranzini E, Nakamura R, Tori R. Haptic interaction for needle insertion training in medical applications: The state-of-the-art. Medical Engineering and physics, Volume 65, 2019, pages 6-25

[4] J. Iqbal, N.G. Tsagarakis and D.G. Caldwell, Design of a wearable direct-driven optimized hand exoskeleton device, 4th International Conference on Advance in Computer-Human Interaction (ACHI), France, 2011, pp. 142-146.

[5] Katić, D., Spengler, P., Bodenstedt, S., Castrillon-Oberndorfer, G., Seeberger, R., Hoffmann, J., ... & Speidel, S. (2015). A system for context-aware intraoperative augmented reality in dental implant surgery. International journal of computer assisted radiology and surgery, 10(1), 101-108.

[6] Kusumoto, N., Sohmura, T., Yamada, S., Wakabayashi, K., Nakamura, T., & Yatani, H. (2006). Application of virtual reality force feedback haptic device for oral implant surgery. Clinical oral implants research, 17(6), 708-713.

[7] Lin, Y. K., Yau, H. T., Wang, I. C., Zheng, C., & Chung, K. H. (2015). A novel dental implant guided surgery based on integration of surgical template and augmented reality. Clinical implant dentistry and related research, 17(3), 543-553.

[8] Lungu, A. J., Swinkels, W., Claesen, L., Tu, P., Egger, J., & Chen, X. (2021). A review on the applications of virtual reality, augmented reality and mixed reality in surgical simulation: an extension to different kinds of surgery. Expert review of medical devices, 18(1), 47-62.

[9] Sohmura, T., Hojo, H., Nakajima, M., Wakabayashi, K., Nagao, M., Iida, S., ... & Takahashi, J. (2004). Prototype of simulation of orthognathic surgery using a virtual reality haptic device. International journal of oral and maxillofacial surgery, 33(8), 740-750.

[10] Steinberg, A. D., Bashook, P. G., Drummond, J., Ashrafi, S., & Zefran, M. (2007). Assessment of Faculty Perception of Content Validity of PerioSim©, a Haptic-3D Virtual Reality Dental Training Simulator. Journal of dental education, 71(12), 1574-1582.

[11] Sukotjo C, Schreiber S, Li J, Zhang M, Chia-Chun Yuan J, Santoso M. Development and Student Perception of Virtual Reality for Implant Surgery. *Education Sciences*. 2021; 11(4):176.

[12] Zhu, M., Liu, F., Chai, G., Pan, J. J., Jiang, T., Lin, L., ... & Li, Q. (2017). A novel augmented reality system for displaying inferior alveolar nerve bundles in maxillofacial surgery. Scientific Reports, 7(1), 1-11.

Keyword Extraction for Local Foods from Restaurant Menus of Roadside Stations

Yoko Nishihara
College of Information Science and Engineering
Ritsumeikan University
Shiga, Japan
email: nisihara@fc.ritsumei.ac.jp

Hirofumi Noguchi
College of Information Science and Engineering
Ritsumeikan University
Shiga, Japan

Ryosuke Yamanishi
Faculty of Informatics
Kansai University
Osaka, Japan

***Abstract*—Some foods are only consumed and available in some regions; these foods are called local foods. For example, B.C. roll is one of the local foods in Canada. The local foods are a form of tourism and are expected to attract more tourists. People in the region are so accustomed to the local foods that they may have difficulty in identifying their values, which means they are unsure whether a particular food is local or not. If they success to choose appropriate local foods, they may get more tourists. Therefore, they should know which food should be sold as a local food. Previous studies have proposed statistical methods for extracting keywords for local foods from restaurant menus on the Internet. However, the restaurant menus often exclude local foods. This study applies the previous statistical method to restaurant menus of roadside stations and extracts keywords for their local foods. These roadside stations are government-designated rest areas located along Japanese roads. They sell local foods for promotion, while the restaurants provide menus of the local foods. Thus, if we apply the statistical method to the restaurant menus of roadside stations, we may obtain menus of the local foods. First, we developed a dataset of restaurant menus of roadside stations. Then, we apply the previous method to the dataset to extract keywords for the local foods. We invited participants to our experiment and they evaluated whether the extracted keywords were related to the local foods. The average rate of keywords for the local foods was 21.1%. Furthermore, we discovered that the extracted keywords were not only for foods but also place names, dish names, and their combinations.**

Keywords-local food; roadside station; restaurant menu; food tourism; TF-IDF

I. INTRODUCTION

People enjoy not only sightseeing on their vacation but also food tourism[1][2]. Some foods are only eaten and available in specific regions. These are called local foods. B. C. roll (a kind of sushi containing barbecued salmon and cucumber), Nanaimo bar (butter tarts), and Rocky road (chocolate ice cream with almond and marshmallow) are examples of food only eaten in Canada. Lanzhou Ramen (a kind of Chinese noodle), Tianjin Xiao Long Bao (a type of soup dumpling), and Peking duck (roast duck), which are local Chinese foods, can be found in foreign countries. However, if people want to experience their authentic taste, they would have to get the dishes from their original region. Local foods have been receiving a lot of attention in recent years: the example is the Slow Food movement in Italy [3]. The Slow Food Association in Italy published guidebooks titled "Osterie D'Italia," which list restaurants offering local foods. Tourists expect to enjoy the local food on their vacations. The tourism industry must advertise local foods that can be eaten in their region and consider how to make them appealing to tourists [4].

Although local foods are only eaten and available in specific regions, people may be confused about which foods are local. This is because people in these regions are accustomed to these foods that they are unaware of their origin. If they success to choose appropriate local foods, they may get more tourists. Therefore, they should know which food should be sold as a local food. Several studies have been conducted to survey the local foods in restaurant menus[5][6]. Further studies have been conducted to discover local foods automatically by applying statistical methods to restaurant menus [7]. The previous methods achieved the automatic evaluation of the locality of food.

The previous study [7] applied their method to restaurant menus on the websites of restaurants, such as Yelp. However, the restaurant menus on the website do not necessarily include local foods. We discover more local foods if the previous method is applied to restaurant menus that include more local foods. Thus, this study applies the previous method to restaurant menus in Japanese roadside stations to extract keywords for the local foods. As the roadside stations provide foods produced in those regions, the restaurants may offer menus that include the local foods. We explain how to extract keywords for the local foods and show the experimental results in the next sections.

The contributions of this study are as follows:

1) We developed a dataset of restaurant menus in Japanese roadside stations. The dataset has 8,707 menus from 1,109 roadside stations in 47 prefectures (regions) (Please contact the 1st author if the database is needed.)
2) We discovered that the keywords for the local foods were not only foods but also place names, dish names, and their combinations.

In Section 2, we propose a keyword extraction method. In Section 3, we explain experiments and experimental results. In Section 4, we discuss the experimental results. In Section 5, we conclude the paper.

II. KEYWORD EXTRACTION METHOD

Figure 1 illustrates the outline of the keyword extraction method. The method is based on restaurant menus of roadside stations. Furthermore, the texts of restaurant menus are parsed into words. The words are evaluated based on their locality and assigned evaluation values. The method extracts keywords with a high locality for the local foods. The following sections will introduce how to develop a dataset and extract keywords.

TABLE I: DATASET EXAMPLE OF RESTAURANT MENUS IN ROADSIDE STATIONS. THE AUTHORS TRANSLATED JAPANESE MENUS INTO ENGLISH.

Menu	Roadside station	Prefecture
Chinese noodle with horse meat	Shichinohe	Aomori
Chinese noodle with boiled strawberry	Hashikami	Aomori
Curry with Murakami (place name) beef	Asahi	Nigata
Rice with tea poured and a sea bream in Kashiwazaki (place name)	Nigata furusato mura	Nigata
Meal of fried pork with Japanese miso	Fuji	Shizuoka
Japanese mustard flavored ice cream	Amagi goe	Shizuoka
Meal of fried pork of Fujisakura (place name)	Mitomi	Yamanashi
Row salmon of Shinshu (place name)	Kotani	Yamanashi
Meal of fried chicken of Choshu (place name) with vinegar and tartar sauce	Abucho	Yamaguchi
Meal of rice bowl with fried shrimp of Hagi (place name) and Japanese noodle	Hagi jyukan	Yamaguchi
Cold Japanese soba of Reiwa (era name of Japan's official calendar)	Adachi	Fukushima
Meal of Aizu (place name) DE Jyaran	Kita no sato	Fukushima
Rice bowl of fried gamecock with vinegar and tartar sauce	Nangoku furari	Kochi
Rice bowl of shiitake mushroom	Birafu	Kochi
Ice cream with fig flavored	Buzen okoshikake	Fukuoka
Ice cream with salt and Yame (place name) tea flavored	Tachibana	Fukuoka
Curry with Japanese pepper	Shimizu	Wakayama
Fried chicken	San Pin Nakatsu	Wakayama
Curry with loquat	Tomiura	Chiba
Meal of preserved fish	Kamogawa ocean park	Chiba

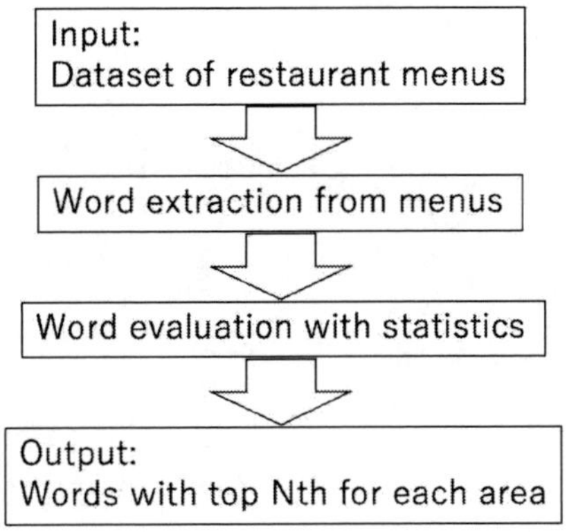

Figure 1. Outline of the proposed method.

A. Dataset of restaurant menus in roadside stations

We focus on the restaurant menus at roadside stations that may provide menus of local foods. These roadside stations are government-designated rest areas located along Japanese roads [8]. There are shops, rest areas, and restaurants that people can use 24 hours a day. Drivers use the facilities since these stations are along roads. However, these stations are used to promote and make local areas active. They provide services using the local culture, famous places, and specialties; the local food is a specialty. Although ingredients for the local foods can be bought at the market, these items must be cooked before they can be eaten. For example, B. C. roll is indigenous to Canada. Salmon, cucumber, rice, and some sauce can be bought at markets but must be cooked before being eaten as B. C. roll. Since the roadside stations provide the ingredients for the local foods and have restaurants, their restaurants may offer menus that include these ingredients for the local foods. Thus, we use restaurant menus at roadside stations to extract keywords for the local foods.

TABLE II: STATISTICAL DATA OF DATASET.

Item	Value
Number of prefectures	47
Number of roadside stations	1,109
Number of menus	8,707
Average of menus per a prefecture	184.8
Minimum of menus among prefectures	0
Maximum of menus among prefectures	561
Average of menus per a roadside station	24.9
Minimum of menus among roadside stations	0
Maximum of menus among roadside stations	102

These roadside stations have Web pages that provide information about their services. We develop a dataset of restaurant menus in roadside stations using the following attributes:

1) Restaurant menu.
2) Roadside station of the restaurant offering the menu.
3) Prefecture, where the roadside station is located.

We choose prefectures in Japan as the regions. The dataset has the three attributes in one line that are separated by commas. TABLE I shows a part of the dataset.

TABLE II shows the statistical information of the dataset. The dataset has 8,707 menus from 1,109 roadside stations in 47 prefectures. The average of menus per prefecture and roadside station is 184.8 and 24.9, respectively.

B. Keyword extraction for a local food

Restaurant menus in the dataset are parsed into words. The words are evaluated in their locality and extracted as keywords for the local foods. Keyword extraction is performed by the previous method [7] using a statistical index called Term Frequency and Inverse Document Frequency (TF-IDF). TF-IDF is an index for word importance in a document [9]; it is a product of two indices: TF (term frequency) and IDF (inverse document frequency).

Although a document contains numerous words, word distributions are not uniform. Some words appear frequently while others do not. Since a document consists of messages by the author, words of high frequency must be more significant for a document. Thus, the word frequency is used to evaluate word importance in a document; this is called a TF value. However, when looking at a set of documents, some words appear in most of the documents while others do not. Therefore, words that appear in particular documents must be more important for the documents. Thus, the inverse document frequency is used to evaluate the word importance for a document; this is called an IDF value. The two values are multiplied to obtain a TF-IDF value using (1).

$$TF - IDF(w, d) = tf(w, d) \times log\frac{N+1}{df(w, D)+1}, \quad (1)$$

where w is a word, d is a document that includes word w, N denotes the number of documents, and D is a set of N documents.

The previous study [7] applied TF-IDF to extract keywords for the local foods. It is assumed that the keywords for the local foods frequently appear in the menus of the area. In contrast, the keywords for the local foods do not frequently appear in those from other areas. Based on this assumption, Restaurant Frequency (RF) and Inverse Local Frequency (ILF) were adopted instead of TF and IDF. The product of the two values becomes RF-ILF, which is given by (2).

$$RF - ILF(w, a) = rf(w, a) \times log\frac{M+1}{lf(w, A)+1}, \quad (2)$$

where a is a menu that includes the word w, M denotes the number of prefectures, and A is a set of M prefectures.

In this study, we employ words that are nouns, verbs, adjectives, and adverbs. For parsing, we used MeCab and the NeologD as a dictionary. Words with a high locality for each prefecture are extracted as keywords for the local foods.

III. EXPERIMENT

We conducted experiments with participants.

A. Experimental settings

Experimental procedures were as follows:

1) An experimenter extracts keywords using the method introduced in Section II.
2) The experimenter asks participants to evaluate whether or not the extracted keywords are for the local foods.
3) The experimenter evaluates the rate of keywords for the local foods.

The experimenter is the second author of this study. We chose prefectures as the regions. In procedure 1), the experimenter extracted 20 keywords for each of the 47 prefectures in Japan, totaling 940 keywords.

In procedure 2), 92 Japanese participated in the experiment. Their ages ranged from 10 to 80, which includes 45 men and 47 women. The experimenter asked the participants to choose prefectures from which they were born and resided for a long time. Then, the participants evaluated the keywords of the chosen prefectures based on their locality. We obtained 100 answers for 29 prefectures because some participants chose a few prefectures. The average answer was 1.08 for each participant. The experimenter evaluated the rate of keywords for the local foods for each prefecture in Japan (in procedure 3)). The experiments were conducted on December, 2021.

TABLE III: EXPERIMENTAL RESULT: RATES OF KEYWORDS FOR LOCAL FOODS. THE TOP AND BOTTOM FIVE PREFECTURES ARE DEPICTED.

Prefecture	Rate
Hokkaido	68%
Nagasaki	64%
Okinawa	39%
Gifu	30%
Aomori	28%
Hiroshima	4%
Ibaragi	5%
Miyazaki	6%
Kanagawa	8%
Yamaguchi	10%
Average	21.1%

TABLE IV: EXAMPLES OF EXTRACTED KEYWORD FOR HOKKAIDO PREFECTURE AND THEIR APPROVAL RATES. PLACE NAME MEANS A KEYWORD TYPE.

Keyword	Rate	Type
Siretoko	100%	Place name
Rausu	66%	Place name
Chinese noodle	100%	Dish name
Ice cream	33%	Dish name
Curry	0%	Dish name
Oyster	100%	Food name
Scallop	66%	Food name
Fried noodles with starchy sauce	33%	Dish name
Hanamaka	100%	Place name
Kelp	100%	Food name
Crab	66%	Food name
Traditional Fried Chicken	100%	Dish name
Dosan	100%	Place name
Lunch	33%	Others (meal style)
Salmon roe	100%	Food name
Mongolian mutton barbecue	100%	Dish name
Sun flower	33%	Others (plant name)
Atsukeshi	0%	Place name
Uryu	66%	Place name
Vegetable	66%	Food name

B. Experimental results

TABLE III shows experimental results, which illustrates the top and bottom five prefectures of the approval rate of keywords for the local food. We obtained answers from 29 of the 47 prefectures. The highest, lowest, and average approval rates were 68%, 4%, and 21.1%, respectively. The approval rate was the rate of approval numbers versus answer numbers.

IV. DISCUSSION

We discuss a prefecture with the highest rate of keywords for the local foods. TABLE IV shows the extracted keywords and approval rates by the participants. We obtained answers from three participants. More than half of the participants approved 14 of the 20 keywords. We extracted the top 20 keywords with a high locality. However, some keywords were judged as not the local foods (for example, curry and ice cream).

TABLE V: TYPES OF KEYWORDS WITH THE HIGHEST LOCALITY FOR 47 PREFECTURES.

Type	Rate (total 47 prefectures)
Place name	40%
Dish name	26%
Food name	17%
Combination of place and food names	11%
Person name	4%
Adjective	2%

The extracted keywords are for food and non-food items. We analyzed different types of keywords. The third column of TABLE IV shows the types of keywords. We observed that the keywords were not only for foods but also for place names, dish names, meal styles, and plant names. Furthermore, we assumed that other prefectures had similar trends in keyword types. The same analysis of keywords with the highest locality in each prefecture was conducted. TABLE V shows the analysis result. We observed that the different types of keywords were place names (40%), dish names (26%), food names (17%), combinations of place and food names (11%), and others (person names and adjectives were 4% and 2%, respectively). The results indicated that the keywords for the local foods were not necessarily foods. People can feel the locality from keywords for place and dish names.

V. Conclusions

This study applied a basic statistical method for extracting keywords for local foods from restaurant menus of roadside stations. First, we developed a dataset of restaurant menus of roadside stations. The dataset included 8,707 menus from 1,109 roadside stations in 47 Japanese prefectures. Then, we applied the previous method to the dataset to extract keywords for the local foods. We asked participants to evaluate whether or not the extracted keywords were for the local foods. The average of keywords for the local foods was 21.1%. We found that the results might be significant because keywords for local foods could be extracted but the extraction rates were not high. We would like to improve the proposed method to obtain keywords for local foods with a higher accuracy. Furthermore, we observed that the extracted keywords were not only for foods but also place names, dish names, and their combinations. We haven't compare the results with those of previous study [7] because the evaluation method was not the same. We will evaluate the consistency of the proposed method by comparing the results of [7].

Acknowledgement

This paper was partly supported by Ritsumeikan Global Innovation Research Organization. We show our great appreciation.

References

[1] T. Sengel, A. Karagoz, G. Cetin, F. I. Dincer, S. M. Ertugral, and M. Balik, "Tourists ' Approach to Local Food," Procedia - Social and Behavioral Sciences, vol. 195, pp. 429-437, 2015.

[2] F. J. Jimenez Beltran, F. Santa-Cruz, and T. Lopez-Guzman, "Gastronomy as a Factor of Tourism Development: Case Study of the City of Cordoba in Spain, " Journal of Gastronomy and Tourism, vol.2. pp.1-14, 2016

[3] J. Chrzan, "Slow food: What, why, and to where?" Food, Culture & Society, vol. 7, no. 2, pp. 117-132, 2004.

[4] E. Latham, "Food tourism in oceania: Telling the stories," Tourism Culture & Communication, vol. 21, no. 3, pp. 221-234, 2021.

[5] H. R. Yurtseven and O.Kaya, "Local food in local menus: The case of gokceada," Tourismos: An International Multidisciplinary Journal of Tourism, vol. 6, no. 2, pp. 263-275, 2011.

[6] M. Nummedal and C. M. Hall, "Local food in tourism: An investigation of the new zealand south island ' s bed and breakfast sector ' s use and perception of local food," Tourism Review International, vol. 9, no. 4, pp. 365-378, 2006.

[7] Y. Tanaka, R. Yamanishi, and Y. Nishihara, "A study on regional characteristics of food by statistical analysis of menus on restaurant search websites (in japanese)," In ARG the 13th Web Intelligenceand Interaction Domestic Conference, no. 13, pp. 61-64, 2018.

[8] Roadside station, https://en.wikipedia.org/wiki/Roadside station.

[9] G. Salton and M. J. McGill, "Introduction to modern information retrieval," McGrow-Hill Book Company, 1983.

Integrating Active Learning and Analysis with Near-Infrared Spectroscopy into Virtual English for Specific Purposes Classes

Rumi Tobita
Center for Liberal Arts and Sciences
Ashikaga University
Tochigi, Japan
email : tobita.rumi@g.ashikaga.ac.jp

***Abstract*— This study introduces an effective online course design adopting active learning and analysis with Near-Infrared Spectroscopy from a brain science and educational technology perspective to meet English for Specific Purposes Curriculum goals for Japanese engineering students and develop global engineers. Before introducing active learning into English for Specific Purposes classes, an experimental study using Near-Infrared Spectroscopy was conducted to clarify preferable combinations of learners' characteristics and the pedagogical methods. Based on its results, project-based learning was successfully integrated into face-to-face English for Specific Purposes classes as active learning. This new attempt obtained favorable outcomes, enhancing learners' collaborative skills, and critical and creative thinking. The results show the effects of adapting active learning strategy into the online English for specific purposes classes.**

Keywords- Near-Infrared Spectroscopy (NIRS); English for Specific Purposes (ESP); Active Learning (AL); project-based learning (PBL); online

I. INTRODUCTION

English for Specific Purposes (ESP) is often defined as English language teaching which is designed to meet specified needs and related in content to particular disciplines, occupations, and activities of learners. ESP also requires careful research and design of pedagogical materials and activities for an identifiable group of adult learners within a specific learning context [1]. According to a theoretical framework of ESP, Needs Analysis-based researches and experiments had been conducted to develop global engineers. In previous studies, the outcomes revealed that many Japanese engineering students tend to be anxious about expressing themselves in English and less motivated to improve their communication skills [2][3]. To solve these concerns, several studies have been implemented integrating data from brain activities and the pedagogical concept to verify an effective ESP course design [4][5]. Before the COVID-19 pandemic, Active Learning (AL) had been introduced as in-person ESP classes and obtained favorable outcomes, such as, raising students' motivation and attitudes to engage tasks and activities [6]. In this study, to develop an effective online ESP course design, AL was embedded into ESP classes using a virtual meeting platform.

Section II briefly introduces pedagogical methods related to brain science and educational technology. In Sections III and IV, implementing AL strategies in ESP classes is described, and Section V presents the conclusions and future remarks.

II. APPLYING BRAIN DATA TO COURSE DESIGN

In the field of educational technology, Aptitude Treatment Interaction suggests that pedagogical strategies work effectively when the instructions match to the learners' aptitudes [7]. Recently, brain activity has become subject to monitoring by technologically innovative instruments, such as Near-Infrared Spectroscopy (NIRS) [8]. NIRS is recognized as a practical non-invasive optical technique to detect hemoglobin density dynamics response during functional activation of the cerebral cortex [9]. Accordingly, to develop an effective ESP course design, Aptitude Treatment Interaction based experiments using NIRS data have been conducted to examine the interaction of learners' aptitudes and instructions in previous studies. In these experiments, participants' listening proficiencies were adopted as learners' aptitudes, and silent and oral reading were adopted as instructions to investigate the difference of brain activity during practice to verify effective AL strategy [6].

III. ACTIVE LEARNING METHODOLOGY

Recently, The Ministry of Education, Science and Technology attempted to integrate AL methodology to Japanese education. Thus, AL frequently appears in university syllabi and textbooks used by instructors. Methodologically, there are various terms used to describe AL, including: student-centered learning, collaborative learning (team, peer or group learning), and participatory learning in which students are actively engaged in building their understanding of facts, ideas, and skills through the completion of instructor- directed tasks and activities [10]. Moreover, AL has a number of benefits for students, for instance, raising motivation, engaging in tasks and activities and, in higher order thinking skills such as synthesis, and evaluation, and avoiding passive listening.

IV. APPLYING PROJECT- BASED LEARNING

Acquiring English communication skills is a critical need so as to develop global engineers who can work in the real-world environment and exchange ideas globally. Thus, in this study, Project-Based Learning (PBL) is implemented to develop global engineers. PBL is a pedagogical approach encouraging learners to gain knowledge and skills through engaging tasks; therefore, in this study, adapted material was task-based themed, in addition to applying a communicative approach to improve communication skills. The material is ideal for building English communicative fluency and confidence while developing practical workplace knowledge and skills. Especially through this material, learners imagined that they were new interns at a fictional company where they worked together in small teams to perform a series of linked tasks and projects to develop new products such as SWOT analysis and focus group. Therefore, integrating PBL material enabled the learners to develop fluency and confidence in speaking, listening, reading, and writing via highly-contextualized tasks (as shown in Table 1), including discussions, presentations, self and team evaluations, report writing, and viewing video instructions using online meeting platform. In addition to PBL, assignments for improving reading and vocabulary-building skills were given to the learners. Due to the COVID-19 pandemic, PBL had to be integrated into virtual ESP classes. This online ESP classes conducted for about 150 engineering students at Japanese technical colleges in 2020 and 2021.

TABLE I. PBL: PROJECT SEQUENCE.

Stage 1	Inters join the company orientation
Stage 2	Teams prepare new product proposals
Stage 3	Teams discuss and evaluate product proposal
Stage 4	Teams perform market research on the product
Stage 5	Teams plan a multimedia advertising campaign
Stage 6	Interns prepare a resume and interview for a job

Table 2 shows the implementation of PBL strategies in ESP classes with Zoom. Having learners in shared small groups could foster a deeper level of connection and communication through breakout rooms.

TABLE II. PBL: INSTRUCTIONSL SEQUENCE USING ZOOM.

Intro-duction and review (10min.)	Viewing video instruction (10min.)	Giving instructions for small group activities (15 min.)	Breakout rooms' activities (30 min.)	Feedback and review (15 min.)

However, breakout rooms' activities enabled learners to engage with small group discussion, presentation, and evaluation, offering opportunities for deeper learning in context and for the development of valuable skills tied to learners' career readiness, instructors' involvement, and support visiting each breakout room is essential. To clarify the effect of integrating AL into virtual ESP classes, the learners were required to submit weekly reflection papers and a final reflection report, to conduct a Can-Do statement and take The Test of English for International Communication (TOEIC) at the end of the semester.

V. CONCLUSION

Learners' feedback gathered from the reflection papers was mainly positive. Significant improvements were also noted in students' competence to communicate using engineering terms and capability of team-work skills to attain the tasks such as SWOT analysis and focus group. Accordingly, it can be said that continuously implementing an AL pedagogical framework into virtual ESP classes could result in effective outcomes and enhance and promote learners' qualities as global engineers. This study and its findings could be relevant to online AL classes. There are still some limitations that need to be addressed. In further study, the latest data of NIRS should be integrated to clarify the effectiveness of AL.

ACKNOWLEDGMENT

This study is supported by a Grant-in-Aid for Scientific Research (C) (No. 18K00788), from 2018 to 2022.

REFERECES

[1] T. Dudley-Evans, "Developments in English for Specific Purposes: A multi-disciplinary approach". Cambridge University Press, 1998.

[2] R. Tobita and H. Kuniyoshi, "The Needs Analysis of English Learners in a Technological College" in Ashikaga Institute of Technology Collaborative Research Center Annual Review. Vol.7, pp.160- 174, 2006.

[3] R. Tobita, M. Miyazaki and M. Ochiai, " Curriculum Development based on Needs Analysis of English Education –Comparison between Technical and Co-medical Universities-", in Ashikaga Institute of Technology Collaborative Research Center Annual Review. Vol. 8, pp.161 -178, 2007.

[4] R. Tobita, "Effectiveness of Analysis with Near-Infrared Spectroscopy for EFL Learners in Japan", HCI International 2016 - Posters' Extended Abstracts - 18th International Conference, HCI International 2016, Toronto, Canada, Proceedings, Part II pp.201-206, 2016.

[5] R. Tobita, "Development of effective ESP course design integrating analysis with near-infrared spectroscopy" ICSIT 2017 - 8th International Conference on Society and Information Technologies, Proceedings Volume 2017-March, Orlando; United States, pp. 183-186, 2017.

[6] R. Tobita, E. Takahashi and T. Okoda, " Effective usage of NIRS data for Japanese EFL Course Design", in Ashikaga University Collaborative Research Center Annual Review. Vol.20 , pp.91-96, 2019.

[7] L. J. Cronbach and R. E. Snow, "Aptitudes and Instructional Methods: A Handbook for Research in Interactions". John Wiley & Sons Inc, New Jersey, 1977.

[8] T. Shimura ed., "Prefrontal Lobe Measurement Using Near Infraraed Spectroscopy – Evaluation of Early Detection Methods and Rehabilitation Methods of Dementia — ", CORONA Publishing, 2009.

[9] Shimadzu. LABNIRS. [Online]. Available from: http://www.an.shimadzu.co.jp/bio/nirs/nirs2.htm /2022.03.21.

[10] K. Y. Zewdu, "Active Learning in Teaching English Language Support Courses to First-Year Students in Some Ethiopian Universities," Doctorate Thesis of Unicersity of South Africa, 2017.

Suitability of Immersive 2D Environments for Tertiary Education using the Gather Environment as an Example

Gerhard Hube, Kevin Pfeffel
Faculty of Economics and Business Administration and
Faculty of Computer Science and Business Information Systems
University of Applied Sciences Würzburg-Schweinfurt
Würzburg, Germany
e-mail: gerhard.hube@fhws.de
e-mail: kevin.pfeffel@fhws.de

***Abstract*— In the last two years, university teaching has been strongly influenced by online formats, mainly by video conference systems. Beyond that, there are also some practical examples for the use of immersive environments in higher education, mainly focused on the usage of virtual reality (VR) or augmented reality (AR) environments. However, this study aims to see if immersive 2D environments are also holistically suitable for teaching in terms of presence, participation, collaboration, and active learning for higher education, as they can offer advantages over video conferencing systems, but are not as costly as VR and AR solutions. A Master's program at the University of Applied Sciences Würzburg-Schweinfurt was chosen for the study. The selected course was held completely in an immersive 2D environment over one semester. Accompanying the course, subjects were asked to complete the Online Learning Environment Survey (OLLES) questionnaire weekly for analysis. Thereby a descriptive evaluation of the questionnaire takes place. All dimensions of the OLLES questionnaire achieve high to very high values. From a purely descriptive point of view, it can therefore be assumed that the used immersive 2D environment is holistically suitable as a learning environment in the tertiary sector. Nevertheless, this should be further explored in future studies by also comparing different courses (immersive 2D environments, video conferencing systems, VR/AR environments, and real-world teaching lectures) to make even stronger statements.**

Keywords-Virtual Learning Environments; Online Teaching; Tertiary Education; 2D Environments; Desktop virtual reality

I. INTRODUCTION

University teaching has been heavily influenced by online teaching over the past two years as a result of the COVID 19 pandemic measures. Besides the isolated usage of VR or AR environments [1], primarily the classic video conferencing tools such as "zoom", "GoToWebinar" or "Cisco Webex" were used, according to their market shares [2]. All of the classic video conferencing tools use video and audio transmission in a simple representation of the participants on the screen of the end device. Due to the continuous and time-consuming use of these systems, signs of fatigue and weariness could be observed, often referred to as "zoom fatigue" [3] [4] also and especially for university students within online courses [5]. However, it can be assumed that online communication and events will continue in the future after COVID 19 pandemic [6]. Therefore, alternatives or additions to classic video conferencing systems such as VR should also be analyzed in order to check their suitability, especially for online university lectures. A first pilot study showed higher spatial and social presence for VR group meetings in comparison with video conference systems [7]. In contrast to video conferencing systems, the representation of the participant in VR is integrated into a virtual world and allows to explore and interact within a dynamic virtual environment [8].

Further, within this introduction there are given some definitions and explanations about the basic terms like VR and immersion and the status quo of VR in education and virtual learning environments (VLE). Section 2 shows the related works for VR and VLE in higher education and especially in tertiary education. Section 3 presents the virtual learning environment gather.town and their specific software features which are used in the study and also the measuring instrument OLLES [9] for analyzing the different dimensions. Section 4 resumes the results, which are then discussed in detail in Section 5. The paper is finished with Section 6 to describe limitations and give an outlook to further work.

A. VR/immersion

VR can be distinguished between immersive VR (I-VR) including additional devices like a head mounted display (HMD) and non-immersive VR on the screen of some end devices, also declared as desktop VR (D-VR) [10]-[13]. Di Natale even suggest a three-way division between non-immersive systems like desktop VR (D-VR), semi-immersive systems like AR or wide field displays and immersive systems like HMD or special designed rooms with projected walls (CAVE) [14]. While the definition for VR seems to be clear in literature, the term of immersion is a multifaceted concept without clarification [1]. On the one side, immersion is viewed as a kind of objective characteristics in terms of technical systems and affordances [15] or a psychological subjective characterized by one's perception of presence and interaction [16]. While Bergstrom defines immersion as an objective property of the platform environment and presence as a subjective feeling [17], it seems that the term of immersion started to become synonymous with "presence" [18]. Despite the strict separation between non-immersive and immersive VR, recent studies tend to consider immersion as a kind of continuum from highly immersive or high-end for I-VR and low immersive or low-end for desktop VR systems (D-VR) [18]-[20]. This is probably because there can be some kind of immersion and spatial presence on desktop VR systems as well.

B. VR in education

The high-end immersive VR seems to fascinate and inspire people in their first reaction, probably because of the high level of immersion and appearance [21]. Especially in terms of education, there were several announcements about ground breaking improvements by the usage of immersive VR, like increasing memory capacity or making better decisions [23]. Wu et.al. reported that I-VR-lectures are more effective than non-immersive environments [24] and Gao assumes better learning outcomes because I-VR is more engaging than traditional methods [25]. A meta-study found that the majority of studies on immersive learning environments from 2014-2019 used AR or VR applications, although all forms of immersion in learning and education were explicitly included. Among other things, the study shows the need for more research on less immersive learning environments with higher narrative and greater challenge [1]. Although the level of immersion in desktop VR systems is not as intense as fully immersive VR technologies, it is not the case that higher immersion and presence directly lead to better learning performance [19]. Johnson-Glenberg discovered, that the main effect for better learning is not the level of immersion between 2D or 3D virtual environment but the level of embodiment. The study compared the learning outcomes between groups learning with a low immersion platform on a desktop and a high immersive platform with an HMD (I-VR). The low embodied I-VR group performed significantly worse than the desktop group with high level embodying [18]. Radianti, states that immersive VR technologies are particularly used in education, even if their level of maturity still seems questionable and there are several research gaps [26]. Hamilton found in his literature review that in most I-VR studies between 2013 and 2019, there was a significant benefit of using I-VR in education. But he also restrict that most studies used short interventions and were mainly focused on scientific topics such as biology or physics [13]. Additionally, there are still limitations remaining, while using immersive VR. Besides higher costs for immersive VR, above all cyber sickness in terms of e.g. headache, blurred vision or dizziness are effects of using HMD technologies [27]. This is one reason why such systems should be used only for a limited span of time [28]. Due to this and considering the specific requirements and accommodations for university lectures, desktop VR applications appear to be more suitable for online education [9] [29] [20].

C. Virtual learning environment (VLE)

Another keyword often used in connection with virtual learning is virtual learning environment (VLE). This term includes a wide range of systems like simple web pages, learning management systems like MOODLE but also three-dimensional learning environments like Second Life or OpenSim [30]. Reisoğlu, following Zuiker, defines the term "3D Virtual Learning Environment (3DVLE)" and describes it as platforms for virtual worlds with avatars as representatives and the ability to communicate via audio or text, such as Second Life or OpenSim [31] [32]. Other authors use the term of "immersive 3D virtual world" or "immersive 3D virtual environment" for similar systems to describe computer based simulated environments in which users are able to immerse themselves through avatars [33] [34]. We will follow the wording of "immersive 3D/2D virtual environment" to describe desktop VR with different levels of immersion. Within this paper we do not include learning management platforms (LMS) for distribution of contents, messages, notices and communication via forums and chats, like e.g. Moodle although they are included in the term of virtual learning environment (VLE) [35] [36]. We want to focus on low immersion desktop solutions that provide the ability to move, interact, collaborate, and communicate in a kind of virtual environment using an avatar. The aim is to use them for online master lectures at universities.

II. RELATED WORK

There are already a number of studies and experiences for the use of virtual learning environments in higher education which are presented below.

A. Immersive VR (I-VR) in higher education

There are several studies on the impact of mainly immersive VR (I-VR) in higher education. Chien et.al. stated that a VR environment increases the motivation and critical thinking skills [37]. Tepe concluded that a VR environment increases performance and professional skill development [38]. Other studies also showed several positive effects on the academic success and motivation [39] [40]. Wen-Yu Lee discovered higher scores in science concepts for sixth-grade students learning with I-VR systems in comparison to students without the help of immersive systems [41]. In the field of higher education, a meta-study analyzed studies on desktop-based virtual environments, games and simulations in particular. They concluded that these virtual tools could be effective in improving learning outcomes [12]. Mystakidis et. al. conducted a literature review analyzing the outcomes of distant learning and their effect on various criteria of "deep and meaningful learning" such as cognitive, social or affective aspects for K-12 high school students. As a result, positive outcomes were found, especially in terms of performance, satisfaction, cooperation and motivation. Although it is also emphasized that insufficient didactic quality cannot be compensated by online formats [42]. In a metastudy on the effects of immersive VR on students' academic performance, Akgün concluded that there are many positive effects on students' abilities, such as an increase in motivation and other positive contributions to learning. Despite to these positive results, the study also determined that there are still technical and health problems to be solved [43].

B. Virtual learning environment (VLE) in higher education

In addition, studies with desktop VR in higher education detected better performance achieved in groups using desktop

VR. However dependent from the individual spatial ability [44]. Reisoğlu analyzed studies between 2000 and 2015 on 3D virtual learning environments (3DVLEs) and various aspects such as platforms used, research topics, and achievements. He found that the Second Life platform is the most used platform and that studies on 3DVLEs peaked around 2012 for simulation and learning support. He concluded some overall positive emotional and cognitive achievements on presence, satisfaction, communication skills and engagement [31]. Coffey also analyzed the second life platform against a normal computer surface for comparing the impact on intercultural sensitivity and reveals significant gains with the usage of a virtual environment [34]. Another study analyzed the effects of collaborative learning in virtual environments with the use of 3D avatars in a virtual learning environment (VLE). The results showed that regardless of a collaborative group or an individual group, learning improved, but participation in a collaborative group had a significant positive effect on academic achievement and satisfaction in higher education [45]. In a systematic literature review on "simulation games", it was discovered that better results in terms of declarative knowledge, procedural knowledge and knowledge retention could be achieved through the use of desktop-based immersive environments for the education of trainees [46].

C. *VR/VLE in tertiary education:*

One of the early publications on "desktop 3D learning environments" without the use of head-up displays in tertiary education comes from Charles Sturt University. Here it is already pointed out that a desktop application is easier for the users and reduces physical and psychological stress compared to immersive virtual worlds with head-mounted displays [47]. A combination of learning management system with Moodle and 3D desktop environment with OpenSim was used in a study to design and evaluate a VLE for teaching with undergraduate students. There were effects on learning skills and understanding of sociocultural aspects that have a strong impact on social interaction when students participate and collaborate in common tasks and activities [30]. Collaboration and interaction seemed to be a high demanded factor influencing VLE systems, either by students and also academic staff [48]. A special form of 3D virtual learning environment is used for analyzing dental students' performance. When comparing stereoscopic 3D vision with passive circular polarized glasses to 2D vision on screen, significantly better results and higher appreciation for the 3D vision were found [49]. Another specific anatomy medical study about the role of stereopsis in virtual and mixed reality conducted that virtual and mixed reality is inferior to physical models [50].

Overall, there are several studies of desktop VR (D-VR) respectively VLE for specific topics, often computer science or medicine [28] [49]-[51]. These studies include various intensities of immersion, but still lack an evaluation of the overall and holistic suitability of 2D desktop learning environments for higher education, including the new immersive 2D environments that have appeared in the last three years.

III. METHOD

In the following we present the immersive learning environment gather town, in which the course took place and the measuring instrument OLLES, which was used for the assessment.

A. *Immersive 2D environment gather.town*

The software gather.town [52] was used as an immersive 2D environment. This is a web conferencing software that allows to create a complete virtual replica of the teaching building. Within this virtual space, users can move around using avatars and interact with each other and their environment. Similar to real life. If the avatars now walk around in the virtual environment and then meet each other at a certain distance, the camera and the microphone of the computers are automatically switched on and the users have the opportunity to communicate. The graphical user interface is quite simple and it does not demand any special requirements to run on a variety of computers. In preparation, the entire real seminar building was recreated in the gather.town environment and the following virtual environment settings and software features were used:

1) *Podium:*

The podium is the classic teaching situation (see Fig. 1). Within the gather.town environment, all students and the tutor are in one large room. The tutor stands in front at the lectern, while the students take their places at the tables. All students can see, hear and of course communicate with each other via camera and microphone. It is possible to share the screen to provide lecture slides or other content to all participants in the plenum area. In this way, the tutor can use lecture slides in addition to a verbal execution of the learning topic, as they would be used in a real teaching situation.

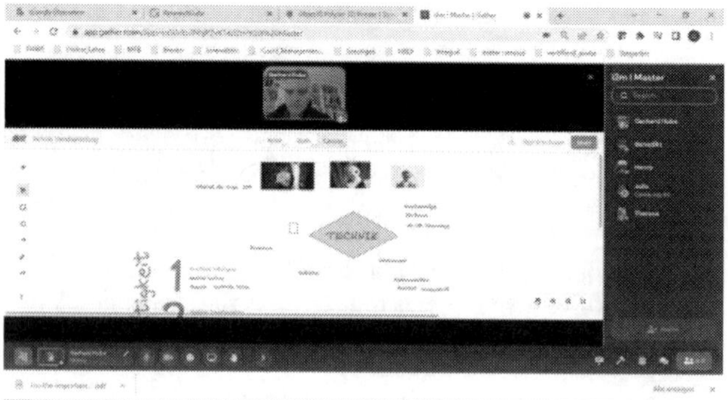

Figure 1. This is the podium. You can see a classic teaching situation in a shared space.

2) *Whiteboard:*

The whiteboard (see Fig. 2) provides an opportunity for collaborative work. To do this, the whiteboard must first be activated. After that, all users who access the whiteboard at the same time can work together on it. This means that all users get write permissions and can interact with the whiteboard. In addition, a video and audio function for communication is available for the workgroup to discuss and exchange while working on the board.

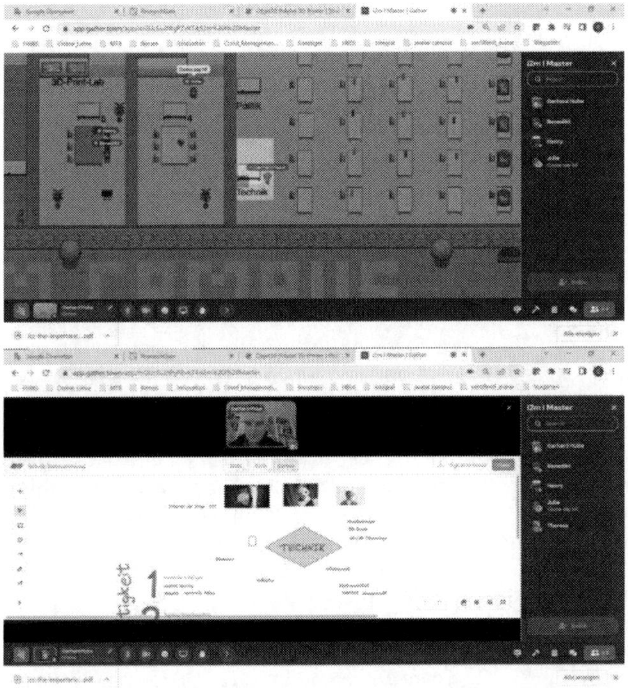

Figure 2. In the upper part of the picture, you can see the whiteboard placed in the room. Below you can see the view when using the interactive whiteboard.

3) Workshops:

Workshops are smaller rooms that provide fewer seats than the large seminar rooms. Here, there are tables with seats and a whiteboard (see Fig. 3). Thus, the users have the possibility to do smaller group work. They can use the table for meetings via the camera, or the whiteboard for joint work or screen sharing for presentation.

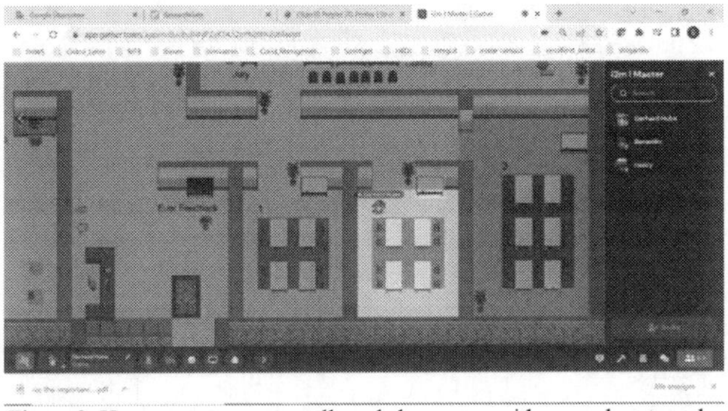

Figure 3. Here you can see a small workshop room with several seats and a whiteboard in the room.

4) Group discussion:

This is a room that is designed in such a way that a pro and a con side can sit opposite each other and participate in a group discussion by means of the camera (see Fig. 4). The whole setting is accompanied by possible viewers, but would also be monitored by a jury that rules the discussion and evaluates the individual arguments.

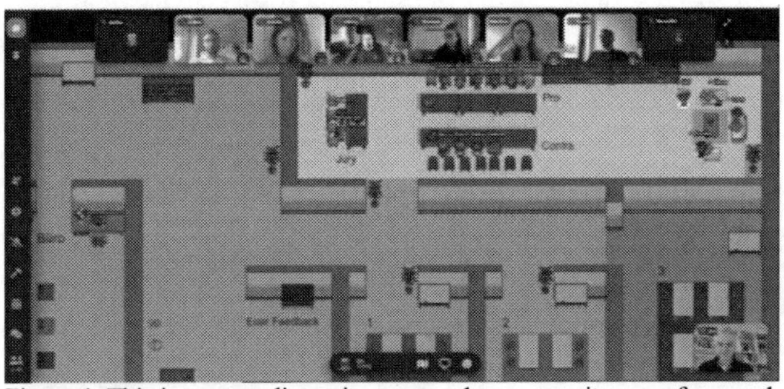

Figure 4. This is a group discussion room, where users sit across from each other in teams and a jury sits in the middle.

5) Break rooms:

In the break rooms, users can stay between the individual seminars and have the opportunity to play various card games at a game table, making music or watching videos (see Fig. 5). In another break room, users have the opportunity to get on a yoga mat. A 10-minute instructional video is then played so users can join in on the yoga session from home.

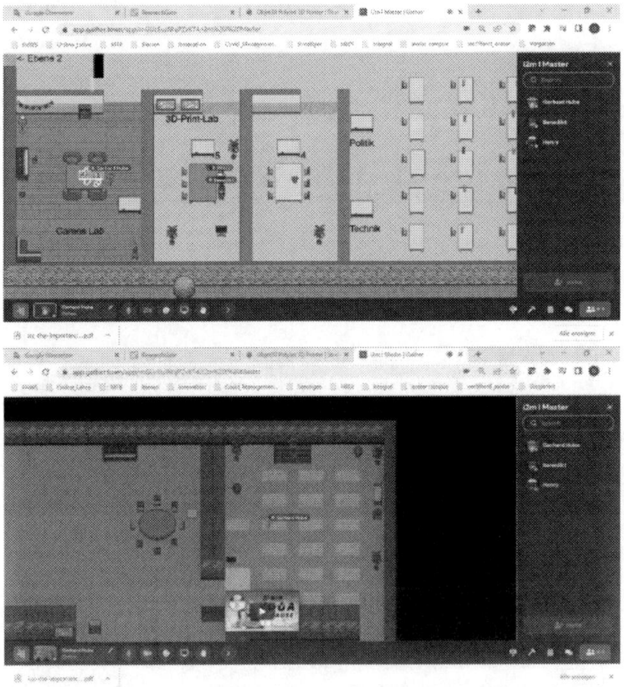

Figure 5. Here you can see the break rooms, where multiple users can gather and share interactive applications like a gaming table or a yoga room where a yoga tutorial is played as a video as soon as you step onto one of the green mats.

6) Other Interactive Objects:

Within the environment, other interactive objects are stationed in the individual rooms or corridors. In the entrance area, for example, there is a blackboard on which the timetable can be viewed, and next door, there is a tutorial that once again describes the functionality of the gather.town environment in a video. There is also a bookcase. If you use it, you get a web window within the gather.town environment, which leads you to the online catalog of the university (see Fig. 6). There the literature search can be accomplished.

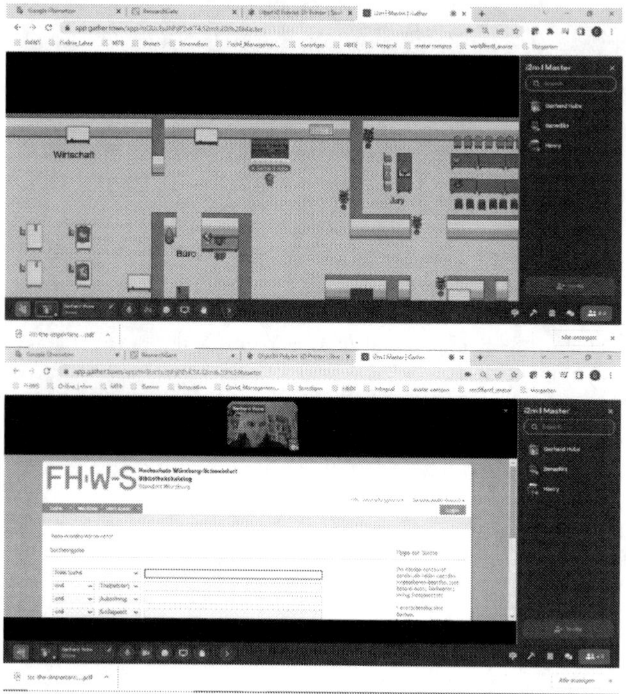

Figure 6. In the upper part of the picture, you can see a bookshelf, which stands freely in the room. Below is the view when you use the bookshelf. This is the online catalog of the university.

B. Measuring instrument

The OLLES questionnaire in its modified 35-item form was used as the measurement instrument [9]. The OLLES questionnaire is a web-based survey instrument for use in online learning environments in tertiary education. In this context, the OLLES questionnaire provides inferences about students' perceptions of interaction opportunities within an online environment in terms of economy and efficiency. The dimensions of the OLLES are Student Collaboration (SC), Computer Competence (CC), Active Learning (AL), Tutor Support (TS), Information Design and Appeal (IDA), Material Environment (ME), and Reflective Thinking (RT). In addition, questions about general computer use and Internet use were also recorded. All items were measured using a 5-point Likert scale.

C. Experimental procedure

Even before the first seminar, all test persons were familiarized with the gather.town environment. Especially the basic functions were tested, so that everybody knows them and can use them independently. In addition, the OLLES questionnaire was introduced, since this was used in its original language English, but the test persons were not native English speakers.

There were a total of four measurement time points. The seminar duration was always from 8:15 am to 13:15 pm. From the start of the test, the seminar was always first held in the gather.town environment and at all four measurement times the entire questionnaire was completed online directly afterwards.

D. Sample

All data were collected at the University of Applied Sciences Würzburg-Schweinfurt within the seminar “trend analysis and innovation assessment” of the master study program “Innovation for small and medium Enterprises”. A total of 17 subjects participated in the study. However, there were not measured values from all subjects at all four measurement time points. From two subjects there were only three measured values and from four subjects there were only two measured values. This is still sufficient to form an arithmetic mean. Nevertheless, one subject was excluded from the final analysis because he produced outlier values on three dimensions. This leaves n = 16 valid subjects for the final analysis. The average age of the subjects is 24.44 years, with a minimum of 22 years and a maximum of 30 years. Of the n = 16 subjects, 7 are female and 9 are male.

IV. RESULTS

The first part of the evaluation is purely descriptive and refers exclusively to the mean values of the dimensions of the OLLES questionnaire, as well as the further questions on computer use and Internet use.

In the case of computer use, it was found that all subjects use their computers daily or at least several times a week. In the case of Internet use, it was found that all subjects used the Internet on a daily basis.

When tested for normal distribution with respect to the dimensions of the OLLES, Student Collaboration (SC), Computer Competence (CC), Active Learning (AL), Tutor Support (TS), Information Design and Appeal (IDA), Material Environment (ME), and Reflective Thinking (RT), all were found to be normally distributed. Those descriptive values can be seen in Table 1.

In the second part of the evaluation, the Wilcoxon signed-ranked test was used to examine whether there were differences between the individual measurement points and thus whether there was a change in the evaluation with regard to the repetition of the use of the gather.town environment.

Since a normal distribution could not be determined for all variables, even after the exclusion of six subjects with partly missing values, the Wilcoxon test was used. Here, all requirements were met.

There were only significant differences between measurement time point 3 and measurement time point 4 for the dimensions Student Collaboration (Exact Wilcoxon Test: $z = -2.09$, $p = .037$, $n = 12$) and Material Environment (Exact Wilcoxon Test: $z = -2.41$, $p = .016$, $n = 12$). Otherwise, there were no other significant differences between measurement time points.

TABLE I. DESCRITIVE ANALYSIS

Descriptive Analysis					
Dimension	*Mean Value*	*Standard Error of the Mean*	*Standard Deviation*	*Minimum Value*	*Maximum Value*
Student Collaboartion (SC)	3,76	0,11	0,42	3,10	4,60
Computer Competence (CC)	4,57	0,11	0,44	3,55	5,00
Active Learning (AL)	3,64	0,13	0,46	2,70	4,60
Tutor Support (TS)	4,10	0,12	0,55	3,20	4,80
Information Design and Appeal (IDA)	3,73	0,12	0,47	2,93	4,80
Material Environment (ME)	3,84	0,07	0,28	3,50	4,45
Reflective Thinking (RT)	3,19	0,16	0,62	2,25	4,10

V. DISCUSSION

In the dimensions of computer use and Internet use, the subjects indicated that they use this on a daily basis. In addition, the gather.town environment and all basic functions were sufficiently explained before the start of the study. Thus, we assume that there were no poor ratings for the environment due to possible lack of technical skills.

All dimensions of the OLLES questionnaire reach high to very high scores. From a purely descriptive point of view, it can therefore be assumed that the gather.town environment is holistically suitable as a learning environment in the tertiary sector. Nevertheless, the individual dimensions will be examined below.

The Student Collaboration (SC) dimension asks in particular about the frequency of communication between students. This includes the question of help and feedback as well as the mutual exchange of information and resources. As already mentioned, studies have shown that collaboration [42] [45] [48] and communication [31] [48] have positive effects on users within a VLE. Therefore, this is an important factor for learning. It can be assumed that high values were achieved here in the evaluation, since gather.town provides enough possibilities, especially through the functions whiteboard, workshops, group discussion and informal encountering, that this can also be used profitably.

The dimension Computer Competence (CC) asks in particular about the assessed competence of one's own computer and Internet use and also the ability to solve minor problems oneself. Since the highest values were achieved here, this further supports the assumption that all subjects had more than sufficient technical skills to use the gather.town environment to its full extent.

The Active Learning (AL) dimension specifically asks about the motivation created, as well as the feedback received through the activities or the teaching unit within the environment itself. Again, various studies already showed that motivation [37] [39] [40] [42] [43] is a crucial factor in the use of VLE's. We assume that especially the varied design of the gather.town environment, but also the use of break rooms led to good scores on this dimension.

The dimension Tutor Support (TS) asks in particular about the participation and accessibility of the tutor. In this respect, the response time to questions and feedback play an important role. Good communication [31] and interaction [48] lead to positively perceived VLEs. The second highest score was obtained for this dimension. This may be due to constant availability and timely communication, as the tutor himself was also always present and responsive within the environment. Therefore, from this perspective, the gather.town environment is well suited for interactive teaching.

The dimension Information Design and Appeal (IDA) asks in particular how creative and original presented teaching materials are and whether graphics used are helpful and visually appealing. This mainly refers to the teaching slides presented as if they were in a presentation. Nevertheless, the colors and walking around within the environment can also have an impact on visual perception and lead to improved learning. In addition, there are the varied break rooms, so that there is also a fairly high rating here.

The dimension Material Environment (ME) asks in particular about the installation process and clarity in using the software. Since very high values were also achieved here, this further supports the point that all test subjects had more than sufficient technical skills to use the gather.town environment to its full extent. In addition, it can also be assumed that the environment is easy to learn and therefore has a high practical value. In general, it can be assumed that VLEs must be accessible and not have too many hurdles to ensure a successful learning environment.

The dimension Reflective Thinking (RT) asks in particular how well subjects were able to learn within the online environment, but also for a comparison to a real classroom. Since the scores here are also good, but lowest, it can be deduced that an online environment can be a sufficient substitute despite having sufficient features that are rated very positively in other dimensions, but real-world classrooms are still the most suitable form of teaching.

Repeated measurement of user ratings of the gather.town environment showed that there was virtually no difference. Although a meta-study by Merchant et al. [12] found small effects in simulation studies in terms of number of sessions, these were measures of learning outcome and not an assessment of the immersive environment as in this study. Therefore, it can be assumed that a one-time survey after the first unit or even after the last unit is quite sufficient.

VI. CONCLUSION

This study was exploratory in nature with the primary goal of seeing if an immersive 2D environment is holistically suitable for teaching in terms of presence, participation, collaboration, and active learning, and thus an enhancement over classic video transmission tools such as "zoom", "GoToWebinar" or "Cisco Webex", and the like. Thus, for now, only an overview of the use of an immersive 2D environment as a learning tool could be provided through this study. Group comparisons with other teaching formats could not yet be made. However, this is the next step in the research. For the next winter semester it is planned to complete the same lecture with a classical video conference tool and to run the same questionnaire. Afterwards a comparison of the two forms of teaching can be made. In addition, it seems to make sense to run another questionnaire in the form of the igroup presence questionnaire (IPQ) to see if there are differences in the sense of presence and how they affect the use. Furthermore, it was found that subsequent interviews may well provide additional important insights. In conversations with students, for example, we found that the gather.town environment was also used by students outside of the seminar to complete other group tasks. In further subsequent studies, I-VR environments can then also be tested in order to be able to make a comparison for this as well. At the moment, there are many indications that hybrid forms of teaching and learning will be used in the future.

REFERENCES

[1] D. Beck, L. Morgado, P. OShea, "Finding the Gaps about Uses of Immersive Learning Environments: A Survey of Surveys in: Journal of Universal Computer Science, vol. 26, no. 8, pp. 1043-1073, 2020. [Online]. Available from: https://repositorioaberto.uab.pt/bitstream/10400.2/10070/1/jucs_26_08_1043_1073_beck.pdf 2022.04.28

[2] Datanyze, LLC: zoom, top competitors of zoom, [Online]. Available from: https://www.datanyze.com/market-share/web-conferencing--52/zoom-market-share 2022.04.28

[3] G. Fauville, et al. (2021) "Nonverbal Mechanisms Predict Zoom Fatigue and Explain Why Women Experience Higher Levels, than Men," SSRN Electronic Journal. [Online]. Available from: https://papers.ssrn.com/sol3/Delivery.cfm/SSRN_ID3820035code4557167.pdf?abstractid=3820035&mirid=1K. 2022.04.28

[4] J. Rump, M.Brandt, "Zoom-Fatigue," 2020. [Online]. Available from: https://www.ibe-ludwigshafen.de/wp-content/uploads/2020/09/EN_IBE-Studie-Zoom-Fatigue.pdf 2022.04.28

[5] E. Peper, V. Wilson, M. Martin, E. Rosegard, R. Harvey, "Avoid Zoom Fatigue, Be Present and Learn," International society for neurofeedback ans research ISNR, 2021. [Online]. Available from: https://www.neuroregulation.org/article/view/21206/13976 2022.04.28

[6] S. Lund, A.Madgavkar, J .J. Manyika, S. S. Smit, K. Ellingrud, M. Robinson, O. Meaney, "The future of work after COVID-19," McKinsey Global Institute, 2021 [Online]. Available from: https://www.mckinsey.com/featured-insights/future-of-work/the-future-of-work-after-covid-19 2022.04.28

[7] F. Steinicke, N. Lehmann-Willenbrock, and A. L. Meinecke, "A First Pilot Study to Compare Virtual Group Meetings using Video Conferences and (Immersive) virtual reality," In Symposium on Spatial User Interaction (SUI '20). Association for Computing Machinery, New York, NY, USA, Article 19, pp. 1–2, 2020. DOI:https://doi.org/10.1145/3385959.3422699

[8] K. M. Chuah, C. J. Chen, and C. S. Teh, "Incorporating Kansei engineering in instructional design: designing virtual reality based learning environments from a novel, perspective," Themes in Science and Technology Education, 1(1), pp. 37-48, 2008.

[9] J. Clayton, "Development and Validation of an Instrument for Assessing Online Learning Environments in Tertiary Education: The Online Learning Environment Survey (OLLES)," doctoral thesis at Curtin university, 2007, [Online]. Available from: https://espace.curtin.edu.au/handle/20.500.11937/550 2022.04.28

[10] G. G. Robertson, S. K. Card, and J. Mackinlay, "Three views of virtual reality: nonimmersive virtual reality," Computer, 26(2), pp. 81, 1993. [Online]. Available from: https://ieeexplore.ieee.org/stamp/stamp.jsp?tp=&arnumber=192002 2022.04.28

[11] C. J. Chen, S. C. Toh, and M. F. Wan, "The theoretical framework for designing desktop virtual reality-based learning environments," Journal of Interactive Learning Research, 15(2), pp. 147.167, 2004.

[12] Z. Merchant, E. T. Goetz, L. Cifuentes, W. Keeney-Kennicutt, T. J. Davis, "Effectiveness of virtual reality-based instruction on students' learning outcomes in K-12 and higher education: A meta-analysis," in: Computers & Education 70 pp. 29–40, 2014. [Online]. Available from: https://www.sciencedirect.com/science/article/pii/S0360131513002108 2022.04.28

[13] D. Hamilton, J. McKechnie, E. Edgerton, and C. Wilson, "Immersive virtual reality as a pedagogical tool in education: a systematic literature review of quantitative learning outcomes and experimental design," in J. Comput. Educ. 8 (1), pp. 1–32, 2021. DOI: 10.1007/s40692-020-00169-2

[14] A. F. Di Natale, C. Repetto, G. Riva, and D. Villani, "Immersive virtual reality in K-12 and higher education: A 10-year systematic review of empirical research," in: Br. J. Educ. Technol. 51 (6), pp. 2006–2033, 2020. DOI: 10.1111/bjet.13030

[15] M. Slater, "Place illusion and plausibility can lead to realistic behaviour in immersive virtual environments," Philosophical Transactions of the Royal Society B: Biological Sciences, Vol. 36, pp. 3549-3557, 2009. https://doi.org/10.1098/rstb.2009.0138

[16] B. G. Witmer, M. J. Singer, "Measuring Presence in Virtual Environments: A Presence Questionnaire," Presence: Teleoperators and Virtual Environments, 1998 Vol. 7, No. 3 p. 22, 1998. https://doi.org/10.1162/105474698565686

[17] I. Bergstrom, S. Azevedo, P.Papiotis, N.Saldanha, and M. Slater, "The plausibility of a string quartet performance in virtual reality," IEEE Xplore, 23(4), pp. 1352–1359, 2017. https://doi.org/10.1109/TVCG.2017.2657138

[18] M. C. Johnson-Glenberg, H. Bartolomea, and E. Kalina, "Platform is not destiny: Embodiedlearning effects comparing 2D desktop to 3D virtual reality," STEM experiences Journal of Computer Assisted Learning, 37(5), pp. 1263–1284, 2021. https://doi.org/10.1111/jcal.12567

[19] J. Zhao , T. Sensibaugh , B. Bodenheimer , T. P. McNamara , A. Nazareth , N. Newcombe , M. Minear and A. Klippel

"Desktop versus immersive virtual environments: effects on spatial learning, Spatial Cognition & Computation," 2020. DOI: 10.1080/13875868.2020.1817925

[20] M. N. Selzer, N. F. Gazcon, M. L. Larrea, "Effects of virtual presence and learning outcome using low-end virtual reality systems," Displays, vol. 59, pp. 9-15, 2019. ISSN 0141-9382, https://doi.org/10.1016/j.displa.2019.04.002.

[21] S. S. Sundar, D. J. Tamul, and M. Wu, "Capturing "cool": Measures for assessing coolness of technological products," International Journal of Human-computer Studies, 72(2), pp. 169–180, 2014. doi:10.1016/j.ijhcs.2013.09.008

[22] D. Quesnel, B. E. Riecke, "Awestruck: Natural interaction with virtual reality on eliciting awe. In B. Thomas, R. J. Teather, & M. Marchal (Eds.), 2017 IEEE symposium on 3D user interfaces (3DUI): Proceedings," March 18- 19,2017, Los Angeles, CA, USA pp. 205–206, 2017. Piscataway, NJ: IEEE. doi:10.1109/3DUI.2017.7893343

[23] N. Elmquaddem, "Augmented and virtual reality in education. Myth or reality?" International Journal of Emerging Technologies in Learning, 14(3), pp. 234–242, 2019. https://doi.org/10.3991/ijet.v14i03.9289

[24] Y. Wu, Z. Yuan, D. Zhou, and Y. Cai, "A mobile Chinese calligraphic training system using virtual reality technology," AASRI Procedia, 5, pp. 200-208, 2013.

[25] Y. Gao, V. A. Gonzalez, and T. W. Yiu, "The effectiveness of traditional tools and computer-aided technologies for health and safety training in the construction sector: A systematic review," Computers & Education, 138, pp. 101–115, 2019. https://doi.org/10.1016/j.compedu.2019.05.003

[26] J. Radianti, T. Majchrzak, J. Fromm, and I. Wohlgenannt, "A systematic review of immersive virtual reality applications for higher education: Design elements, lessons learned, and research," in Computers & Education 147, 2020. [Online]. Available from: https://www.sciencedirect.com/science/article/pii/S0360131513002108?casa_token=oYLDmPnweSsAAAAA:f7mfbkxcymyb5Rsg6zjEkGKbLz2DNqygucsG7bQNEsOUMiuVSGWFkGwelugo8BDvSZ9f1A76z 08 2020.04.28

[27] T. M. Porcino, E. Clua, D. Trevisan, C. N. Vasconcelos, and L.Valente, "Minimizing cyber sickness in head mounted display systems: Design guidelines and applications," in IEEE 5th International Conference on Serious Games and Applications for Health (SeGAH) pp. 1–6, 2017. doi:10.1109/SeGAH.2017.7939283 .

[28] L. Freina, M. Ott, "A Literature Review on Immersive virtual reality in Education: State Of The Art and Perspectives," in: LE@D - Laboratório de Educação a Distância e Elearning | Artigos em revistas / Papers in journals, [Online]. Available from: https://www.researchgate.net/publication/280566372_A_Literature_Review_on_Immersive_Virtual_Reality_in_Education_State_Of_The_Art_and_Perspectives 2022.04.28

[29] H.-M. Huang, U. Rauch, and S.-S. Liaw, "Investigating learners' attitudes toward virtual reality learning environments: based on a constructivist approach," Computers & Education, 55(3), pp. 1171-1182, 2010.

[30] J. Khlaisang, N. Songkram, "Designing a Virtual Learning Environment System for Teaching Twenty-First Century Skills to Higher Education Students in ASEAN," Technology, Knowledge and Learning, 24, pp. 41-63, 2019. https://link.springer.com/article/10.1007/s10758-017-9310-7

[31] I. Reisoğlu, B. Topu, R. Yılmaz, T. K. Yılmaz, Y. Göktaş, "3D virtual learning environments in education: a meta-review," in: Asia Pacific Educ. Rev. 18 (1), pp. 81–100, 2017. DOI: 10.1007/s12564-016-9467-0

[32] S. J. Zuiker, "Educational virtual environments as a lens for understanding both precise repeatability and specific variation in learning ecologies," British Journal of Educational Technology. 2012. doi:10.1111/j.1467-8535.2011.01266.x

[33] B. Dalgarno, M. J. W. Lee, L.Carlson, S.Gregory, and B.Tynan, "Institutional support for and barriers to the use of 3D immersive virtual worlds in higher education," in G. Williams, P. Statham, N. Brown & B. Cleland (Eds), Changing Demands, Changing Directions. Proceedings ascilite Hobart 2011 pp. 316-330, 2011. http://www.ascilite.org.au/conferences/hobart11/procs/dalgarnofull.pdf

[34] A. J. Coffey, R. Kamhawi,P. Fishwick, and J. Henderson, "The efficacy of an immersive 3D virtual versus 2D web environment in intercultural sensitivity acquisition," in: Education Tech Research Dev 65 (2), pp. 455–479, 2017. DOI: 10.1007/s11423-017-9510-9

[35] P. Alves, L. Miranda, C. Morais, "The Influence of Virtual Learning Environments in Students' Performance," in: ujer 5 (3), pp. 517–527, 2017 DOI: 10.13189/ujer.2017.050325

[36] L. V. Magalhães, L. M. Li, "Web-Based Undergraduate Medical Education in a Virtual Learning Environment Using an Original Pedagogical Approach: an Observational Longitudinal Study," Revista Brasileira de Educação Médica, 2019. https://www.scielo.br/j/rbem/a/TcFDTxnxzMgrbLyCRPmhnXd/?format=pdf&lang=en

[37] S. Y. Chien, G. J. Hwang, and M. S. Y. Jong, "Effects of peer assessment within the context of spherical video-based virtual reality on EFL students' English-Speaking performance and learning perceptions," Computers & Education, 146, 103751, 2020.

[38] T. Tepe, "Başa Takılan Görüntüleyiciler İçin Geliştirilmiş Sanal Gerçeklik Ortamlarının Öğrenme ve Buradalık Algısı Üzerine Etkilerinin İncelenmesi [Investigating The Effects of virtual reality Environments Developed for HeadMounted Display on Learning and Presence]". (Unpublished Doctoral Thesis). Hacettepe University. Institute of Education Sciences. Ankara, 2019.

[39] M. H. Kim, "Effects of Collaborative Learning in a Virtual Environment on Students' Academic Achievement and Satisfaction," Journal of Digital Convergence, 19(4), pp 1–8, 2021. https://doi.org/10.14400/JDC.2021.19.4.001 .

[40] B. Yildirim, E. Sahin-Topalcengiz, G. Arikan, and S. Timur, "Using virtual reality in the classroom: Reflections of STEM teachers on the use of teaching and learning tools," Journal of Education in Science, Environment and Health (JESEH), 6(3), pp. 231-245, 2020. DOI:10.21891/jeseh.711779

[41] S. W.-Y. Lee, Y.-T. Hsu, K.-H. Cheng, "Do curious students learn more science in an immersive virtual reality environment? Exploring the impact of advance organizers and epistemic curiosity," Computers & Education, vol. 182, 2022, 104456, ISSN 0360-1315, https://doi.org/10.1016/j.compedu.2022.104456

[42] S. Mystakidis, E. Berki, J. Valtanen, "Deep and Meaningful E-Learning with Social virtual reality Environments in Higher Education: A Systematic Literature Review," MDPI, Appl. Sci. 2021, 11, 2412. [Online]. Available from: https://doi.org/10.3390/app11052412 2022.04.28

[43] M. Akgün, B. Atıcı, "The Effects of Immersive virtual reality Environments on Students' Academic Achievement: A Meta-analytical and Meta-thematic Study," Participatory Educational Research , 9 (3) , pp. 111-131, 2022. DOI: 10.17275/per.22.57.9.3

[44] E. A.-L. Lee, K. W. Wong, "Learning with desktop VR: Low spatial ability learners are more positively affected," Computers & Education, vol.79, pp. 49-58, 2014. ISSN 0360-1315, https://doi.org/10.1016/j.compedu.2014.07.010.

[45] D. Kim, D. Jo, "Effects on Co-Presence of a Virtual Human: A Comparison of Display and Interaction Types," in: Electronics

2022, 11, 367. [Online]. Available from: https://doi.org/10.3390/electronics11030367 2022.04.28

[46] T. Sitzmann, "A meta-analytic examination of the instructional effectiveness of computer-based simulation games," Pers. Psychol. 64, pp. 489–528, 2011. [Online]. Available from: https://onlinelibrary.wiley.com/doi/epdf/10.1111/j.1744-6570.2011.01190.x 2022.04.28

[47] B. Dalgarno, J. Hedberg, "3D learning environments in tertiary education," paper published at 18th Annual Conference of thje Australasian Society for Computers in Learning in Tertiary Education (ASCILITE), Publisher: BMU, University Melbourne, 2001. [Online]. Available from: https://researchoutput.csu.edu.au/ws/portalfiles/portal/9632917/PID%26%2320%3B6456%26%2320%3Bpre-pub.pdf 2022.04.28

[48] R. Charanya, M. Kesavan, "Analysis of Factors Influencing the Virtual Learning Environment in a Sri Lankan Higher Studies Institution," 2019 International Research Conference on Smart Computing and Systems Engineering (SCSE), 2019. DOI: 240-244 https://ieeexplore.ieee.org/document/8842719

[49] I. R. Boer, P. R. Wesselink, and J. M. Vervoorn, "Student performance and appreciation using 3D vs. 2D vision in a virtual learning environment," in: European Journal of Dental Education 20 (3), pp. 142–147, 2016. DOI:10.1111/eje.12152.

[50] B. Wainman, G. Pukas, L. Wolak, S. Mohanraj, J. Lamb, G. R. Norman, "The Critical Role of Stereopsis in Virtual and Mixed Reality Learning Environments," in: Anatomical Sciences Education 13 (3), pp. 401–412, 2020. DOI:10.1002/ase.1928.

[51] Y.-P. Chao, H.-H. Chuang, L.-J. Hsin, C.-J. Kang, T.-J. Fang, H.-Y. Li, C.-G. Huang, T. Kuo, C. Yang, H.-Y. Shyu, S.-L. Wang, L.-Y. Shyu, and L.-A. Lee, "Using a 360° virtual reality or 2D Video to Learn History Taking and Physical Examination Skills for Undergraduate Medical Students: Pilot Randomized Controlled Trial," JMIR Serious Games. 9. e13124. 10.2196/13124, 2021.

[52] Gather Presence, Inc. (2022). gather.town. [Online]. Available from https://www.gather.town 2022.04.28

Comparison of Vibrotactile Display and Pseudo-mastication Sound Display on Food Texture Perception

Yuki Nishi
Faculty of Engineering
Kumamoto University
2-39-1, Kurokami, Chuo-ku, Kumamoto, Japan
Email: nishi@saga-lab.org

Satoshi Saga
Faculty of Advanced Scinence and Technology
Kumamoto University
2-39-1, Kurokami, Chuo-ku, Kumamoto, Japan
Email: saga@saga-lab.org

***Abstract*—Several cross-modal augmentation research on food texture has been conducted in recent years. These results revealed that pseudo-mastication sound can affect the perception of food texture. However, there have been few studies on food texture using vibrotactile stimuli to the whole body. Thus, we proposed a method of presenting vibrotactile stimuli using mastication sound or myoelectric potential under mastication. Twelve subjects participated in the experiment and were asked to rate nine adjective-pairs related to the food texture of two types of food. The results showed that the proposed method affects the perception of the hardness, crispiness, chewiness, freshness, and thickness of certain foods.**

Keywords*—*Food Texture; Cross-modal; Vibrotactile Stimuli; Mastication Sound.

I. Introduction

In recent years, several research efforts have been conducted to improve the experience of eating by making full use of Virtual Reality (VR) technology. When people eat food, they taste the flavor, appearance, aroma, texture, mastication sound, and other elements. Therefore, eating is a cross-modal experience of the five senses. The presentation of auditory, tactile, and other information using multisensory interactions has been reported to affect the perception of food texture during the eating experience. Zampini et al. [1] proposed a method to affect the perception of the crispiness and chewiness of potato chips by amplifying and returning the high-frequency component of the mastication sound generated when eating potato chips. Endo et al. [2] reported that participants felt hardness in soft foods by presenting pseudo-mastication sound generated from electromyogram (EMG) signals of chewing movement. These studies have investigated methods for presenting sensory information, such as auditory and tactile sensation, to specific body parts.

However, few studies evaluated method of presenting vibrotactile information to the entire body. This study focuses on vibrotactile stimuli, and proposes a method to present vibrotactile stimuli by employing mastication sound or electromyogram as input signal in real-time. For comparison, we also generated pseudo-mastication sound from the two input signals described above and presented it under mastication. We conducted psychophysical experiments on two types of food to compare the effects of vibrotactile stimuli and pseudo-mastication sound on food texture perception.

The structure of this paper is as follows. This section explains the background and our approach. In Section II, we present related work. Section III describes our proposed method. Section IV describes a psychophysical experiment. Section V shows the result of the experiment. Section VI discuss the effect of proposed method on food texture. Section VII draws a conclusion.

II. Related work

The International Organization for Standardization (ISO 11036:2020) defines texture as "all the mechanical, geometrical, and surface attributes of a product perceptible by means of mechanical, tactile, and, where appropriate, visual and auditory receptors" [3]. Thus, tactile and auditory senses are considered to play a significant role in food texture perception.

Eating is not only an essential activity for a living but also an experience of sharing the taste, enjoyment, and pleasure of food. Meals can also be viewed as a form of entertainment. Therefore, improving the dining experience makes food more palatable and improves quality of life. Therefore, various studies have been conducted to improve the dining experience considering meals as entertainment and amusement.

Nakaoka et al. proposed a system called eat2pic [4] that encourages users to develop healthy eating habits. Chopstick sensors recognize what and how much the user eats, and the digital campus is colored according to the type of food. Chewing food slowly and consuming a well-balanced diet will result in the painting reflecting attractive colors and motivating healthy eating habits.

Narumi et al. proposed MetaCookie+ [5] that uses visual and olfactory senses to change the flavor of cookies. For example, the system superimposed a cookie of a different color than the actual one on the Head Mounted Display (HMD) wearer's field of vision, and added an odor by olfactory display to make him perceive the same cookie as tasting differently. Many of the participants in the experiment tasted chocolate cookies even though they were eating butter cookies.

Other studies have focused on food texture. It has been suggested that the bubble structure of bread affects the food texture [6]. The brittleness of sweet potatoes varies depending on the cooking method, affecting their texture [7].

Physical feedback-based food texture display has also been reported. Uemura et al. [8] constructed a device employing a crank mechanism and presented the texture of each food by controlling the torque. Hashimoto et al. [9] proposed a straw device, which vibrates the suction pressure in the straw and can reproduce the suction sensation of foods. Niijima et al. [10] presented food texture by presenting Electrical Muscle Stimulation (EMS) to the masseter muscle.

While the physical presence of texture has been proposed, there are also cross-modal approaches to texture. Several studies indicate that cross-modal texture can affect appetite [11] [12]. In general, the elderly have less ability to masticate food than the young. Especially elderly people with impaired masticatory and swallowing functions often have difficulty eating hard foods and are restricted to soft foods only. However, constantaneous eating of soft foods without a crisp texture can cause appetite attenuation. Endo et al. [13] amplified the 250 Hz to 1000 Hz frequency component of the EMG acquired from the masseter muscle under mastication and generated pseudo-mastication sound feedback to the user. They reported that feedback of pseudo-mastication sound by the timing of mastication increased the perception of food hardness, the sense of comfort and satisfaction. Chewing JOCKEY [14] by Koizumi et al. is designed for a typical home dining experience. The system acquires mastication sound and provides audio feedback via bone-conducting headphones, making it less susceptible to ambient noise and conversation. The design does not obstruct conversation during meals by not covering the ears.

III. METHODS

This section explains the two display methods, pseudo-mastication sound and vibrotactile stimuli. The mastication sounds or electromyograms were used as input signals of vibrotactile stimuli.

A. *Vibrotactile stimuli*

Our proposed method employs whole-body vibrotactile display to enhance the food texture perception. To realize the method, we built a large vibration device by mounting a transducer and amplifier on a wooden chair. The device vibrates the user's whole body from his thighs. By employing the chair-type device, user can feel the vibration without wearing some kind of vibration motors. We used a TST239Silver Transducer (CLARK SYNTHESIS INC.) and a Nobsound TA-21 MiniBluetooth 5.0 DSP digital amplifier for the vibration device. In this study, myoelectric potential or mastication sound were used as input signals of mastication. The myoelectric potential is obtained from an electrode attached to the masseter muscle of the participant, and the mastication sound signal is obtained from a condenser microphone attached to the other masseter muscle. The input signal, either myoelectric potential or mastication sound, is amplified by an amplifier and output from the transducer as vibrotactile stimuli. When seated on a large vibrating device, users can perceive vibrotactile stimuli from their thighs to their whole body according to the timing of mastication. Figure 1 shows the large vibration device created in this study and Figure 2 shows the system configuration of the proposed method.

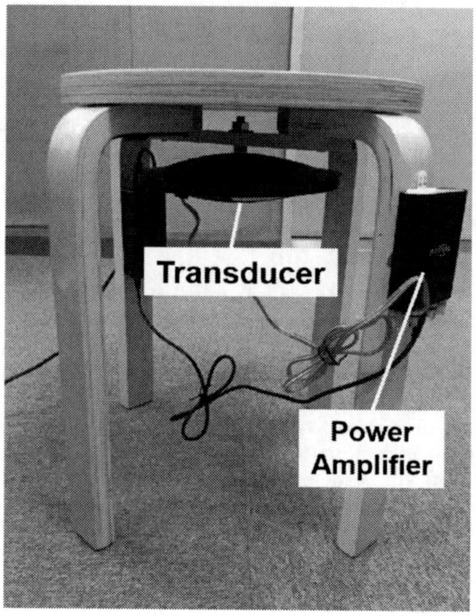

Figure 1. Vibration device

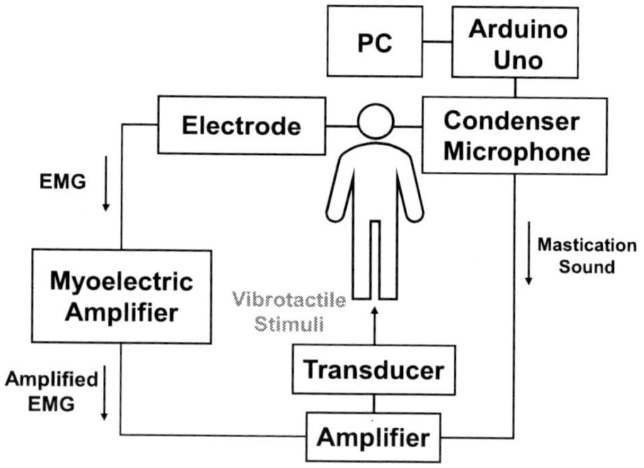

Figure 2. Presenting vibrotactile stimuli

B. *Pseudo-mastication sound*

We also investigated auditory stimuli for comparison with vibrotactile stimuli. We generated pseudo-mastication sound using a simplified method based on Endo et al [2]. The EMG signal detected under mastication sounds like a noise or the sound of the wind. Endo et al. generated pseudo-mastication sound by amplifying the amplitude with an equalizer using the 250 Hz to 1000 Hz frequency components of the EMG. This study applied a high-pass filter of 250 Hz to the input signals, such as myoelectric potential obtained from an electrode attached to the masseter muscle of the participant, or mastication sound obtained from a condenser microphone attached to the other masseter muscle, and output to headphones as pseudo-mastication sound. Figure 3 shows the system configuration for presenting pseudo-mastication sound.

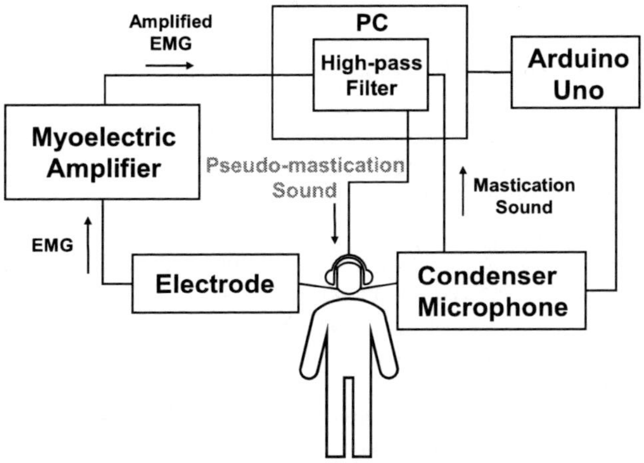

Figure 3. Presenting pseudo-mastication sound

IV. EXPERIMENT

We conducted an experiment to investigate whether the food texture perception of two kinds of foods can be affected by presenting vibrotactile stimuli or pseudo-mastication sound under mastication. Twelve participants (9 males and 3 females, with ages ranging from 18 to 22 years and an average age of 21.25 years) took part in this experiment. The same explanation was given to each participant to keep the experimental environment the same. The participants wore an eye mask to shut the visual information out. Further, the experiment was conducted in a soundproof room so that ambient noise information would not affect the perception of food texture.

First, participants were seated at the chair, and were asked to masticate food without listening to any sound by wearing the noise-cancelling headphone (BOSE QuietComfort 15). The condition was treated as control condition and named as condition A. Next, the participants experienced vibrotactile information or pseudo-mastication sound based on their own mastication sound or myoelectric potential during mastication. The conditions of each pair were named as condition B, C, D, and E (Table I).

After the experiment of each condition, they were asked to rate the following nine adjective-pairs on a 7-point Likert scale; "soft - hard," "not crispy - crispy," "sparse - dense," "thin - thick, "not chewy - chewy," "unnatural - natural," "stale - fresh," "uncomfort - comfort," and "not sticky - sticky." The conditions B to E were performed in a random order to eliminate the order effect.

As described in Section II, some foods have different textures depending on the cooking method and bubble structure. Thus, it is desirable to use foods that have already been processed and have little difference in food texture from one individual to another. We chose rice cracker (Setonosioage, KURIYAMABEIKA Co., Ltd.) and gummy (Meiji fruit gummy candy grape, Meiji Co., Ltd.). The characteristic of the rice cracker we chose is soft and crispy texture, and gummy's is elastic, but not too soft. In the experiment, we split the rice cracker in a half and made it into bite-size pieces for easy mastication.

In the experiment during mastication of gummy, the condenser microphone could not collect mastication sound. Thus, we held experiments under mastication of gummy with conditions A, D, and E, except for conditions B and C. Figure 4a and Figure 4b show the overview of experimental scenes and Table II shows the adjective pairs of questionnaires. As a caveat, this experiment was not blind to the food items because the experiments on rice cracker and gummy were conducted independently. In addition, this experiment may not be generalizable because of the male bias of the participants, the lack of control variables for age and ethnicity, and the use of specific foods.

TABLE I. EXPERIMENTAL CONDITIONS

condition	input	output
A	none	none
B	mastication sound	vibrotactile stimuli
C	mastication sound	pseudo-mastication sound
D	myoelectric potential	vibrotactile stimuli
E	myoelectric potential	pseudo-mastication sound

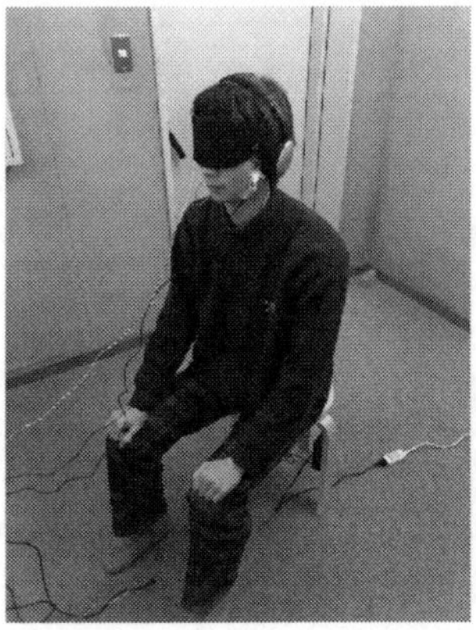

(a). Participant is sitting on the vibrotactile chair

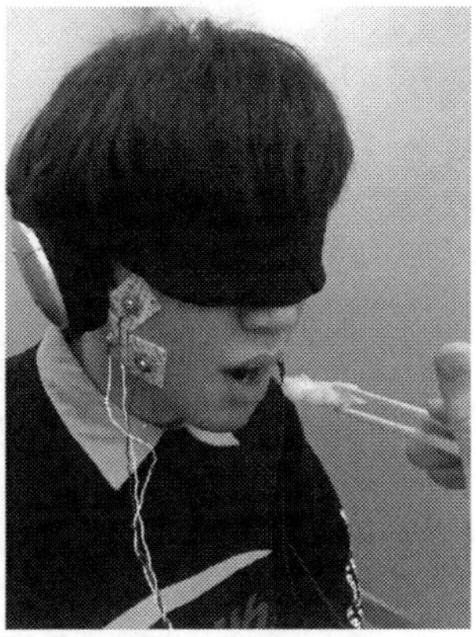

(b). Participant is masticating food

Figure 4. Experimental scene

TABLE II. ADJECTIVE PAIRS OF QUESTIONNAIRES

Question	Item	Scale	Item
Q1 Hardness	Soft	1-2-3-4-5-6-7	Hard
Q2 Crispness	Not crispy	1-2-3-4-5-6-7	Crispy
Q3 Dense	Sparse	1-2-3-4-5-6-7	Dense
Q4 Thickness	Thin	1-2-3-4-5-6-7	Thick
Q5 Chewiness	Not chewy	1-2-3-4-5-6-7	Chewy
Q6 Naturalness of sound	Unnatural	1-2-3-4-5-6-7	Natural
Q7 Freshness	Stale	1-2-3-4-5-6-7	Fresh
Q8 Comfort	Uncomfort	1-2-3-4-5-6-7	Comfort
Q9 Stickiness	Not sticky	1-2-3-4-5-6-7	Sticky

V. Result

In this section we explain each result of the experiment. First we describe the result of rice cracker, followed by gummy texture result.

A. Perception of rice cracker texture

The distributions of the evaluation score in the conditions A to E under rice cracker mastication are shown in Figure 5a to Figure 5h. The triangle in the figure represents the mean, and the black line represents the median. The circle points indicate outlier. Questionnaire data were analyzed between control condition A and other conditions using Wilcoxon signed-rank test. $*$ indicates a significant difference. (p-value was 0.05.)

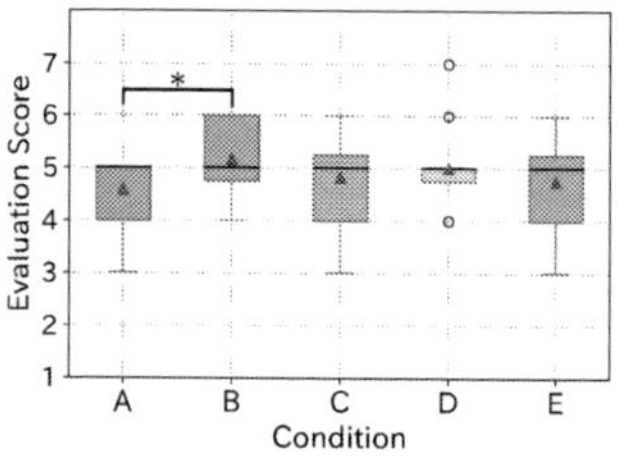

(a). Q1 Hardness

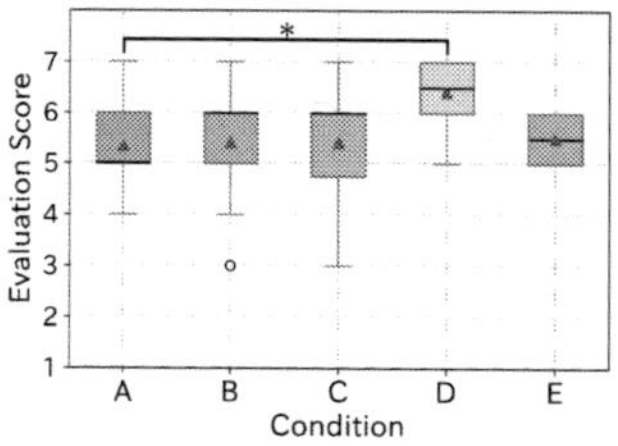

(b). Q2 Crispness

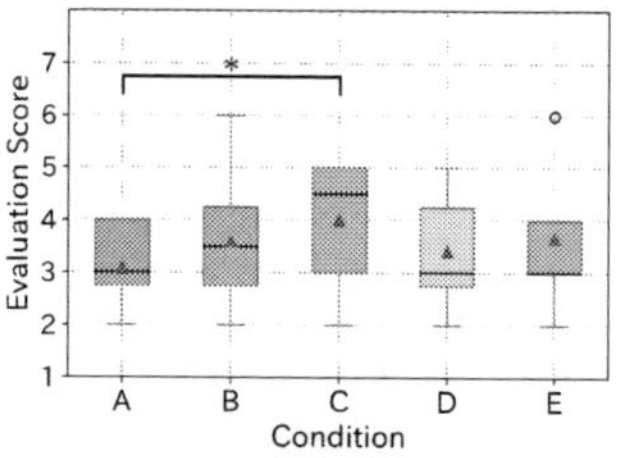

(c). Q3 Dense

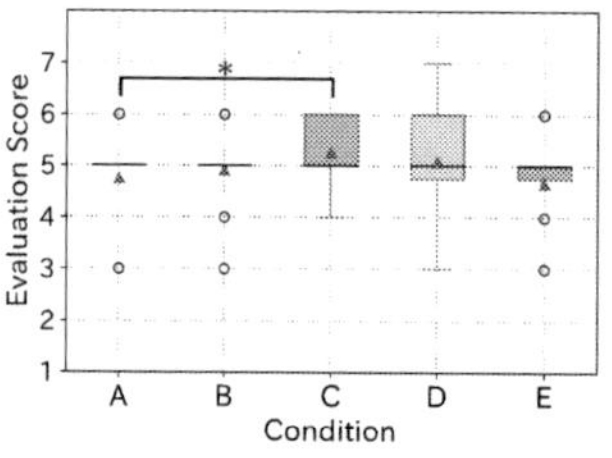

(d). Q4 Thickness

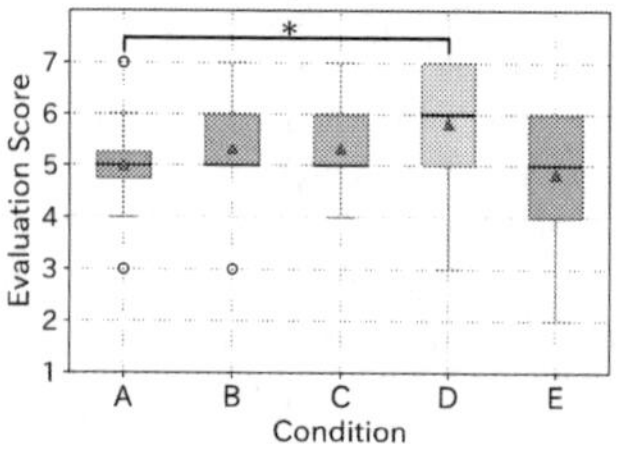

(e). Q5 Chewiness

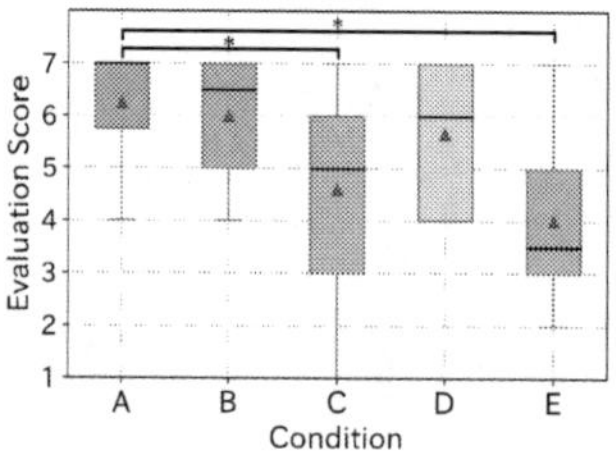

(f). Q6 Naturalness

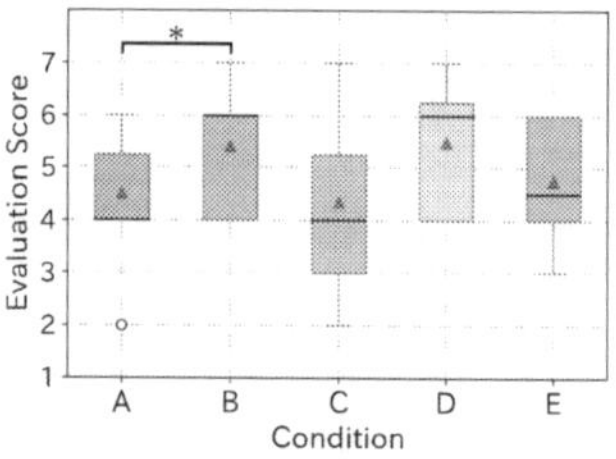

(g). Q7 Freshness

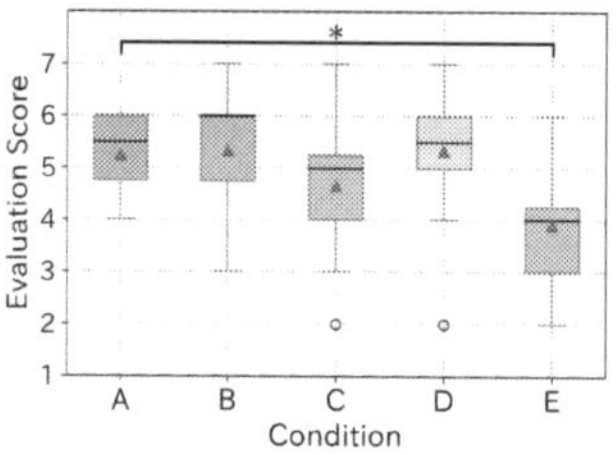

(h). Q8 Comfort

Figure 5. Evaluation score of each condition during rice cracker mastication

Comparing the conditions of A and B, the perceived hardness (questionnaire 1: "soft - hard") was shown significantly greater in condition B ($p = 0.0196$). Also, perceived freshness (questionnaire 7: "stale - fresh") was significantly greater in condition B ($p = 0.0412$). Comparing the conditions of A and C, although food texture of rice cracker was perceived as dense (questionnaire 3: "sparse - dense" ($p = 0.00496$)) and thick (questionnaire 4: "thin - thick" ($p = 0.0339$)) in condition C, participants perceived the sounds of pseudo-mastication sound as unnatural (questionnaire 6: "unnatural - natural" ($p = 0.0313$)).

Furthermore, among the conditions of A and D, the judged crispness (questionnaire 2: "not crispy - crispy") was presented significantly greater ($p = 0.00589$), and the judged chewiness (questionnaire 5: "not chewy - chewy") was shown significantly greater ($p = 0.00830$) in condition D. In condition E, participants perceived the sound of the rice crackers as unnatural (questionnaire 6: "unnatural - natural" ($p = 0.00310$)) and perceived uncomfort (questionnaire 8: "uncomfort - comfort" ($p = 0.0199$)). Therefore, the analysis revealed that vibrotactile stimuli and pseudo-mastication sound presented during mastication affected the food texture perception of rice cracker.

B. Perception of gummy texture

The distributions of the evaluation score given by the participants in conditions A, D, and E during gummy mastication are shown in Figure 6a to Figure 6c. The triangle in the figure represents the mean, and the black line represents the median. The circle points indicate outlier. Questionnaire data were analyzed between control condition A and other conditions using Wilcoxon signed-rank test. $*$ indicates a significant difference. (p-value was 0.05.)

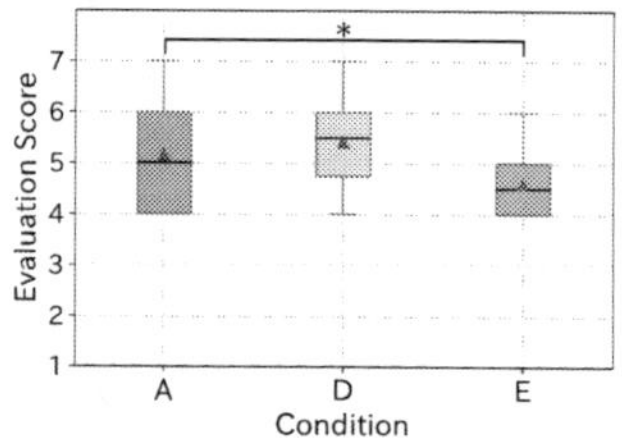

(a). Q4 Thickness

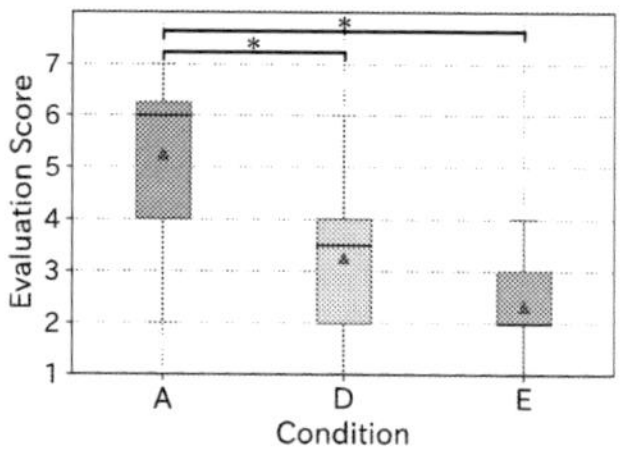

(b). Q6 Naturalness

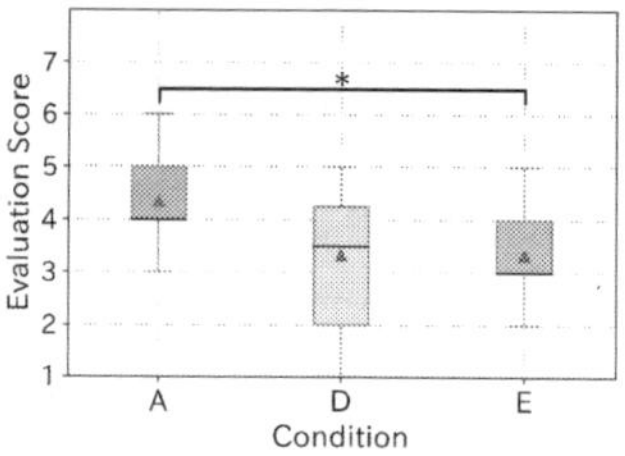

(c). Q8 Comfort

Figure 6. Evaluation score of each condition during gummy mastication

Among the conditions of A and D, participants perceived the sound as unnatural (questionnaire 6: "unnatural - natural" ($p = 0.0311$)) in condition D. Moreover, among the conditions of A and E, the perceived thickness (questionnaire 4: "thin - thick") was shown significantly greater ($p = 0.0384$) ,and participants perceived pseudo-masticaion sound as unnatural (questionnaire 6: "unnatural - natural" (p = 0.00210)), and uncomfort (questionnaire 8: "uncomfort - comfort" (p = 0.0422)). Thus, the analysis showed that vibrotactile stimuli and pseudo-mastication sound presented during mastication affected the food texture perception of gummy.

VI. Discussion

Our results show that the perception of rice cracker and gummy texture are affected both by the vibrotactile stimuli and pseudo-mastication sound during mastication. In particular, vibrotactile stimuli affected food texture perception, which is different from that of pseudo-mastication sound.

A. Effect of vibrotactile stimuli on food texture

When the vibrotactile stimuli were provided, participants were more likely to evaluate rice cracker as having the property of hardness, crispness, chewiness, and freshness. Condition B, in which mastication sound was used as the input signal, affected the perception of the hardness and freshness of the rice cracker. Under the condition B, some participants commented that "I felt the food to be hard more than usual." and "I felt vibration from the chair as if something hit the bottom of the chair."

Condition D, in which a myoelectric potential was used as the input signal, affected the perception of the crispness and chewiness of the rice cracker. Under the condition D, some participants reported that "I felt like I was eating with my whole body." and "I felt the enhanced chewiness of rice cracker."

Regarding the gummy texture, when the vibrotactile stimuli were provided, participants evaluated the perceived sound as more unnatural. Under the condition D, some participants reported that "I felt strange between the vibrotactile stimuli and gummy texture." Since gummy is relatively soft food, the vibrotactile stimuli presented during mastication was different from that of the usual eating environment, and it is thought that some participants felt a sense of discomfort. Under the condition in which vibrotactile stimuli were presented, there was no commonality among the texture perception that showed significant difference between rice cracker and gummy. This suggests that the low-frequency component (0-200 Hz) is significant in these texture perceptions, and affected them differently for rice cracker and gummy.

B. Effect of pseudo-mastication sound on food texture

When the pseudo-mastication sound was provided, participants tended to evaluate rice cracker as denser, thicker, unnatural sounding, and uncomfort. Under the condition C, some participants commented that they heard a chewing sound and felt that the volume of rice cracker had increased when masticating rice cracker.

The pseudo-mastication sound was generated from the air-conducted sound of masticating rice cracker and presented to the headphones of participants. Thus, it is likely that the pseudo-mastication sound modified by the high-pass filter enhanced the perception of density and thickness in condition C. Under the condition E, some participants commented that the pseudo-mastication sound was uncomfort and sounded like an ASMR (Autonomous Sensory Meridian Response) of earpick. The pseudo-mastication sound is generated by applying high-pass filter to myoelectric potential in condition E.

Under the condition E, some participants reported that they felt the pseudo-mastication sound was unnatural, and that they perceived gummy texture more than no sound.

Under the condition in which pseudo-mastication sound was presented, the texture perception, "unnaturalness of sound" and "discomfort" that showed significant difference have a commonality between rice cracker and gummy. This suggests that the high-frequency component of the auditory information may have influenced these texture perceptions. As described in Section VI-A, there was no commonality among the affected texture perception in rice cracker and gummy. Therefore, different frequency bands in vibrotactile information auditory information could have led to differences in affected attributes. In addition, this experiment did not blind to the food items. Since this may have little influence on the result, we consider conducting the study under blind conditions such as randomly presenting food items.

VII. Conclusion

This study proposed a method to present vibrotactile stimuli to the whole body by employing mastication sound or electromyogram as input signal. We investigated whether the food texture of rice cracker or gummy can be affected by presenting vibrotactile stimuli or pseudo-mastication sound during mastication.

The analysis revealed that when the vibrotactile stimuli were provided, participants tended to be perceived the rice cracker texture as harder, crisper, fresher, and the sound as unnatural compared to control condition. In the case of gummy texture, they perceived the sound as unnatural more than usual.

On the other hand, under the presentation of pseudo-mastication sound, participants tended to be perceived the rice cracker texture as denser, thicker, unnatural sounding and uncomfort compared to control condition. In the case of gummy, they were more likely to perceive gummy texture as thicker, unnatural sounding, and uncomfort.

Consequently, our research showed that proposed method affects the food texture perception, and presenting vibrotactile information throughout the body has the potential to improve the eating experience.

Acknowledgement

This study was partly supported by JSPS KAKENHI 18H04104 (Grant-in-Aid for Scientific Research (A)), 19K22879 (Grant-in-Aid for Challenging Exploratory Research), and the Asahi Glass Foundation.

References

[1] Z. Massimiliano and C. Spence, "The role of auditory cues in modulating the perceived crispness and staleness of potato chips," *Journal of sensory studies*, vol. 19, no. 5, pp. 347–363, 2004.

[2] H. Endo, S. Ino, and W. Fujisaki, "The effect of a crunchy pseudo-chewing sound on perceived texture of softened foods," *Physiology & behavior*, vol. 167, pp. 324–331, 2016.
[3] ISO, "Sensory analysis - Methology - Texture profile," https://www.iso.org/obp/ui/#iso:std:76668:en, [retrieved: May, 2022].
[4] R. Nakaoka, Y. Nakamura, Y. Matsuda, S. Misaki, and K. Yasumoto, "eat2pic: Food-tech design as a healthy nudge with smart chopsticks and canvas," in *2021 IEEE International Conference on Pervasive Computing and Communications Workshops and other Affiliated Events (PerCom Workshops)*. IEEE Computer Society, 2021, pp. 389–391.
[5] T. Narumi, S. Nishizaka, T. Kajinami, T. Tanikawa, and M. Hirose, "Augmented reality flavors: gustatory display based on edible marker and cross-modal interaction," in *Proceedings of the SIGCHI conference on human factors in computing systems*, 2011, pp. 93–102.
[6] E. N. C. Mills, P. J. Wilde, L. J. Salt, and P. Skeggs, "Bubble formation and stabilization in bread dough," *Food and bioproducts processing*, vol. 81, no. 3, pp. 189–193, 2003.
[7] A. Andersson *et al.*, "Effect of preheating on potato texture," *Critical Reviews in Food Science & Nutrition*, vol. 34, no. 3, pp. 229–251, 1994.
[8] H. Iwata, H. Yano, T. Uemura, and T. Moriya, "Food simulator: A haptic interface for biting," in *IEEE virtual reality 2004*. IEEE, 2004, pp. 51–57.
[9] Y. Hashimoto *et al.*, "Straw-like user interface: virtual experience of the sensation of drinking using a straw," in *Proceedings of the 2006 ACM SIGCHI international conference on Advances in computer entertainment technology*, 2006, pp. 50–es.
[10] A. Niijima and T. Ogawa, "Virtual food texture by electrical muscle stimulation," in *Proceedings of the 2016 ACM International Symposium on Wearable Computers*, 2016, pp. 48–49.
[11] L. Mioche, P. Bourdiol, and M. Peyron, "Influence of age on mastication: effects on eating behaviour," *Nutrition research reviews*, vol. 17, no. 1, pp. 43–54, 2004.
[12] K. Swan, R. Speyer, B. J. Heijnen, B. Wagg, and R. Cordier, "Living with oropharyngeal dysphagia: effects of bolus modification on health-related quality of life—a systematic review," *Quality of Life Research*, vol. 24, no. 10, pp. 2447–2456, 2015.
[13] H. Endo, S. Ino, and W. Fujisaki, "Texture-dependent effects of pseudo-chewing sound on perceived food texture and evoked feelings in response to nursing care foods," *Appetite*, vol. 116, pp. 493–501, 2017.
[14] N. Koizumi, H. Tanaka, Y. Uema, and M. Inami, "Chewing jockey: augmented food texture by using sound based on the cross-modal effect," in *Proceedings of the 8th international conference on advances in computer entertainment technology*, 2011, pp. 1–4.

Predicting Rapid Shifts in Cognitive Resource Allocation

Justin Brooks
D-Prime LLC
Washington, D.C., USA
email: justin.brooks@dprime.ai

Philip Dyer
D-Prime LLC
Wading River, NY, USA
email: phil.dyer@dprime.ai

Katherine Cox
Human Research and Engineering Directorate
The U.S. Combat Capabilities Development Command
Army Research Laboratory
Aberdeen Proving Ground, MD, USA
email: katherine.r.cox11.civ@army.mil

Jonroy Canady
Human Research and Engineering Directorate
The U.S. Combat Capabilities Development Command
Army Research Laboratory
Aberdeen Proving Ground, MD, USA
email: jonroy.d.canady.civ@army.mil

Kanika Bansal
Human Research and Engineering Directorate
The U.S. Combat Capabilities Development Command
Army Research Laboratory
Aberdeen Proving Ground, MD, USA
email: phy.kanika@gmail.com

Javier Garcia
Human Research and Engineering Directorate
The U.S. Combat Capabilities Development Command
Army Research Laboratory
Aberdeen Proving Ground, MD, USA
email: javier.o.garcia.civ@army.mil

***Abstract*—Human cognition is the set of abilities humans possess to intelligently interact with the world through goal-directed behaviors and is an essential component of daily life. As with several other processes (e.g., physical exertion), cognitive resources are inherently limited. Moreover, as the systems with which humans interact become more complex (e.g., artificial intelligence), the degree and rate of the associated depletion of these cognitive resources can vary dramatically. A real-time signal of cognitive depletion can be used to moderate task demands imposed on humans to enable high-performing human and complex system interactions; however, previous attempts have identified generalizability across both individuals and a variety of tasks to be a significant challenge in modeling cognitive depletion. Here, we present a model that uses physiological measurements and that generalizes across three different real-world tasks and across heterogeneous samples of participants. Specifically using features that are implicated in autonomic and central nervous system activity, our model detects cognitive resource depletion in multiple tasks, including mental arithmetic, simulated navigation/decision-making, and visuospatial/sensorimotor processing. The model makes second-by-second predictions of cognitive resource depletion, which can be used in real-time human-in-the loop systems.**

***Index Terms*—cognitive resource depletion; humans and complex systems**

I. Introduction

Our perceptual experiences coupled with our intrinsic goals guide our subsequent actions. This requires a series of complex perceptual interpretations, sensorimotor processes, and rapid decisions. While this complex cognitive coordination is often completed with relative ease, there are inherent limitations to each one of these constructs. Notable limitations have been observed in working memory [1] and visual attention (e.g., see [2] but see [3]); importantly, these limitations can have an inherent fluctuations independent of ongoing task demands [3] and a wide range of individual differences [4]. Moreover, fluctuating individual states like changes in stress, fatigue, and other physiological factors can impact these limitations in complex ways and sometimes with dramatic consequences [5].

Real-time monitoring of cognitive resources can facilitate optimal performance by providing actionable insights that can be used to trigger individualized adaptations [6]. These individualized interventions could, for example, take the form of retasking to another cognitive domain or a forced intermission of inactivity if a particular individual's cognitive resources are depleted.

The ways in which cognitive resources have been monitored, however, are somewhat limited. For example, at one extreme, subjective measures like the validated NASA-TLX [7] are widely used; however, they require interruption of the ongoing task and are impossible to use in a real-time state assessment system. At the other end of the spectrum, researchers have developed cognitive workload models using a variety of deep learning and machine learning approaches [8]. Some of the biggest challenges with this latter approach are 1) the lack of generalizability across various tasks and 2) the limited application or utility outside of artificially constrained laboratory-based tasks.

Here, we introduce a model of Cognitive Resource Depletion (CRD) which is built on the physiological features extracted during a realistic multi-task dataset and is tested in two independent but similarly realistic task paradigms. The physiological measures are derived from electroencephalography (EEG) and electrocardiography (ECG) and were chosen because of their specificity to central nervous system (CNS) and autonomic nervous system (ANS) functions, both of which have been related to cognitive workload in other studies.

The model accounted for significant sources of variability in performance in all tasks, regardless of individual differences or the variety of sensorimotor actions and complex decisions required for each task. Due to the complex interplay between the ANS, the CNS (measures derived from EEG), and the most predictive measurement features extracted within the model, the model appears to be predictive of cognitive depletion in a subject- and task- agnostic fashion, suggesting the critical role the relationship between the CNS and the ANS plays in cognitive resource depletion.

In Section II, the experimental approaches including the types of data and sensors used are described. In Section III the approach to model development and validation and provided. In Section IV, the modeling results including results for each dataset are presented. In Section V a discussion of the results in the context of CRD are described. In Section VI, we present general conclusions and suggested future research directions.

II. Methods and Materials

In this section, we describe the experimental methods used to collect the data and how the model was derived from those data.

A. Overview

For an overview of the model development and deployment, Figure. 1 displays the training, testing, and validation stages of the model. As shown in 1, a single model was developed with the DualTask data and then applied to the independent but similarly dynamic and realistic TeamTask and VisualTargetTask, which were collected in separate populations and at different experimental sites. Validation of the model was initially performed within the DualTask (tan) using a leave-one-out (LOO) procedure. External validation was performed using the TeamTask and VisualTargetTask (green). Descriptions of the datasets are provided in subsequent sections. Briefly, the DualTask dataset was analyzed and used to develop a real-time model of cognitive resource depletion which was hypothesized to occur during the dual task phase of the experiment (i.e., when participants were performing the simultaneous navigation and mental arithmetic tasks). The model was validated with that dataset using a LOO cross-validation approach. Once trained and tested, the model in DualTask was then applied to the TeamTask and VisualTargetTask datasets.

In the TeamTask, the model output was compared to subjective ratings from the NASA-TLX. To validate the model, the continuous model probabilities were thresholded and then integrated over time, resulting in a cumulative amount of time that the model predicted a participant was cognitively depleted. This cumulative number of seconds was correlated with each NASA-TLX subscore and total score.

In the VisualTargetTask, the percentage of time that the model predicted cognitive resource depletion was compared between high and low difficulty conditions. The length of time that participants experienced the low difficulty condition was longer than the high difficulty condition, so it was necessary to compare this normalization.

All protocols were approved by the U.S. Combat Capabilities Development Command Army Research Laboratory (ARL) Human Research Protection Program.

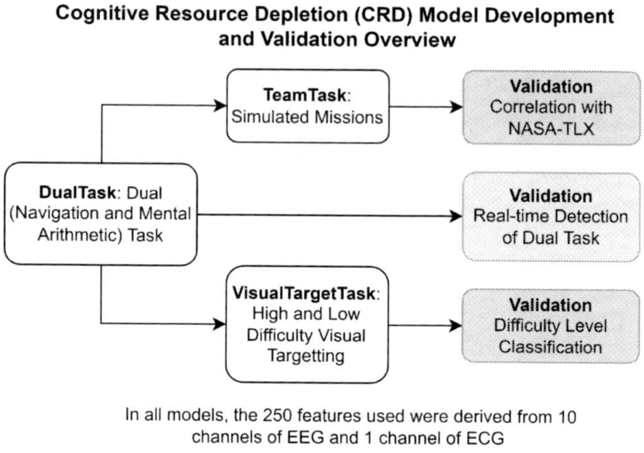

Fig. 1: An overview of the methods presented in the current manuscript.

B. DualTask

Forty-five subjects, recruited from the Los Angeles area, participated in this study [17 females with mean age ± standard deviation (SD) = 36.8 ± 12.3 years; 28 males with mean age ± SD = 41.6 ± 14.4 years]. All subjects were at least 18 years of age or older and able to speak, read, and write English. All subjects signed an Institutional Review Board-approved informed consent form prior to participation and were compensated for their time.

The overarching study aim was to examine physiological markers (i.e., EEG, ECG) of cognitive resource depletion in the context of an experimentally imposed dual-task paradigm. Participants were asked to count the number of target objects in a visual search task. All participants were exposed to all the same target objects, but they were asked to focus on different target objects. Participants were randomly assigned to one out of four target object conditions (1 – Motorcycle, 2 – Humvee, 3 – Furniture, 4 – Aircraft). In addition, the environment also contained non-targets that were used as distractors.

While participants performed the continuous target identification and navigation task, they were simultaneously required to complete a math task. This math task was given approximately 8 minutes into the experiment and required the addition of a series of 3-4 numbers that were read aloud. Participants were then asked to report the sum aloud while continuing to navigate the virtual environment and count targets. While performing the task, participants wore a 64-lead EEG and 2-lead ECG; the complete description of the data collection has been previously published [9].

C. TeamTask

Participants were seven U.S. Army Soldiers. Six Soldiers were members of the Minnesota U.S. Army National Guard, and one Soldier was assigned to the Army Evaluation Center under the U.S. Army Test and Evaluation Command. The Soldiers were aged 37.71 ± 10.16 (29 – 57 years) and had 19.71 ± 9.52 (12 – 39) years of experience in the Army.

Zephyr BioHarnesses were used to collect ECG data. The BioHarness is a lightweight (50g) belt that is worn around the upper torso, directly against the skin. The 2-lead BioHarness enables the capture and wireless transmission of ECG, torso accelerometry, and respiration data. EEG data were collected using Advanced Brain Monitoring (ABM) X24 EEG Systems. The ABM X24 is a commercial EEG system designed for measuring EEG in an untethered, free-moving manner with minimal impact on the wearer. The system has 20 leads and mounts to the head using an elastic headband.

Subjective measures have been found to be useful in characterizing individual workload and are often used as a validation of other measures. The NASA-TLX [10] has been used extensively to assess individual ratings of overall workload, as well as a breakdown of six categories that are seen as contributing to this overall workload (mental demand, physical demand, temporal demand, performance, effort, and frustration).

In this study, participants completed a set of simulated missions in which vehicle crews navigated to objectives and performed various offensive and defensive maneuvers. Within each mission, participants had to consider multiple factors, including mission completion, enemy engagements, terrain, troops, time, and civilians. The crew was responsible for multiple tasks within each vehicle, including driving, maintaining situational awareness, using the weapon to engage with human-operated opposition forces, and completing mission objectives. Movement through the environment was dynamic and consisted of formations, battle drills, or movements coordinated by the commander and among the team. Participants were fully trained on each of the tasks that they were asked to perform. At the conclusion of each simulated mission, participants completed an electronic version of the NASA-TLX.

D. Visual Target Task

Participants were seventeen students (7 women, 10 men) from a university in the Mid-Atlantic region of the United States. All participants were volunteers recruited through flyers and word-of-mouth on campus, and they provided informed consent in accord with the university's Institutional Review Board. The sample had a mean age of 26.18 years (SD = 3.70).

The dataset used for this analysis came from a neurofeedback study whose methods have been previously published [11]. Briefly, participants wore 64-lead EEG and 2-lead ECG monitors. The task performed was a high difficulty and low difficulty shooting virtual reality simulation in which participants had to shoot enemy targets and refrain from shooting friendly targets. Difficulty was manipulated by target exposure time. In the high difficulty condition, targets were presented very briefly, forcing participants to make a decision on whether to shoot or not very quickly. In the low difficulty condition, the target exposure time was longer, permitting easier discrimination between friendly and enemy targets.

III. Model Development

In the DualTask experiment, the objective was to determine on a second-by-second basis if the participant was in the dual task state or not, which was interpreted as cognitive resource utilization. The model was developed using EEG and ECG features. The EEG features were specifically chosen to characterize frontal/parietal interactions, and the ECG features were chosen to characterize the autonomic nervous system response.

The inputs to the model are features derived from ECG and EEG data. The EEG electrodes used were P3, P4, O1, O2, FP1, FP2, F3, F4, F7, and F8. The output of the model for the DualTask is the predicted probability that the subject was performing the math task. For binary outcomes, the probability was thresholded at 0.5.

Raw ECG data was cleaned using the Neurokit2 package for Python. Raw EEG data was cleaned by low-pass filtering at 30 Hz and then mean-centering across the frontal and parietal channels of interest. ECG features were calculated over 30-second windows, while EEG features were calculated over 3-second windows.

The ECG features calculated were heart rate: min, max, mean, and variability. EEG features calculated were: power of alpha-band frequencies over parietal channels, power of theta-band frequencies over frontal channels, Pearson correlation coefficients between all EEG channel pairs, and functional connectivity features (using the weighted phase lag index) between alpha- and theta-band-passed channels. These frequencies were chosen because of their relationship to mental arithmetic performance.

Subjects were excluded from the dataset if their data suggested either ECG or EEG electrodes were not securely attached, determined by visual inspection of the data. Out of 64 subjects, 19 were excluded. Constraints were applied to heart rate and heart rate variability calculations: heart rates outside the window [25, 175] BPM were deemed invalid; heart rate variabilities greater than 300ms were also deemed invalid. Where invalid values were present, the previous (valid) value was used.

A feed-forward neural network with 2 dense hidden layers and 20 nodes per layer was used. Dropout layers were used but replaced in favor of L1 and L2 regularization with factors of 0.003 and 0.01 respectively. ReLU activations were used on the hidden layers, and the final activation was a sigmoid function. Weighted binary cross entropy was used for the loss function, with a weight such that false negatives were penalized twice as much as false positives. Learning curves were used to tune the hyperparameters to prevent overfitting and maximize performance. The final, tuned model was then applied to the TeamTask and VisualTargetTask datasets. In Figure. 2 an example out of the model is provided with a threshold of 0.5. The prediction from the model (blue line) is shown with the Dual Task (mental arithmetic). The model outputs a probability ranging from 0-1 at each second. The probabilities provided by the model were thresholded at different values (dashed lines) to create a binarized time series for subsequent analyses.

A. *Exploratory Analysis: Thresholding*

As part of our exploratory analyses in the external validation datasets (TeamTask and VisualTargetTask), we examined the effect of various thresholds for the model predictions. This was motivated by the observations that 1) the tasks in each dataset were markedly different and therefore likely had different cognitive demands, and 2) the subjects used in each dataset were different. Thus, we wanted to examine whether different thresholds might result in different model predictions based on the differences in tasks and the individuals performing them. For these analyses, we varied the threshold for the model prediction from 0.1 to 0.9 in increments of 0.1. At each threshold level, we binarized the models' probability output and computed a prediction. In TeamTask, these varied threshold predictions were compared with the NASA-TLX subscores and total score, and in VisualTargetTask these thresholds were used to compare the differences across high and low difficulty conditions. In Figure. 3, the results of this analysis are shown across NASA-TLX subscores and various thereshold is provided. Mental demand and Temporal Demand were highly correlated with the model output across a wide range of thresholds. This statistically significant correlation over a range of thresholds was not evident for the other subscales of the NASA-TLX nor the total score.

IV. Results

In this section, results of the model output are discussed separately and concludes with a discussion of the dynamic thresholding results.

A. *Dual Task*

The model presented in this manuscript was developed and fit to DualTask using the Matthews Correlation Coefficient (MCC) as the objective function. This was chosen because of its ability to better assess the performance of the model on unbalanced data.

The performance of the model using a LOO cross validation was evaluated with accuracy, precision, recall, F1 score, and the Matthews Correlation Coefficient. These values (mean +/- standard deviation) were: 0.72 +/- 0.06; 0.30 +/- 0.12; 0.40 +/- 0.18; 0.336 +/- 0.12; 0.18 +/- 0.15, respectively.

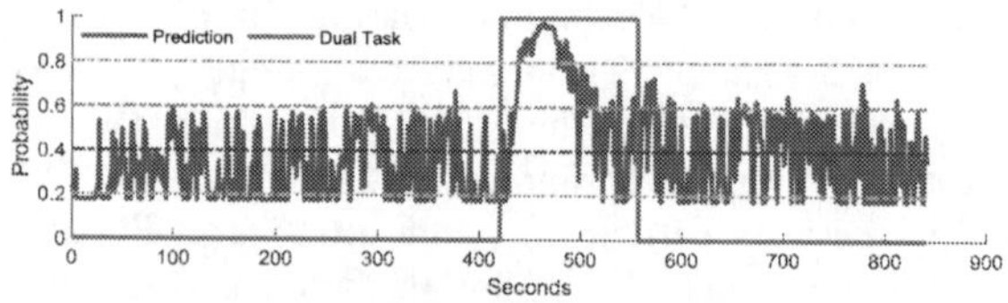

Fig. 2: Example dynamics in prediction of the DualTask and thresholding.

Feature importances were determined to understand what physiological parameters contributed to the prediction of being in the DualTask. Of the 250 features used in the full model, we report the 10 most important features in order of most-to-least important: mean heart rate, minimum heart rate, maximum heart rate, heart rate variability, FP1T, FP2-F4 correlation, O1-F4 correlation, F7-FP2 correlation, O2-FP2 correlation, theta band P3-FP2 WPLI.

B. *Team Task*

In TeamTask, participants performed realistic military missions (e.g., area defense) in a simulated environment. At the conclusion of each mission (75 minutes), participants completed a NASA-TLX survey. Our model, trained on DualTask, was used to create second-by-second predictions. These binarized predictions were integrated over time and used to correlate with NASA-TLX subscores and total score, as we expected a survey response to be based on perceived lasting cognitive burden throughout the task.

Using a threshold of 0.5 (that was used to train the model in the DualTask), significant correlations were observed for the mental demand ($r = 0.42$, $p = 0.0197$) and temporal demand ($r = 0.42$, $p = 0.0201$) components of the NASA-TLX. This was an expected finding, considering known difficulties in multitasking and validated estimates of workload determined by NASA-TLX. However, we also explored additional thresholds in deploying the model in TeamTask, as the demand and burden could have been considerably different from the DualTask procedures. It is likely that different tasks would have different levels of workload and thus, thresholds should be adapted. We show this exploratory analysis below.

Over a range of thresholds, mental demand and temporal demand showed statistically significant correlations (r = 0.38-0.50; all p ¡ .05). At the very highest thresholds, additional components of the NASA-TLX were correlated, including the NASA-TLX total score with the highest noted correlation ($r = 0.5536$, $p = 0.01$).

C. *Visual Target Task*

In the VisualTargetTask experiment, participants performed a simulated shooting task in high difficulty and low difficulty conditions. The model output was compared between the difficulty conditions. At a threshold of 0.5, there was a significant difference between the model predictions for

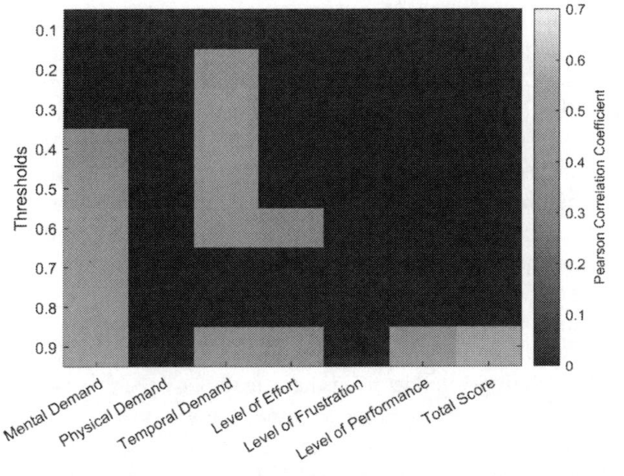

Fig. 3: Correlations between the amount of time cognitively depleted and the various subscores of the NASA-TLX (x-axis) across a number of thresholds (y-axis).

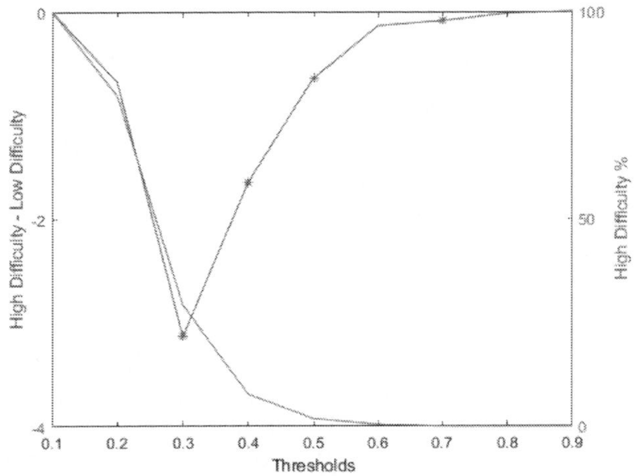

Fig. 4: Exploratory analysis was performed to investigate relative thresholding of probabilities and its effect on discriminating high and low difficulty conditions.

the high and low difficulty conditions. In the low difficulty condition, the model estimated that participants experienced cognitive resource depletion 2.5% of the time compared to 1.86% in the high difficulty condition (difference = 0.64%, p = 0.0013, via t-test). This was somewhat unexpected, as we predicted that there would be greater model-determined CRD for the high difficulty compared to the low difficulty condition; however, the unexpected result may be due to peculiarities in the design of this task. Specifically, accurately shooting the targets was made more difficult by less exposure time to the target, which then could have impacted the way in which resources are deployed (e.g., more reflexive responses). Despite this peculiarity, the CRD model can successfully classify difficulty across task conditions.

We also performed an exploratory analysis over thresholds as was done for the TeamTask (Figure 4). In Figure. 4, the mean differences between high and low difficulty are plotted for various thresholds (blue line). The blue line shows the difference between the model predictions, while the orange shows just the high difficulty predictions. Starting at a threshold probability of 0.3, there is a statistically significant difference between the model predictions for the two conditions (asterisks) which were determined by t-test. For all comparisons, the low difficulty condition had higher levels of cognitive resource depletion predictions. This number represents the difference in time (expressed as a percentage) between the time spent in a CRD state for both difficulty conditions. For thresholds of 0.3, 0.4, 0.5, and 0.6, a significant difference was observed wherein the model predicted more CRD in the low difficulty condition than in the high difficulty condition (asterisks). As a reference, the percentage of time in spent in a CRD state is shown for the high difficulty task alone without the low task difficulty percentages subtracted (orange).

V. DISCUSSION

We have developed a continuous and generalizable Cognitive Resource Depletion (CRD) model that successfully estimates resource depletion in a variety of realistic tasks and that is robust to individual differences from non-invasively collected physiological signals. Physiological signals collected during three different realistic tasks were used as predictors to train and test the model, and the reliable and validated NASA-TLX survey [7], [10] or experimental manipulations were used to validate the cognitive burden of each individual subject. The CRD model, trained on a dataset where subjects were continuously monitoring an environment and occasionally asked to perform an additional task, the DualTask dataset, was able to be deployed on two independent datasets: a team-based navigation and decision making task (TeamTask) and an individual visual target detection task (VisualTargetTask) with different levels of difficulty. This model, and the underlying physiological signals used as predictors, appears to successfully predict a state that underlies each one of these tasks and is behaviorally relevant.

A. Generalizability of the CRD Model

Generalizability of models in human state assessment is often quite challenging, as there are many contributing factors that deter these models from being generalizable, including individual differences in cognitive strategy, measurement noise, and task-specific physiological targets. Our CRD model was trained on a single dataset that involved monitoring an environment and performing mental arithmetic and that was purposely designed to engage multiple systems and burden subjects. In this model, we attempted to predict whether there was a single task being completed or subjects were engaged in the dual task. Model output was then validated with NASA-TLX subscales when the model was deployed on the TeamTask, a challenging and complex realistic navigation and decision making task that required coordination between individuals. Interestingly, the estimated total time of cognitive depletion was significantly correlated with multiple subscales of the NASA-TLX and most robustly (across many thresholds) with the mental and temporal demand subscales. Moreover, in the VisualTargetTask, this time of cognitive depletion was also associated with task difficulty, however in a way that was opposite of what was predicted. Perhaps due to the implementation of "difficulty" in this task and different cognitive resource deployment compared to the other tasks, the CRD model did not relate to task difficulty as predicted, but it still predicted a difference in these conditions. Thus, it appears as though the CRD model may be tracking a cognitive construct that changes continuously and is sensitive to multi-tasking, perceived mental and temporal demand, and task difficulty, which we call cognitive depletion.

The training set, a dual visual monitoring and math task, appears to sufficiently engage cognitive depletion such that the CRD Model does not need additional training for robustness. This dual task robustness is unique in its use of mathematics and visual processing and general multi-tasking. Performing arithmetic calculations in one's mind involves a complex coordination of different brain regions and networks [12] and a level of abstraction that separates itself from both the object and social world in which we live and interact [13] but paradoxically may be applied to both [14]. Multi-tasking is also a specialized state that recruits more neural resources than a single task alone [15] and can potentially lead to distraction, overload, and information loss. These properties, coupled with current notions of general intelligence within the brain [16], could suggest that the training task (DualTask) is uniquely suited for a generalized model of cognitive depletion, as it engages resources within the mind (through the mathematics component) that can be applied to a variety of experiences and to multitasking. Future studies may further test the generalizability of the model, perhaps using more abstract tasks and parametrically modulating the number of tasks.

Interestingly, the CRD model is also robust to individual differences, as it does not need to be calibrated to each subject. This result of robustness to individual differences underlying the construct of cognitive depletion is quite surprising. Intuitively, one might understand that cognitive depletion would require individual calibration, especially when considering the model is based on physiological signals that often suffer from nuisance signals, especially in a realistic non-laboratory setting [17], [18]. It may be, however, that special properties of the features extracted and used in the model may have substantially contributed to the generalizability across subjects.

B. Covert physiological events and the CRD Model

Physiological monitoring of covert mental events is commonly used to understand the mechanistic properties of thought, including a variety of cognitive phenomena (e.g., perception, emotions, etc.) and fleeting mental states (e.g., fatigue, stress). Within the CRD Model, heart rate information and specific EEG features (i.e., connectivity) were the most diagnostic to this cognitive depletion.

The most informative features of the ANS were those associated mostly with fluctuations in sympathetic and parasympathetic nervous system activity; specifically, modulation of heart rate and heart rate variability [19], [20]. Interestingly, these features were among the most important among the 250 features tested. While the relationships between cognitive workload and autonomic metrics have been studied extensively [21], cardiovascular metrics such as those used here vary significantly with age, and our participants varied quite dramatically in age. This may suggest that the CRD model learns complex relationships between these features which transcend this inherent limitation in cardiovascular metrics.

The most informative EEG features involved not the commonly used power fluctuations in EEG, but rather the statistical dependence between different sensors, especially involving the frontal cortex (see Results). This interesting finding is perhaps not surprising, as power fluctuations in EEG are often susceptible to many different sources of noise [22], especially in a realistic environment in which subjects may move more freely or perform continuous tasks in which eyeblinks and other movements are difficult to control. We have recently shown that in another realistic tasks (i.e., driving), a synchronization metric between EEG sensors was also more sensitive to task demands than fluctuations in power [23] to the extent that if power alone were used, no neural differences would have been observed. Moreover, fluctuations in neural networks underlying a large variety of tasks has been shown to be predictive of a large and growing list of behaviors including multitasking [24] and adaptations to new stimuli or stress [25].

Thus, in addition to the idiosyncrasies of evoked task demands, underlying physiological features of the CRD Model appear to have a substantial contribution to its generalizability. Future studies may be able to deploy this model in different settings and contexts, using additional features that may capture the dynamic physiological processes more broadly and perhaps extending the simple statistical dependencies between sensors used here to more complex systems or network science approaches known to capture physiological behavior at a variety of scales.

C. Temporal Resolution and Thresholding

An overarching concept that emerges between the tasks, model fit, physiological sensors, and underlying construct which we suggest we are predicting is that of temporal resolution. The convergence of these items into a successful and robust model suggests a waxing and waning of cognitive depletion across time, and while our thresholding and correlational analyses suggest a pathway in which it may be calibrated for individual tasks, this model could also provide a framework in which to detect other potential states of interest. Currently, we suggest that thresholds will need to be determined on a per task basis which is congruent with the notion that various tasks impose varying levels of cognitive demand. In order to support generalizability across tasks we suggest two future research directions. First, the model output can be thresholded at varying levels and an integration across those thresholds performed to identify robust periods of CRD detection. This would generate additional parameterization (e.g., continuity of significant differences across thresholds). This type of analysis is similar to cluster-based statistical testing [26]. A second approach could involve empirical derivation of appropriate thresholds for a dictionary of task types (e.g., visuospatial demanding task, mental arithmetic, etc.). This second approach has some traction in the cognitive ergonomics literature that examine different types of naturalistic tasks [27]. With respect to timescales, the EEG and ECG features were extracted in 3 sec and 30 sec windows respectively, thus limiting the fluctuations which may be diagnostic for other states or limiting the generalizability of the model. Rather than a limitation, these two different timescales could also have contributed to the model's robustness. Future studies may explore the complex dynamics between the length and dynamics underlying cognitive constructs, the measurement resolution, and the need for temporally flexible or scale-free feature extractions for covert physiological recordings.

VI. Conclusions and Future Directions

The continuous, generalizable, and robust CRD Model successfully estimates resource depletion in a variety of realistic tasks and is resilient to individual differences from non-invasively collected physiological signals; however, the deployment of this model is still limited. Future investigations of the CRD Model robustness may inspect its success in non-visual tasks and expand the context to additional real-world applications. Additionally, future research may include additional physiological sensor types and features including fNIRS and pupillometry (although the latter is difficult without measurement of ambient luminence). Finally, more psychological assessments will be useful to understand its uses and limitations. Future applications may use this model in a closed-loop fashion where real-time assessments are used to drive adaptations between humans and complex systems.

Acknowledgements

Research was sponsored by the U.S. Army Research Laboratory's (ARL) Human Research and Engineering Directorate (HRED) and was accomplished under Cooperative Agreement Number W911NF-21-2-0108. The views and conclusions contained in this document are those of the authors and should not be interpreted as representing the official policies, either expressed or implied, of the U.S. Army Research Laboratory's (ARL) Human Research and Engineering Directorate. The U.S. Government is authorized to reproduce and distribute reprints for Government purposes notwithstanding any copyright notation herein.

References

[1] G. A. Miller, "The magical number seven, plus or minus two: Some limits on our capacity for processing information." *Psychological Review*, vol. 63, no. 2, pp. 81–97, Mar. 1956. [Online]. Available: http://doi.apa.org/getdoi.cfm?doi=10.1037/h0043158

[2] J. M. Wolfe, "The binding problem lives on: comment on Di Lollo," *Trends in Cognitive Sciences*, vol. 16, no. 6, pp. 307–308; author reply 308–309, Jun. 2012.

[3] V. Di Lollo, "The feature-binding problem is an ill-posed problem," *Trends in Cognitive Sciences*, vol. 16, no. 6, pp. 317–321, Jun. 2012. [Online]. Available: https://linkinghub.elsevier.com/retrieve/pii/S1364661312000988

[4] E. Hunt, J. W. Pellegrino, and P. L. Yee, "Individual Differences in Attention," in *Psychology of Learning and Motivation.* Elsevier, 1989, vol. 24, pp. 285–310. [Online]. Available: https://linkinghub.elsevier.com/retrieve/pii/S007974210860540X

[5] A. H. Taylor and L. Dorn, "Stress, Fatigue, Health, and Risk of Road Traffic Accident among Professional Drivers: The Contribution of Physical Inactivity," *Annual Review of Public Health*, vol. 27, no. 1, pp. 371–391, Apr. 2006. [Online]. Available: https://www.annualreviews.org/doi/10.1146/annurev.publhealth.27.021405.102117

[6] X. Gu, Z. Cao, A. Jolfaei, P. Xu, D. Wu, T.-P. Jung, and C.-T. Lin, "EEG-Based Brain-Computer Interfaces (BCIs): A Survey of Recent Studies on Signal Sensing Technologies and Computational Intelligence Approaches and Their Applications," *IEEE/ACM Transactions on Computational Biology and Bioinformatics*, vol. 18, no. 5, pp. 1645–1666, Sep. 2021. [Online]. Available: https://ieeexplore.ieee.org/document/9328561/

[7] S. G. Hart, "Nasa-Task Load Index (NASA-TLX); 20 Years Later," *Proceedings of the Human Factors and Ergonomics Society Annual Meeting*, vol. 50, no. 9, pp. 904–908, Oct. 2006. [Online]. Available: http://journals.sagepub.com/doi/10.1177/154193120605000909

[8] Y. Zhou, S. Huang, Z. Xu, P. Wang, X. Wu, and D. Zhang, "Cognitive Workload Recognition Using EEG Signals and Machine Learning: A Review," *IEEE Transactions on Cognitive and Developmental Systems*, pp. 1–1, 2021. [Online]. Available: https://ieeexplore.ieee.org/document/9458953/

[9] L. R. Enders, R. J. Smith, S. M. Gordon, A. J. Ries, and J. Touryan, "Gaze Behavior During Navigation and Visual Search of an Open-World Virtual Environment," *Frontiers in Psychology*, vol. 12, p. 681042, 2021.

[10] S. G. Hart and L. E. Staveland, "Development of NASA-TLX (Task Load Index): Results of Empirical and Theoretical Research," in *Advances in Psychology*. Elsevier, 1988, vol. 52, pp. 139–183. [Online]. Available: https://linkinghub.elsevier.com/retrieve/pii/S0166411508623869

[11] D. P. Spangler, S. Alam, S. Rahman, J. Crone, R. Robucci, N. Banerjee, S. E. Kerick, and J. R. Brooks, "Multilevel Longitudinal Analysis of Shooting Performance as a Function of Stress and Cardiovascular Responses," *IEEE Transactions on Affective Computing*, vol. 12, no. 3, pp. 648–665, Jul. 2021. [Online]. Available: https://ieeexplore.ieee.org/document/9097281/

[12] M. Delazer, F. Domahs, L. Bartha, C. Brenneis, A. Lochy, T. Trieb, and T. Benke, "Learning complex arithmetic—an fMRI study," *Cognitive Brain Research*, vol. 18, no. 1, pp. 76–88, Dec. 2003. [Online]. Available: https://linkinghub.elsevier.com/retrieve/pii/S0926641003002155

[13] M. Mitchelmore and P. White, "Abstraction in Mathematics and Mathematics Learning," *Proceedings of the 28th Conference of the International Group for the Psychology of Mathematics Education*, vol. 3, pp. 329–336, 2004.

[14] P. L. Ferrari, "Abstraction in mathematics," *Philosophical Transactions of the Royal Society of London. Series B: Biological Sciences*, vol. 358, no. 1435, pp. 1225–1230, Jul. 2003. [Online]. Available: https://royalsocietypublishing.org/doi/10.1098/rstb.2003.1316

[15] K. P. Madore and A. D. Wagner, "Multicosts of Multitasking," *Cerebrum: The Dana Forum on Brain Science*, vol. 2019, pp. cer–04–19, Apr. 2019.

[16] J. Hawkins, M. Lewis, M. Klukas, S. Purdy, and S. Ahmad, "A Framework for Intelligence and Cortical Function Based on Grid Cells in the Neocortex," *Frontiers in Neural Circuits*, vol. 12, p. 121, Jan. 2019. [Online]. Available: https://www.frontiersin.org/article/10.3389/fncir.2018.00121/full

[17] Lun-De Liao, Chin-Teng Lin, K. McDowell, A. E. Wickenden, K. Gramann, Tzyy-Ping Jung, Li-Wei Ko, and Jyh-Yeong Chang, "Biosensor Technologies for Augmented Brain–Computer Interfaces in the Next Decades," *Proceedings of the IEEE*, vol. 100, no. Special Centennial Issue, pp. 1553–1566, May 2012. [Online]. Available: http://ieeexplore.ieee.org/document/6168212/

[18] A. Ortiz-Rosario and H. Adeli, "Brain-computer interface technologies: from signal to action," *Reviews in the Neurosciences*, vol. 24, no. 5, pp. 537–552, Jan. 2013. [Online]. Available: https://www.degruyter.com/document/doi/10.1515/revneuro-2013-0032/html

[19] R. D. Dias, M. C. Ngo-Howard, M. T. Boskovski, M. A. Zenati, and S. J. Yule, "Systematic review of measurement tools to assess surgeons' intraoperative cognitive workload," *British Journal of Surgery*, vol. 105, no. 5, pp. 491–501, Mar. 2018. [Online]. Available: https://academic.oup.com/bjs/article/105/5/491-501/6123151

[20] A. M. Hughes, G. M. Hancock, S. L. Marlow, K. Stowers, and E. Salas, "Cardiac Measures of Cognitive Workload: A Meta-Analysis," *Human Factors: The Journal of the Human Factors and Ergonomics Society*, vol. 61, no. 3, pp. 393–414, May 2019. [Online]. Available: http://journals.sagepub.com/doi/10.1177/0018720819830553

[21] A. R. Hidalgo-Muñoz, D. Mouratille, N. Matton, M. Causse, Y. Rouillard, and R. El-Yagoubi, "Cardiovascular correlates of emotional state, cognitive workload and time-on-task effect during a realistic flight simulation," *International Journal of Psychophysiology*, vol. 128, pp. 62–69, Jun. 2018. [Online]. Available: https://linkinghub.elsevier.com/retrieve/pii/S0167876017306542

[22] N. Bigdely-Shamlo, T. Mullen, C. Kothe, K.-M. Su, and K. A. Robbins, "The PREP pipeline: standardized preprocessing for large-scale EEG analysis," *Frontiers in Neuroinformatics*, vol. 9, Jun. 2015. [Online]. Available: http://journal.frontiersin.org/Article/10.3389/fninf.2015.00016/abstract

[23] E. E. Flynn-Evans, L. R. Wong, Y. Kuriyagawa, N. Gowda, P. F. Cravalho, S. Pradhan, N. H. Feick, N. G. Bathurst, Z. L. Glaros, T. Wilaiprasitporn, K. Bansal, J. O. Garcia, and C. J. Hilditch, "Supervision of a self-driving vehicle unmasks latent sleepiness relative to manually controlled driving," *Scientific Reports*, vol. 11, no. 1, p. 18530, Dec. 2021. [Online]. Available: https://www.nature.com/articles/s41598-021-92914-5

[24] M. Alavash, C. C. Hilgetag, C. M. Thiel, and C. Gießing, "Persistency and flexibility of complex brain networks underlie dual-task interference," *Human Brain Mapping*, vol. 36, no. 9, pp. 3542–3562, Sep. 2015.

[25] V. Paban, J. Modolo, A. Mheich, and M. Hassan, "Psychological resilience correlates with EEG source-space brain network flexibility," *Network Neuroscience*, vol. 3, no. 2, pp. 539–550, Jan. 2019. [Online]. Available: https://direct.mit.edu/netn/article/3/2/539-550/2214

[26] S. H. Kwon, "Threshold selection based on cluster analysis," *Pattern Recognition Letters*, vol. 25, no. 9, pp. 1045–1050, 2004. [Online]. Available: https://www.sciencedirect.com/science/article/pii/S0167865504000674

[27] P. Braarud, "Subjective Task Complexity and Subjective Workload: Criterion Validity for Complex Team Tasks," *International Journal of Cognitive Ergonomics*, vol. 5, no. 3, pp. 261–273, Sep. 2001. [Online]. Available: http://www.tandfonline.com/doi/abs/10.1207/S15327566IJCE0503_7

Common Usability Issues on University's Websites

Reem Alsaeed
Department of Information Technology
College of Computer, Qassim University
Buraydah, Saudi Arabia
e-mail: r.reim@qu.edu.sa

Mohammad Mahdi Hassan
Department of Computer Science
College of Computer, Qassim University
Buraydah, Saudi Arabia
e-mail: mo.hassan@qu.edu.sa

Abstract— **Usability is an important quality factor for the success or failure of any website. Users of university websites encounter various usability problems during the navigation and information searching activities. Studying these problems is a critical issue for the success of the growing higher education market. The main goal of this paper is to identify usability challenges encountered by the users of university websites. We conducted an extensive literature review in this regard. We identified numerous aspects of usability and relevant challenges to those aspects. We also presented proposed solutions from the existing literature. This study will help to have a deeper insight into user requirements to develop usable university websites.**

Keywords- Usability; Usability evaluation methods; Usability issues; University websites.

I. INTRODUCTION

Usability is one of the critical criteria of website quality. Nielsen has defined usability as "a quality attribute that assesses how easy user interfaces are to use"[1]. Another well-known definition of usability given by the International Standards (ISO 9241-11 1998) is the effectiveness, efficiency, and satisfaction with which specified users can achieve goals specified in a specified context of use" (ISO 9241-11 1998). The success or failure of any website relies on that user should not face any obstacles during the website's usage. Web usability has a combination of multiple components to look upon, which are relevant to the amount of time required to learn to navigate a website, how quickly the desired goal is achieved, and the user's perceptions[2].

Numerous studies have employed evaluation techniques to assess the site's usability by measuring user performance and satisfaction and then suggesting enhancements to the site's usability. Researchers proposed several evaluation approaches to assess the usability aspects. Usability Evaluation Methods (UEMs) could be classified into three categories: (1)User-based methods, (2)Experts-based methods, and (3)Tool-Based Methods[3]. User-based methods involve assessing the interface by the users and finding usability issues, such as questionnaires and interviews. Expert-based methods involve having several experts' examinations of the user interface, such as heuristic evaluation. However, both approaches were conducted to evaluate the external attributes of the site (e.g., design consistency). Unlike other methods, tools-based methods aim at assessing the website's internal attributes that users or experts cannot perceive (e.g., the quality of the HTML code).

Nowadays, the importance of universities' websites has increased with the rapid development of technology. Such websites' importance comes from being a gateway to provide information and services. It is also a marketing tool to reach potential students. Most universities' websites provide the same information and services. In order to achieve the aims of such websites, universities should consider usability while developing and improving their websites. Many studies found in the literature evaluated the usability of university websites by employing different usability evaluation methods, such as questionnaires[3]–[6]and heuristic evaluation. Some studies employed two or more evaluation methods [7][8].

This study investigates various usability problems found in university websites and extracts their proposed solutions from existing literature. The paper also aims to understand university websites' specific characteristics and usability aspects. The rest of this paper is organized as follows. Section 2 provides a background of usability evaluation approaches, and we present the methodology used in this study in Section 3. Section 4 presents issues and challenges followed by proposed solutions in Section 5. Finally, Section 6 concludes the paper.

II. BACKGROUND DISCUSSION

Usability evaluation methods mainly aim to identify usability problems on systems evaluated. According to Nielsen[9], usability problems can be defined as the user interface aspects that may have any negative effect on the user. It may negatively affect usability factors, such as ease of understanding, learning, usage, and user satisfaction. Many research studies evaluated the usability of university sites by employing different usability evaluation methods. As a result, various usability problems were detected through experiments.

Several studies[3]–[6][10]–[12] involved users in the usability testing of university sites by using questionnaires, user testing, or/and other methods. Those studies assessed university sites usability' from the students' point of view. For example, Christoun et al. [4] investigated student satisfaction with the usability, aesthetics, content, and technology of a college's site of one of southeastern Massachusetts' public institutions of higher education. Hasan [3] also evaluated the usability of nine Jordanian university sites, while [5] investigated the usability of the Benue State University Website in Nigeria. Jabar et al. [6] measured the usability of the top three Malaysian university websites from students' perspectives. The study [11] used user testing and interviews to assess the effect of the information architecture of Dalhousie University's Website, including how information is categorized, labeled, and presented and how navigation and access are facilitated. Furthermore, Kasli and Avcikurt [12] evaluated 132 educational websites in Turkey using website evaluation forms and interviews.

Other studies employed heuristic evaluation or other expert-based methods to identify university site usability problems. Kostaras and Xenos [13], for example, evaluated the usability of the new site of Hellenic Open University. Similarly, Astani and Elhindi [14] selected the top 50 universities in the U.S to rate by two experts based on the design characteristics of sites. Furthermore, Hasan [7][8][15] investigated the usability of university sites in Jordan using heuristic evaluation based on the set of heuristics proposed by Hasan [16]. Nizamani et al. [17]tested the usability of the top 10 universities of Pakistan by utilizing guideline scoring.

In order to sufficiently identify usability problems on university sites, some studies utilized a combination of two or more approaches. Qasim et al. [18] used questionnaires and heuristic evaluation to assess university sites' usability in Pakistan. The study [19] combined heuristic evaluation and performance measurement to assess the usability of the Hellenic Open University(HOU) Website. Pierce [20] also evaluated the usability of the Harvard University site by heuristic evaluation and user testing. Furthermore, Majrashi and Hamilton [21] used several methods, including usability testing, heuristic evaluation, experts review, and competitive analysis. They evaluated the usability of the Jazan University site in Saudi Arabia and the RMIT University site in Australia. Also, the study investigated the design and content of eight university sites worldwide to identify the necessary content and essential features that should be included in each university site. Erickson et al. [22] evaluated the accessibility and usability of university sites using accessibility and usability evaluation methods.

Some studies found in the literature utilized automated evaluation tools. Al-Ananbeh et al. [23] employed HTML ToolBox, SEO PageRank, and PageRank Checker to evaluate eighty sites for universities in the Arab countries automatically. Islam and Tsuji [24] also combined automated tools and questionnaires to test the usability of some academic sites in Bangladesh. The literature outlined above proved the usefulness of usability evaluation methods regarding their ability to detect various usability problems on university sites. The identified problems were collected and analyzed to provide valuable sources, including the different types of usability problems that could be found on any university site, along with the solutions.

III. METHODOLOGY

In order to get an insight into the usability issues faced by users of university websites, we performed an extensive review of the literature. The goal is to analyze scientific studies related to university site usability', focusing on issues and solutions. We formulated the following research question for our study:

- What are the common usability issues found in university websites and how to resolve those?

To address the research question above, we have completed an extensive literature review. The phases of the study are shown concisely in Figure. 1.

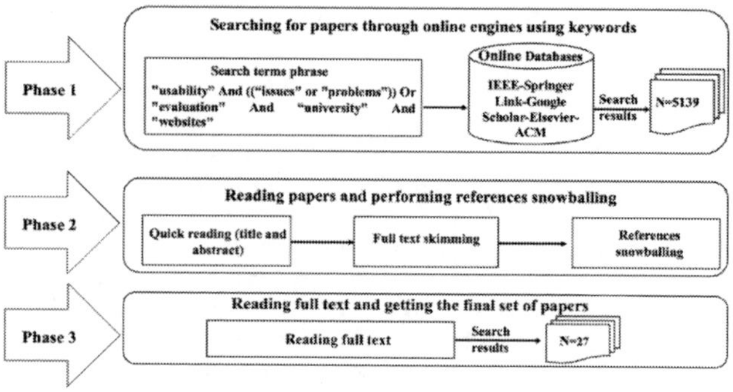

Figure 1. Phases of the Study

In this study, we considered only studies that achieved the following inclusion and exclusion criteria:

- We included studies that discuss university websites' usability or conduct experiments to evaluate university websites' usability worldwide by utilizing different usability evaluation methods and identifying usability problems or providing solutions.
- We excluded studies that have no relation to university websites or those concerned with systems relevant to university websites (e.g., e-learning and e-library).

The methodology phases are explained below:

Phase one: We identified the main search terms: usability, usability issues, usability problems, usability evaluation, and university websites. And then searched through digital databases: Google Scholar, IEEE, Elsevier, ACM, and Springer link using keywords. We focused on highly relevant papers and restrained the search to human-computer interaction/computer science studies if the search engines supported it. As a result, we obtained 5139 papers from the five digital library databases (Google Scholar -1840, IEEE - 1480, Elsevier -159, ACM -1452, and Springer link -208).

Phase Two: We performed a quick reading for the title and abstract of all collected papers to do a preliminary paper classification (relevant, irrelevant, and need further reading). And then, we skimmed papers that needed further reading by reading relevant sections (e.g., the introduction and conclusion). Finally, we performed snowballing on the selected relevant papers, scanning their reference lists to identify additional relevant studies that we did not include. The studies were included or excluded based on the identified criteria.

Phase Three: We read the whole text of the papers and identified the final set of papers, which was 27 papers. And then, we explored papers thoroughly to extract relevant information.

IV. Usability Issues And Challenges

Usability issues mostly lead to a delay in accomplishing users' tasks or preventing achieving their goals, which frustrate them. Some reviewed studies have provided more detailed descriptions of detected usability problems. After the literature survey on usability issues, we collected and classified ninety-two specific usability issues into seventeen categories. Each category of the seventeen categories and relevant usability problems are explained below:

A. Design Issues

Twelve usability problems are relevant to four major design issues: overall web pages design, inconsistency of fonts and images, appearance issues regarding links and elements, and overcrowded elements and information.

- Overall web pages design: Inconsistency of design and layout of web pages color (e.g., an inappropriate combination of background and font colors)[5][7][8]; inconsistency of the interface language (i.e., some pages on the English interface displayed Arabic or English content)[7][8]; inconsistency of the content (e.g., content differed between English and foreign language interfaces)[7][8]; inappropriate page heading[7][8]; inappropriate design of the main menu (e.g., the menu items unseen or could not be selected)[7][8]; unappealing aesthetic features[6].
- Inconsistency of fonts and images: inconsistency in font case (capital and small), size, style (regular and bold), and color[3], [5]–[8], inappropriate number, size, or quality of images[7][8][24], and broken images[5][7].
- Appearance issues regarding links and elements: misleading links (e.g., elements looked like links, but no action is performed when clicked)[21], and inconsistency or incorrect alignment of the headers and content (center, right, or left) [7][8][21].
- An overcrowded element and information (e.g., unnecessary elements and information and an overcrowded advertisement) [6][21].

B. Navigation Issues

- Users get lost within the website pages [5][21].
- Difficulty finding or using a site map (e.g., the site map is not linked to all the website pages) [21].
- Links Errors: broken links [5][7][10]; under construction and maintenance pages [21]; dead node pages (orphan page) [7][8][21]; links not opening the destination pages [7][8]; misleading links [7][8]; and links causing the menu to disappear [7][8].
- Global navigation issues: it is a common navigation pattern located on the top of every page. This section is reserved for links of top-level categories, logos, search bars, and other important elements. This pattern issues include the following: the global navigation disappearance (e.g., university logo, home page link, and other navigation options are disappeared, do not work properly, or does not exist at all) [7][8][21]; poor or inconsistent design of global navigation [21]; elements of global navigation issues (e.g., primary users sections have not included as categories in the global navigation) [21].
- Lack of Navigation Patterns (e.g., breadcrumbs)[21].

C. Ease of Use Issues

- Difficulty in interaction with a website [3][7][18].
- Lack of support in more than one language [3][7].
- Lack of considering the usage for blind and other disabled individuals (e.g., use of an inappropriate color like green which is not suitable for color blinds)[25].

D. Visibility of System Status Issues

Invisibility may cause some issues, mainly if the process consumes time. Users have to be informed about the progress of any processed process, their current location on the website, and where they go next. The category includes the following: the invisibility of search query (e.g., status progress of submitted search) [21]; the invisibility of other processes status (e.g., the progress of downloading files or submitting forms)[21]; and invisibility of selected icons and links status (e.g., icon and link are not highlighted when they selected) [13][24][25].

E. Load Time Issues

The load time of websites should be reasonable. Some websites were evaluated and found to be too slow [5].

F. Compatibility Issues

- Browsers Incompatibility [5][24].
- Devices Incompatibility (e.g., lack of following the platform guidelines for mobile version) [21][23].

G. Content Issues

The most important component of a university website is information content.

- Inadequate Information [5][8][17][20][26].
- Empty Pages [7][8].
- Old Information [7][8][17][26].
- Inappropriate content (e.g., repeated or very concise content) [7][8].
- Information Classification issues (e.g., the contents were not classified by headings and sub-headings)[21].
- Labels of Links and Button issues (e.g., button and link labels did not start with action words) [21].
- Content Errors (e.g., punctuation or grammatical errors) [7][8].
- Lack of Technical Information (e.g., information regarding the file types that will open through links)[8].

H. Search Issues

Earlier studies showed that the most preferred features on educational websites from the user's perspective are useful navigational support and effective search tools [7]. The category comprises the usability issues encountered by users during their search for information.

- Ineffectiveness of search tools [4][7][8][11][17][26].
- Limitation of search scope [21].
- Intolerance of Errors (e.g., misspellings) [21].
- Lack of refining and filtering mechanism [17][21].
- Lack of research suggestions [21].
- Lack of search scope customization [21].
- Lack of support features (e.g., autocomplete) [21].

I. User Support Issues

For users to accomplish their tasks and look for information needed in the website, it is necessary to provide good support for the users to achieve tasks quickly and easily.

- Lack of Help and Documentation (e.g., lack of hints to help navigate or to complete tasks, and lack of tutorials, services documenting, and the FAQ) [12][18][17][21].
- Lack of support for login and authentication processes [21].
- Lack of support for services (e.g., services guide) [12][20][21].
- Lack of Search Support [20][21].
- Lack of helpful error messages [21].
- Use of technical language in error messages (e.g., using “attribute” term rather than “field” term) [21].

J. Information Architecture Issues

The organization and classification of the website's content and pages must be easy for accessing and finding information.

- Labeling issues (e.g., not self-explanatory, perplexed, or generalized labels) [5][11][21].
- Hierarchy issues [11][21].
- Organization system issues(e.g., deep hierarchy) [11][21].

K. Data Entry Forms Issues

- Form Fields and Text Area Problems (e.g., lack of form features that help users input the proper data like default values)[21][27].
- Form button problems: lack of following the standards in labeling and positioning of buttons (e.g., use the label “OK” for the submitting button rather than “Submit” label, buttons are not located based on the natural reading order of the website audience, or two buttons have the same function, but they are located in different places)[21].
- Form Feedback problems (e.g., providing feedback without full description of what is happening, using poor language (like "adding process is done"), or using inappropriate color for a particular message)[21].
- Label alignment problems (e.g., labels are far from the fields) [21].
- Unhelpful error messages [21].
- Form functionality issues (e.g., difficulties regarding correcting errors when submitting an incomplete form or with non-expected data entry, and synchronously validation of the form before being submitted)[21].

L. Accessibility Issues

Among the users of university websites, there are a rising number of disabled users, such as individuals with visual impairments and individuals with reading-related and learning disabilities. As such, it became necessary for the designers of university websites to consider the specific needs of such users and make modifications needed to ensure web content accessibility for all users as possible.

- Accessibility issues regarding performing tasks (e.g., tasks cannot be completed using only the keyboard)[21][22].
- Accessibility issues regarding design (e.g., poor contrast between text and background and lack of meaningful alternate text for inaccessible graphics) [21][22].
- Forms accessibility issues (e.g., labels of form fields do not match the visible text for that element when read by the screen reader) [22].
- Accessibility issues regarding navigation (e.g., lack of helpful skip navigation links)[22].

M. FamiliarityIssues

Information presentation has to be in a logical order and follow real-world convention.

- Matching the real-world convention issues (e.g., registration instructions are displayed at the end of the registration task rather than at the top of tasks to read them first)[21].
- Using unfamiliar terminology (e.g., using unfamiliar words to typical users, such as operational rules term, bursar, and provost[21], and lack providing a reference for the user that contains such terminologies) [20].
- Form issues (e.g., inappropriate or illogical structure and elements alignment) [21].

N. User Control and Freedom Issues

While conducting the tasks on university websites, sometimes users face critical situations, such as making mistakes in previous stages or facing some difficulties. They need some way of going back or undoing[21].

- Lack of ways to undo actions (e.g., cancel button or back button not existing) [21].
- Lack of navigation options (e.g., lack of link of the main page of the category, lack of link of "Back to the top" on the pages that have a too long amount of information[13][19][21], and indirect navigating ways through key topics in the site)[20].

O. ConsistencyIssues

This category is nearly overlapped with all aspects, such as design, navigation, and content, whereby consistency is pivotal for all aspects of a website's usability.

- Unexpected placement of elements (e.g., sign out was not in expected place) [21].
- Navigation Inconsistency (e.g., inconstant navigation bar and different format of menus on the page) [13][20][21].

- Content Inconsistency (e.g., forms buttons labeled inappropriate or very ambiguous names[13], and blank front pages of some categories)[19][21].
- Design Inconsistency (e.g., inconsistent design of website pages in the form of colors, fonts, and languages[3][13][19][21].
- Search Facility Inconsistency(e.g., a search box is not in its standard location)[21].

P. Prevention of ErrorIssues

Users can not always avoid errors while using the sites; therefore, preventing errors upfront from occurring is a good feature for websites [21].

- Lack of preventing errors of forms (e.g., lack of hints clarifying the required data format and permitted length, lack of showing the mandatory fields up front, lack of submission confirmation of critical form)[21].
- Content ambiguity or presentation errors[20](e.g., a single command has different jobs, and a single animation image leads to navigate to two different pages)[21].
- Links errors issues (e.g., invalid and unimplemented links) [21].
- Search facility errors[13][19].

Q. MemorabilityIssues

- Memorization of Information (e.g., need to memorize courses ID when students attempt to enroll in courses or read multiple pages when looking for information relevant to a particular topic)[21].
- Memorization of task's Instructions[21].
- Memorization of navigational paths deep (e.g., menu with 6 levels deep[13][19][20].

V. Observation And Proposed Solutions

This section presents guidelines for designers of university sites to achieve the advantages of usable websites. An essential component of a university site is information. The university sites usually provide information and services for students and staff. Information should be accurate, updated, and consistent. Accessing information should also be quick and easy for students. Logically organize information (e.g., courses classification by degree, school, and campus[21]), follow real-world conventions, and avoid deep hierarchy. Terminology and links labels should be self-explanatory, accurately describe the relevant contents, and be familiar in an academic environment. The site should provide information regarding the file types that open through links (e.g., DOC and PDF files)[8]. Students and staff should be able to contact via contact services(e.g., email and contact forms). Access and search tools should be well worked. The search facility has to offer refining and filtering mechanisms, alternative search suggestions, support features (e.g., autocomplete), customizing search scope, and the search scope should include the entire university site [21]. The university site should support the native of most students and other commonly used languages (e.g., English language).

Since the university sites are too large and have many branches, using navigation patterns, such as breadcrumbs is very useful. Navigation options should be consistent, implemented correctly, and placed obviously on all site pages. Include global navigation in the most frequently visited site's pages and use other navigation patterns (e.g., breadcrumbs) for other pages[21]. The University logo should be linked with the 'Home Page' and be placed in the global navigation area. The global navigation has to include the main content categories (e.g., students, staff, research, and program and courses)[21]. All links should open intended and expected pages. Design site map and a site index (A-Z) appropriately. The site should provide information about under construction and maintenance pages, or redirect users to alternative pages that provide the same information or services[21].

It is necessary to provide good support for students and staff to achieve tasks quickly and easily (e.g., Online enrolment). Provide assistance on pages with high error occurrences[21]. Make users feel in control in many situations. Offer multiple navigation options and help students undo some entries or exit from situations like the cancel button or back button. Provide helpful error messages in familiar terminology to help them recognize, diagnose, and recover. Provide immediate feedback in plain language and use an appropriate color after clicking the link or button (e.g., the color green indicates a successful process)[21]. The site should offer features that help students and staff input the correct data in the form fields (e.g., input hints and default values). The site must prevent potential errors in links (e.g., invalid links and unimplemented links), content (e.g., a single command has different jobs), and forms (e.g., errors of data entering). Students should not have to remember information. System usage instructions should be simple, easy, and visible[28][29]. The site should provide FAQ and documentation (e.g., documentation of student and staff services[21]) obviously and easily. Users should always know the progress of any query or process that is processed (e.g., downloading files or submitting forms), their current location on the site, and where they go next. The site must be accessible for diverse user groups, including disabled. Pages must work or display appropriately under different browsers and devices. Test the sites through common web browsers[23][28] by employing tools(e.g., Browser Shots)[24].

The site design component should reflect its intended function[28]. Make sure menu items and all content of pages should be aligned correctly based on the interface language. The load time of the site's pages should be reasonable. Display what the student need when and where they need it[21]. Do not burden frequently refreshed pages with many multimedia elements[28]. The site must follow navigation standards, forms, and search facilities (e.g., the search box placed in the expected place). Students and staff resources and other elements should be placed in the standard location to make the site easy to learn and remember.

VI. Conclusion

Using any system by actual users reveals some potential weaknesses that suggest usability problems. Users' preferences may affect and cause the classification of some issues as problems while they might never bother the other users. However, it still should be considered as a usability issue if there is an expectation that these issues may bother some actual users during their system usage[30]. Several literature reviews have been conducted on university site usability evaluation, but not many have focused on usability issues and solutions. Those studies discussed specific aspects, such as objectives, methods, and common usability attributes used. This research addressed a gap noted in the literature concerning the lack of a comprehensive source that cataloged different types of usability problems detected in university sites. We have identified and analyzed ninety-two different usability issues mentioned in earlier studies. We classified them into seventeen categories based on usability aspects violations. We also found an agreement among most of the reviewed studies as they mainly focused on some standard usability features, such as design, navigation, and content. This observation may indicate the importance of these features for the usability of university sites.

Our study could be a valuable source for developers and researchers interested in university site usability. The developers could focus on these features to investigate and improve the usability of educational sites. In future work, we intend to develop a new set of usability heuristics that could be used as a comprehensive and reliable instrument for evaluating the usability of university sites. We are planning to have a follow-up empirical study to update the usability problems list and identify the severity and frequency of those problems. We hope that this study will contribute to a recommendation for improving university site usability.

REFERENCES

[1] J. Nielsen, "Usability 101 : introduction to usability why usability is important," Usabilty 101introduction to usabilty, vol. 266, p. 9/2, 2012.

[2] S. Sahni and S. K. Dubey, "Web usability : issues , challenges and solutions," Int. J. Adv. Eng. Res. Sci., vol. 1, no. 2, pp. 61–66, 2014.

[3] L. Hasan, "Evaluating the usability of nine Jordanian university websites," Int. Conf. Commun. Inf. Technol. - Proc., pp. 91–96, 2012.

[4] S. Christoun, H. Aubin, C. Hannon, and R. Wolk, "Web site usability in higher education," Proc. ISECON, vol. 7, no. 110, 2006.

[5] A. Undu and S. Akuma, "Investigating the usability of a university website from the users ' perspective : an empirical study of Benue State University Website," Int. J. Comput. Inf. Eng., vol. 12, no. 10, pp. 922–929, 2018.

[6] M. Jabar, U. Usman, and F. Sidi, "Usability evaluation of universities' websites," International Journal of Information Processing and Management, vol. 5, no. 1, pp. 10–17, 2014.

[7] L. Hasan, "The Website of the University of Jordan: usability evaluation," Int. Arab J. e-Technology, vol. 3, no. 4, pp. 258–269, 2014.

[8] L. Hasan, "Heuristic evaluation of three Jordanian university websites," Informatics Educ., vol. 12, no. 2, pp. 231–251, 2013.

[9] J. Nielsen, "Usability engineering - 1st edition," Morgan Kaufmann, 1994. .

[10] P. Sukmasetya, A. Setiawan, and E. R. Arumi, "Usability evaluation of university website: a case study," J. Phys. Conf. Ser., vol. 1517, no. 1, May 2020.

[11] S. Gullikson et al., "The impact of information architecture on academic web site usability," Electron. Libr., vol. 17, no. 5, pp. 293–304, 1999.

[12] M. Kasli and C. Avcikurt, "An investigation to evaluate the websites of tourism departments of universities in Turkey," J. Hosp. Leis. Sport Tour. Educ., vol. 7, no. 2, pp. 77–92, 2008.

[13] N. Kostaras, N. Kostaras, M. Xenos, and M. Xenos, "Assessing educational web-site usability using heuristic evaluation rules," Evaluation, no. May, pp. 543–550, 2007.

[14] M. Astani and M. A. Elhindi, "An empirical study of university websites," Issues Inf. Syst., vol. 9, no. 2, pp. 460–465, 2008.

[15] L. Hasan, "Using university ranking systems to predict usability of University websites," J. Inf. Syst. Technol. Manag., vol. 10, no. 2, pp. 235–250, 2013.

[16] L. Hasan, "Investigating the relative importance of design criteria in the evaluation of the usability of educational websites from the viewpoint of students," Lect. Notes Eng. Comput. Sci., vol. 2198, pp. 832–837, 2012.

[17] S. Nizamani, K. Khoumbati, S. Nizamani, S. Memon, and S. Nizamani, "Usability evaluation of the top 10 universities of Pakistan through guideline scoring," Sindh Univ. Res. J. - Science Ser., vol. 51, no. 01, pp. 151–158, 2019.

[18] A. Qasim, J. Hassan, and A. Munawar, "Usability analysis of university websites in Pakistan," Lgurjcsit, vol. 4, no. 2. pp. 13–29, 2020.

[19] T. Papadopoulos and M. Xenos, "Quality evaluation of educational websites using heuristic and laboratory methods," 2nd Panhellenic Sci. Student Conf. Informatics, Relat. Technol. Appl., no. September 2008, pp. 43–54, 2008.

[20] K. Pierce, "Web site usability report for Harvard university," Capella Univ., 2005.

[21] K. Majrashi and M. Hamilton, "User experience of university websites," Lambert Academic Publishing, April, 2014.

[22] W. Erickson et al., "The accessibility and usability of college websites: Is your website presenting barriers to potential students?," Community Coll. J. Res. Pract., vol. 37, no. 11, pp. 864–876, 2013.

[23] A. A. Al-Ananbeh, B. A. Ata, M. Al-Kabi, and I. Alsmadi, "Website usability evaluation and search engine optimization for eighty Arab university websites," Basic Sci. Eng., vol. 21, no. 1, pp. 107--122, 2012.

[24] A. Islam and K. Tsuji, "Evaluation of usage of university websites in Bangladesh," DESIDOC J. Libr. Inf. Technol., vol. 31, no. 6, pp. 469–479, 2011.

[25] H. Gul, S. Z. Iqbal, and M. Saqib, "Usability evaluation of an educational website in Saudi Arabia," VAWKUM Trans. Comput. Sci., vol. 8, no. 2, pp. 1–9, 2015.

[26] L. Hasan and E. Abuelrub, "Common usability problems on educational websites," Proc. 2013 Int. Conf. Educ. Educ. Technol., no. July 2013, pp. 172–177, 2013.

[27] M. B. Alotaibi, "Assessing the usability of university websites in Saudi Arabia: a heuristic evaluation approach," Proc. 2013 10th Int. Conf. Inf. Technol. New Gener. ITNG 2013, pp. 138–142, 2013.

[28] U. K. Yusof, L. K. Khaw, H. Y. Ch'ng, and B. J. Neow, "Balancing between usability and aesthetics of web design," Proc. 2010 Int. Symp. Inf. Technol. - Vis. Informatics, ITSim'10, vol. 1, pp. 1–6, 2010.

[29] M. Rolf and J. Nielsen, "Improving a human-computer dialogue," Commun. ACM, vol. 33, no. 3, pp. 338–348, Mar. 1990.

[30] J. Nielsen and R. Molich, "Heuristic evaluation of user interfaces," Conf. Hum. Factors Comput. Syst. - Proc., no. April, pp. 249–256, 1990.

Designing Ụbụrụ: The Alpha Stage

Executive Function Rehabilitation Application for Mild Traumatic Brain Injury

Akuadasuo Ezenyilimba
Human Systems Engineering, Arizona State University
National Science Foundation Research Traineeship
Mesa, United States of America
email: aezenyi1@asu.edu

Jennifer Wethe
Psychiatry/Psychology, Mayo Clinic
Mayo Clinic Arizona Concussion Program
Phoenix, United States of America
email: Wethe.Jennifer@mayo.edu

Nancy J. Cooke
Human Systems Engineering, Arizona State University
Center for Human, Artificial Intelligence & Robot Teaming
Mesa, United States of America
email: Nancy.Cooke@asu.edu

Troy McDaniel
POLY, Arizona State University
Center for Cognitive Ubiquitous Computing (CUbiC)
Mesa, United States of America
email: troy.mcdaniel@asu.edu

***Abstract*— Ụbụrụ is an executive function computerized rehabilitation application specifically designed for mild Traumatic Brain Injury (mTBI) individuals. Ụbụrụ utilizes serious games to train cognitive flexibility, planning, and organization. This paper explores the rationale and components behind the alpha stage of the application's development, and its first design iteration. Currently, individuals with a history of mTBI have limited rehabilitation options as a result of lack of knowledge in terms of available services, access, time, or financial and insurance constraints. Due to the invisible nature of mTBIs, perception of injury severity is diminished, individuals are not properly equipped with how to proceed forward with rehabilitation, and awareness of injury can be inadvertently compromised. The intention behind the Ụbụrụ application is to be a computerized cognitive rehabilitation alternative and additive when limitations such as time, finances, or insurance exist.**

Keywords-mild traumatic brain injury; executive function; serious games; computerized cognitive rehabilitation

I. INTRODUCTION

Non-standardization of care for (mTBI) continues to stagnate an individual's ability to have an effective recovery process. Currently mTBIs account for 70 – 90 % of the 69 million Traumatic Brain Injuries (TBI) that occur each year [8]. The common misconception that continues to persist is that all mTBI patients will make a full recovery within a few days of injury onset. Further research has shown that mTBI individuals can still continue to experience Post Concussive Symptoms (PCS) for years if not decades after injury [1]. Of those deemed recovered, at least 25% present with some form of PCS [1].

Symptoms of this nature can delay an individual's ability to return to work and impede individuals with prolonged Executive Functioning (EF) deficits [8]. Subcortical networks and frontal lobe structures are particularly vulnerable in traumatic brain injury. Damage within these areas of the brain can result in varying levels of Executive Dysfunction (ED) that can make it challenging to complete independent, goal-oriented behavior and tasks; thus, infringing on everyday activities [13]. Having a history of a mTBI has demonstrated that individuals can face decrements related to planning, organization, reasoning, set shifting, and monitoring [13].

Less than 30% of individuals with mTBI report seeking or receiving next line care in terms of rehabilitation [2]. With very few individuals actively seeking or receiving treatment, mTBIs can be deemed an invisible injury, leaving people improperly equipped with tools to improve their overall quality-of-life post injury. For mTBI individuals especially it can be hard to accept the severity of a mTBI injury, due to the lack of diagnostic testing to pinpoint shortcoming, and the lack of concreteness surrounding the injury [4]. In addition to the invisible nature of mTBIs, cognitive processes such as awareness and acceptance can be negatively impacted. Impediments of this nature can limit the recovery process. If these processes are not appropriately engaged, successful recovery is less than likely [2]. Many mTBI individuals, especially athletes, report not seeking help because they initially perceived their injury as not being severe enough; they believed symptoms resolved; they were not sure who to contact; or they were unaware that such services were available [3].

In addition to non-standardized mTBI care, the strain of COVID-19 has shed light on confounding factors in the form of present challenges, such as treatment access and the priority of mTBI patients [9]. COVID-19 has put many medical concerns on the backburner to prioritize public safety. Regardless of the present challenges, the needs of the TBI community are still imminent.

With referral rates being as low as 2% for next line care when a TBI is classified as mild, there are not many available options to further rehabilitation [7]. Additionally, at least 65% of TBI individuals are discharged without any sort of rehabilitation plan or checkups [10].

Although current research is limited, it has been demonstrated that computerized cognitive rehabilitation can be an effective tool in assisting mTBI individuals during their recovery [14]. Presently one of the main focus areas for mTBI rehabilitation, and computerized training is vision-based interventions, for instance oculomotor rehabilitation [5]. Of those interventions that do not solely focus on vision related training, there are only aspects of cognition, for example Lumosity, that do not feature EF specific training [13]. Furthermore, other challenges related to current mTBI interventions include studies being conducted only at the military level that do not include civilians, thus continuing to add to the ongoing limitation of limited knowledge or awareness provided to the general public for mTBI rehabilitation. Lastly, current computerized interventions do not have the ability to equip individuals with the necessary tools to transfer skills learned in rehabilitation to activities of daily living that stem beyond motor skills, such as reading [5].

In order for mTBI individuals to be able to make the most out of their recovery process it is important to be able to: 1. have a sense of individual autonomy, 2. have access to available resources and services, and 3. have knowledge of available services and resources. Furthermore, rehabilitation initiatives and programs need to address dysfunction-specific mechanisms associated with mTBI (i.e., executive function). Tailored programs that pinpoint areas of ED are necessary and would be most beneficial for sustainable long-term outcomes [13]. This paper will further explore how to incorporate the aforementioned needs and objectives to make mTBI rehabilitation more attainable through the implementation of an EF computerized rehabilitation application that utilizes serious games. The proposed application will be described in its alpha stage.

The purpose of this paper is to: 1. further explore rehabilitation limitations facing the traumatic brain injury (mTBI) community 2. address the needs of mild Traumatic Brain Injury (mTBI) individuals specifically, and 3. explore a proposed intervention in its alpha stage.

With the proposed intervention being in its alpha stage a potential limitation to consider moving forward is the fact that the application is internet/Wi-Fi dependent. The following paper will first discuss in section two the application overview related to the proposed application's objectives, the incorporation of EF training through serious gamification, the rationale behind the initial application assessment, and the intended serious games and other application features for EF rehabilitation. The third section of the paper will discuss the anticipated experimental procedures. Finally, the fourth section of this paper will highlight the intended next steps for the development of the application.

II. Application Overview

The following sections will describe the components of the proposed application in detail. Within these sections the application objectives, executive function focus, and serious gamification approach will be explained.

A. *Application Objective*

Ụbụrụ (pronounced Oh-bow-roo; from the Igbo language; English translation: brain; see Figure 1) is an EF rehabilitation application intended to be an alternative and/or additive to rehabilitation for the mTBI community. The aim of Ụbụrụ is to help individuals mitigate common areas of ED for mTBIs through cognitive flexibility, organization, and planning training. The goal of Ụbụrụ is to allow mTBI individuals to have awareness and control during their rehabilitation journey by actively being able to 1. see progress and/or regression, 2. receive feedback, and 3. set realistic goals on a weekly basis.

Figure 1. Ụbụrụ start page.

With many mTBI individuals not being fully aware of their limitations, due to their inherent nature to adapt to their new normal or simply not being aware of the severity of their ailments, Ụbụrụ's design aims to bring awareness to the forefront of its training [4]. In addition to goal setting, Ụbụrụ seeks to overcome awareness challenges through feedback in the form of scores, tips, and weekly self-report surveys. Ụbụrụ is also designed to actively encourage participants to seek and take advantage of other local resources by 1. providing recommendations, if necessary, at the end of each EF game session, and/or 2. having a readily available and accessible resources page built into the application.

B. Executive Function Training Through Serious Gamification

For mTBI individuals, EF is one of the most at-risk cognitive processes [6]. When left untreated, ED via mTBI injury can result in psychological stress that can stem beyond the damage acquired by the initial injury, hindering an individual's ability to engage in everyday functioning. To overcome ED challenges, reduction and monitoring of post concussive symptoms is needed, awareness of available resources within a community are a must, and quality of life needs to actively be considered and improved [6].

To address these concerns, Ụbụrụ takes a serious gamification approach. Through gamification, participant motivation can be increased, and participants will be more willing to participate and are more likely to stay engaged [11]. With Ụbụrụ aiming to be a computerized cognitive rehabilitation alternative when time, access, finances, or insurance are an issue, gamification will allow users to engage in necessary rehabilitation even when a physician is not able to be present. In addition to present limitations hindering recovery, Ụbụrụ aims to have skills acquired during rehabilitation be transferable to activities of daily living. By pinpointing transferability, Ụbụrụ is tailored to reduce the psychosocial stress brought on by vocational, recreational, and / or interpersonal functioning [6].

C. Ụbụrụ Assessment

To begin using Ụbụrụ, all participants will start by taking the initial Ụbụrụ assessment. Upon completing the assessment participants will be able to see firsthand their primary, secondary, and tertiary focus in terms of cognitive flexibility, planning, and organization (see Figure 2).

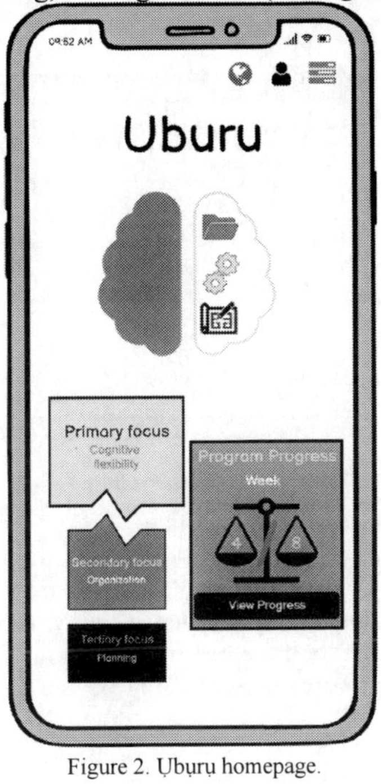

Figure 2. Ụbụrụ homepage.

The initial assessment will contain tasks that test participants ability to engage in the aforementioned EF skills. From here participants will complete weekly EF serious games. There will be a total of five games with varying levels of cognitive flexibility, planning, and organization incorporated.

D. Cognitive Flexibility Games

Challenges brought on by additional psychological stress from mTBI can impair the ability to effectively engage in tasks that are dependent on cognitive flexibility. Cognitive flexibility, much like psychological flexibility, is dependent on shifting perspective to adapt to situational demands [6]. Oftentimes mTBI individuals do not have a full understanding of decrements they are facing, resulting in mTBI individuals avoiding tasks that require engagement of EF skills that have been diminished post-injury. Avoidant behavior of this nature consequently results in a misinterpretation whereby individuals believe that they are fine. Since individuals are not actively training these EF skills, persistent decrements continue to hinder activities of daily living [6].

To address cognitive flexibility challenges, Ụbụrụ has users engage in tasks that are designed to train participants to switch between different tasks, while engaging working memory. Within the app there are three cognitive flexibility specific games (Beat the Value, Keeping Track (also incorporates aspects of planning and organization), and This or That). The aforementioned cognitive flexibility games are designed to encourage users to adapt their thinking in order to adjust to their current environment (i.e., the serious games). By encouraging users to actively change their approach when dealing with ongoing challenges that require problem solving, Ụbụrụ, aims to improve the EF skill of cognitive flexibility through, task switching, attention to detail, and maintaining pertinent information.

Beat the Value. One of the main challenges TBI individuals face is being able to problem solve [1]. Beat the Value is designed to help participants sharpen their problem-solving skills through math, while engaging in task switching. As levels continue to progress users will be responsible for maintaining instructions while completing the task.

Keeping Track. Many mTBI individuals with ED face challenges with maintaining and holding on to information to achieve an overarching goal [13]. Keeping Track focuses on training participants ability to differentiate between items while paying attention to detail. Through the game of Keeping Track participants will be responsible for task switching during a subordinate task in order to acquire information for a superior task.

This or That. This or That builds on task switching with an emphasis on paying attention to instruction detail. The focus of this game is to allow participants to maintain relevant information to achieve an overarching goal. As users continue to progress through the levels of This or That they will need to be abreast of information related to the task, and prioritize the instructions given to them to complete the task at hand.

E. Organization Game

Deficits with organization can be attributed to issues with early stages of encoding, resulting in ineffective processing of information needed to achieve a task [12]. Challenges with organization can impede the ability to follow and create schedules, prioritize and follow logical steps, and coordinate activities. Additionally, organization deficits can hinder mTBI individuals' ability to effectively break down tasks [1].

Rank Order. To address problems with organization, Rank Order focuses on teaching users how to break down an overarching event or goal into smaller tasks. The game of Rank Order has participants look at a list of items and then determine where to start first and order events logically. As levels progress, users will also be responsible for deciphering which events are most urgent, flexible, and/or are able to be rescheduled.

F. Planning Game

mTBI individuals are known to face difficulty when it comes to engaging in activities that require planning. Deficiency in planning can lead to plans that are ineffective or poorly developed, resulting in needing more time to correct and redirect plans [1].

Train of Thoughts. The planning game, Train of Thoughts, provides real world scenarios that allow participants to see the end result of their decisions. During the Train of Thoughts game users are responsible for helping a civilian determine the necessary sequence of events (i.e., making it to a doctor's appointment on time) in order for the 'train to leave the station' while utilizing aspects of working memory and prioritization. These scenarios are designed to resemble activities of daily living so knowledge and skills can be applied to the participant's life.

G. Weekly Survey

Weekly Surveys will be made available at the end of the week for all participants once all tasks and sessions are completed. The survey will consist of three types of questions: Likert scale, multiple choice, and open-ended questions. The self-report nature of the survey serves as a check in for user feedback, keeps users aware of progress, and keeps users accountable of their program.

III. Anticipated Experimental Procedure

Prior to the experimental stage Ụbụrụ will undergo usability testing. Upon completion of usability testing the experimental stage will commence. For the purposes of this study Ụbụrụ will be used as a cognitive rehabilitation additive in the form of a web-based application.

During the experimental stage of Ụbụrụ, participants will be able to access weekly tasks via the Executive Function Dashboard (see Figure 3). Ụbụrụ will track participants' performance on a weekly basis and customize treatment plans in the following weeks accordingly.

A. Duration

The study will take place over the span of eight weeks. Each week will contain three sessions. Every week based on participant performance, the level of difficulty will increase, decrease, or remain the same. For study purposes, all participants will complete all five of the Ụbụrụ games.

B. Levels

At the start of the study, all participants will begin at level one and move through the application's levels from there. Based on participants' weekly performance, progression will be customized to each user based on their scores.

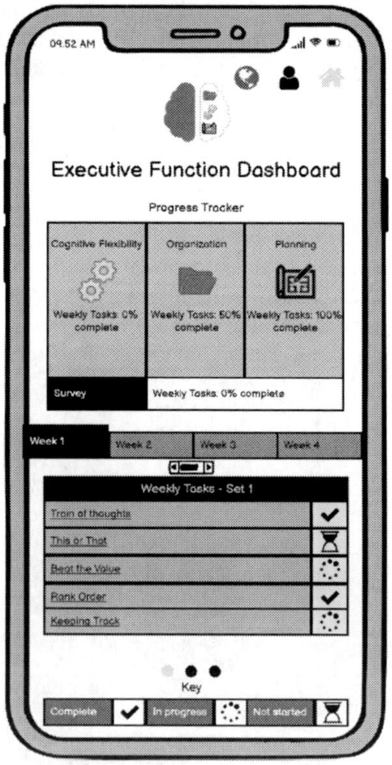

Figure 3. Ụbụrụ executive function dashboard.

In addition to level customization, recommendations for external resources will be provided to participants who need them based on game scores. For participants whose scores do not auto populate an external resource recommendation, a resource page will be readily available throughout the application and provide users with relevant local resources.

C. Measures

Participants' scores on the Ụbụrụ Assessment will be collected at the beginning and end of the study. In addition to assessment scores, participant's weekly individual game scores, time to complete each game, and self-report surveys will be points of measure.

IV. Conclusion

The future of Ụbụrụ is still underway. As Ụbụrụ begins to enter its beta stage, the development of this application allows for a testbed to further explore ED amongst mTBI individuals. The hope for this application is to begin to narrow the gap for rehabilitation limitations and non-standardization of care for the mTBI community, by testing a new computerized cognitive rehabilitation alternative and additive. Ụbụrụ will explore the potential of a new approach for mTBI rehabilitation, by training specific EF decrements to help mitigate extraneous factors that continue to persist as a result of PCS. With Ụbụrụ as an experimental study, the application will be able to further explore user feedback, mTBI rehabilitation needs, and potential shortcomings.

Acknowledgment

This work was supported by a grant from the National Science Foundation [1828010].

References

[1] C. Bottari, N. Gosselin, J. Chen, A. and Ptito, "The impact of symptomatic mild traumatic brain injury on complex everyday activities and the link with alterations in cerebral functioning: Exploratory case studies," *Neuropsychological Rehabilitation*, vol. 27 no. 5, pp. 871-890, April 2015, https://doi.org/10.1080/09602011.2015.1110528

[2] J. Brown, K. Ackley, and K. Knollman-Porter, "Collaborative goal setting: A clinical approach for adults with mild traumatic brain injury," *American Journal of Speech-Language Pathology*, vol. 30, no. 6, pp. 2394–2413, November 2021, https://doi.org/10.1044/2021_ajslp-21-00078

[3] J. Brown, and K. Knollman-Porter, "Continuum of care following sports-related concussion," *American Journal of Speech-Language Pathology*, vol. 29 no. 3, pp. 1389–1403. August 2020, https://doi.org/10.1044/2020_ajslp-19-00131

[4] P. W. Buck, R. G. Laster, J. S. Sagrati, and R. S. Kirzner, "Working with mild traumatic brain injury: Voices from the Field," *Rehabilitation Research and Practice*, vol. 2012, pp. 1–6, February 2012, https://doi.org/10.1155/2012/625621

[5] K. Ciuffreda, N. Yadav, P. Thiagarajan, and D. Ludlam, "A Novel Computer Oculomotor Rehabilitation (COR) program for Mild Traumatic Brain Injury (mTBI)," *Brain Sciences*, vol. 7 no. 99, pp. 1-9,. August 2017, https://doi.org/10.3390/brainsci7080099

[6] J. W. Faulkner, et al., "Psychological flexibility: A psychological mechanism that contributes to persistent symptoms following mild traumatic brain injury?," *Medical Hypotheses*, vol. 143, pp. 1-10, October 2020, https://doi.org/10.1016/j.mehy.2020.110141

[7] K. Knollman-Porter, J. A. Brown, T. Wallace, and S. Spitz, "First-Line Health Care Providers Reported Knowledge of and Referrals to Speech-Language Pathologists for Clients With Mild Traumatic Brain Injury," *American Journal of Speech-Language Pathology*, vol. 30 no. 5, pp. 2214-2227, September 2021, https://doi.org/10.1044/2021_ajslp-20-00373

[8] Y. Kraemer, et al., "Post-traumatic headache after mild traumatic brain injury in a one-year follow up study – risk factors and return to work," *The Journal of Headache and Pain*, [Online], February 2022, https://doi.org/10.21203/rs.3.rs-1117390/v1

[9] S. Manivannan, et al., (2021). "Management of neurotrauma during COVID-19: A single centre experience and lessons for the future," *Brain Injury*, vol. 35, no. 8, pp. 957–963. May 2021, https://doi.org/10.1080/02699052.2021.1934731

[10] J. O'Neil, J.V. Ierssel, and H. Sveistrup, "Remote supervision of rehabilitation interventions for survivors of moderate or severe traumatic brain injury: A scoping review," *Journal of Telemedicine and Telecare*, vol. 26 no. 9, pp. 520-535, May 2019, https://doi.org/10.1177/1357633x19845466

[11] G. Oatley, T. Choudhury, and P. Buckman, (2021). "Smart textiles for improved quality of life and cognitive assessment," *Sensors*, vol. 21 no. 23, [Online], November 2021, https://doi.org/10.3390/s21238008

[12] C. Oldenburg, A. Lundin, G. Edman, C. Nygren-de Boussard, and A. Bartfai, "Cognitive reserve and persistent post-concussion symptoms—a prospective mild traumatic brain injury (mTBI) cohort study," *Brain Injury*, vol. 30 no. 2, pp. 146–155, August 2015, https://doi.org/10.3109/02699052.2015.1089598

[13] E. Pang, "Different Neural Mechanisms Underlie Deficits in Mental Flexibility in Post-Traumatic Stress Disorder Compared to Mild Traumatic Brain Injury," *Frontiers in Psychiatry*, vol. 6, pp. 1-6, December 2021, https://doi.org/10.3389/fpsyt.2015.00170

[14] A. Westphal, et al., "A-140 computer based cognitive rehabilitation interventions for visual attention following mild traumatic brain injury" *Archives of Clinical Neuropsychology*, vol. 36 no. 6, pp. 1193, August 2021, https://doi.org/10.1093/arclin/acab062.158

Unity-Warmth: Positional and Thermal Sensation Presentation System Through a Display

Suguru Sato
Faculty of Engineering
University of the Ryukyus
Okinawa, Japan
e185768@ie.u-ryukyu.ac.jp

Kagura Itokazu
Faculty of Engineering
University of the Ryukyus
Okinawa, Japan
e195709@ie.u-ryukyu.ac.jp

Yuhei Akamine
Faculty of Engineering
University of the Ryukyus
Okinawa, Japan
yuhei@ie.u-ryukyu.ac.jp

Yui Kita
H2L, Inc.
Tokyo, Japan
yui@h2l.jp

Emi Tamaki
University of the Ryukyus
H2L, Inc.
Japan
hoimei@acm.org

***Abstract*—In long-distance relationships, partners experience poor communication between partners because of the lacking physical existence. Current computer-mediated communication causes two types of related discomfort: "visual" and "somatosensory". This study aims to emphasize the existence (of a distant partner) by reducing these discomforts. A hypothesis about reducing these discomforts by adjusting the "visual size ratio", "consistency of position sense", and "thermal sense" was made. In the suggested system, Unity-Warmth, the communication methods are adjusted to be close to those in real life, in terms of body size, hand-contact position, and body temperature. Unity-Warmth consists of a touch panel display that can project half of someone's life-size image and a transparent heater that conveys the body's warmth. An experiment verified the effectiveness of Unity-Warmth by comparing the conventional system (Zoom Meetings) with Unity-Warmth. The results show that Unity-Warmth emphasizes five out of six types of existence: the sense that the interlocutor is "being there", the sense of participating with the interlocutor, the sense of being in the same space as the interlocutor, the realism of the interlocutor, and consistency with real-world communication experience. In the future, Unity-Warmth can be applied to communication between people who struggle to meet in person and express physical intimacy, such as "grandparents and grandchildren" and "celebrities and their fans".**

Keywords*—*HCI; Human Interaction; Human Interface; Telepresence.

I. INTRODUCTION

The transmission of existence is important in long-distance relationships. Computer-mediated communication, such as video calls, is effective in long-distance relationships [1]–[4]. However, video calls cannot transmit much information that concerns human sensation. Therefore, partners experience poor communication because of the lacking physical existence.

The human senses are divided into three main categories: "special", "somatic", and "visceral", as shown in Figure 1. Special senses include sight, hearing, taste, smell, and equilibrium. Somatic senses are roughly divided into cutaneous and deep sensations (intrinsic sensations). These are divided by the depth of the receptors that receive information.

Cutaneous sensations are obtained through receptors near the body's surface, from the superficial layer to the dermis. There are three types of cutaneous sensations: "tactile and pressure", "warmth and cold", and "pain". Tactile and pressure sensations perceive an object's surface texture and shape when touched by a hand. Warmth and cold sensations perceive the warmth and coldness of an object. Pain sensations perceive pain or strong warmth or coldness only on the surface layer.

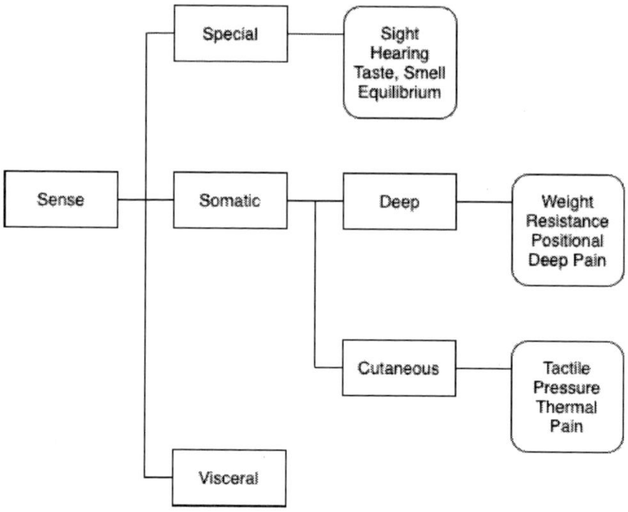

Figure 1. Types of human senses.

Deep sensations (intrinsic sensations) are obtained by receptors intrinsic to joints, muscles, and tendons. There are three types of deep senses: "positional and motor", "resistance and weight", and "pain". Positional and motor senses perceive the position and movement of the joints and body. Resistance and weight senses perceive the stretch and tension of muscles and the position and movement of joints and the body. Pain senses perceive deep pain [5].

Computer-mediated communication is far removed from real-life communication in terms of "visual" and "somatosensory". The visual size ratio (apparent size) of face-to-face users through a computer is different from the visual size ratio of face-to-face users in the real world. This visual difference discomforts users. In addition, communication enabled by touching a display or device is good given that fingertips perceive a resistance sensation presentation. However, this generates somatosensory discomfort because of the lack of "position sensation" consistency or "thermal sensation" presentation. This lack of sensations transfer creates poor communication.

This study aims to emphasize the existence (of a distant partner) by reducing these two discomforts.

The remainder of this paper is organized as follows. Section II describes the three existence senses and current state of computer-based communication with existence. Section III describes the suggested method for reducing the discomfort of "visual" and "somatosensory" sensations in computer-mediated communication. Section IV overviews the experiment and its methods. Section V describes the results. Section VI considers the results. Finally, Section VII summarizes the results of this study and discusses future perspectives.

II. Related Work

When people communicate, they perceive human existence through three types of existence: "environmental objects changed by human action", "somatosensory", and "audiovisual". The next section introduces related research divided into three types of existence.

A. Present Situation of Computer-Mediated Communication with Existence

1) Environmental Objects Changed by Human Action: Several studies have published remote communication systems that provide users with existence of others by remotely manipulating environmental objects [6]–[13].

A study that suggested "SyncDecor", provides a virtual sense of cohabitation by synchronizing the state of remotely located household items, such as lamps and trash cans, as shown in Figure 2 [6]. This system provided a relatively strong sense of connectedness in which partners' actions in their living space impacted each other, as well as shared a weak sense of connectedness similar to conventional awareness sharing systems.

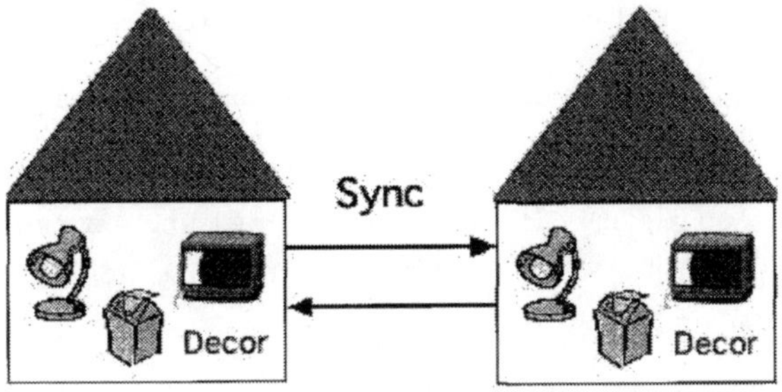

Figure 2. SyncDecor, in which environmental objects (everyday items) in remote locations are changed by human action [6]

'Tsunagari' communication aimed to foster a feeling of connection between people and maintain their social relationships [7]. A system based on this concept, called the Family Planter system, was also developed for family use.

"Lover's Cups" is a drinking-together interface that allows people to remotely share the drinking time with someone they care about [8]. Using a wireless connection, an otherwise ordinary pair of cups become a communication device, amplifying the social aspect of drinking behavior.

A study suggested a new method of communicating "awareness" between people separated by long distances to supplement existing forms of communication, such as telephone and e-mail [9]. By equipping furniture and appliances such as doors, sofas, refrigerators and televisions with sensors, a system wherein these items are connected to remote equivalents was developed, and their near-simultaneous use is communicated.

"ComSlipper" is a lightweight yet expressive sensible slipper that enhances the quality of computer-mediated relationships [10]. This system empowers wearers to create a sense of connection with others. Wearers use body gestures and tactile manipulation to feel and express emotions and availability to distant loved ones.

"Feellight" enables simple and seamless communication between distanced individuals [11].

"Connected Candles" creates awareness and connects people in long-distance relationships [12]. The system consists of a pair of candle stands, which include two candles each, one being a real candle and the other electronic. The candle stands are placed at different locations and are connected through the Internet such that lighting the real candle illuminates the electronic candle.

"Peek-A-Drawer" is a new communication device that uses furniture to support lightweight communication between people [13]. It provides virtual shared drawers that connect distanced family members.

While these systems are adequate for passive communication, they cannot actively communicate existence. They are unsuitable for partners to feel each other's existence through active communication involving contact.

2) Existence through Somatosensory: Numerous methods have been investigated to invoke existence by transmitting somatic sensations such as touch or temperature [14]–[21].

People prefer to use haptic (encompassed by somatosensory) communication devices, primarily with people close to them. A study on haptic modality shows that Haptics could be used for practical purposes and emotional communication, for example, in mimicking touch between partners [14].

A study that explored the importance of the touch modality on affect conveyance shows that the story accompanied by communicative touch resulted in a significant increase in the sense of connectedness with the storyteller over the speech-only condition and trended toward greater affective conveyance [15].

A study on the effectiveness of remote contact in a video meeting, where a robot hand was used to shake hands remotely, shows that two-way remote contact, between the user and device, substituting for the other person's body, are in contact at the same time on the other person's side, creating a high degree of social telepresence [16]. This study showed that creating social telepresence and giving the other person a sense of closeness is possible.

Remote hugs have also been investigated [17]. A study on the alleviating effect of virtual interpersonal touch on social judgment shows that a virtual hug reduces the negative inferences in recalling information about a target person [18]. In a study that presented the hugging device with thermal sensation, a significant difference in social presence between those that received thermal 'hugs' and those that did not was observed [19].

As a device that provides more intimate contact, the interactive device provides a physical interface for transmitting a kiss between two remotely connected people [20], [21].

These devices can invoke existence by eliciting somatosensory sensations through contact. However, input and output location information is inconsistent with visual feedback owing to using a device with or without a display.

3) Audiovisual Presence: Capcom Co., Ltd. developed an adventure game for women called "Prisoner's Palma" based on the concept of "experiential love adventure through glass" [22]. In this game, a smartphone screen is used as the glass of a visiting room to realize natural physical intimacy through the display. However, the following disadvantages exist. The small screen size makes it difficult to perceive a realistic impression. The touch panel feels cold in contrast to the character's reactions, resulting in a sense of discomfort owing to the lack of "thermal sense". In a scene where the character and user hold out their hands to each other, the character's reaction does not change, whether touching the character's hand or other places, making the user feel uncomfortable because of the absent "positional sense".

A study that designed and evaluated "MyEyes", a First Person View (FPV) video streaming technology probe made with cardboard goggles and a smartphone, compared the three different views with couples to explore the effect on social presence and body ownership [23]. Distance-separated partners see each other's view on their screen, where it can overlap their own view (Overlapped), be placed above it (Horizontal), or presented in parallel such that each is seen with a different eye (Split). Couples most preferred the Overlapped View, as it provided the strongest feeling of co-presence, whereas a Horizontal View provided the greatest sense of mutual understanding. These qualitative results showed couples valued performing synchronized acts together and doing activities "in" the remote location. However, because it does not involve physical contact, it causes discomfort in the sense of touch and resistance.

B. Hypothesis

Table I compares related work for each sense.

TABLE I. COMPARISON WITH RELATED WORK

	Visual	Position Sense	Thermal Sense
SyncDecor			
Remote Handshaking	✓		✓
Toraware no Palm		✓	
Ours	✓	✓	✓

From the present situation of computer-based communication with existence, discomfort is thought to be caused by differences in "visual size ratio", "consistency of positional sensation", and "thermal sensation" compared to the real world.

Therefore, if these differences and present "audiovisual" and "existence through somatic sensation" are eliminated, the system can reduce communication discomfort remotely.

III. Method

Adjust the visual size ratio such that the scale of the user's image on display is the actual size to reduce "visual" discomfort. In addition, by presenting "position sense" and "thermal sense" on the display contact surface between users, the discomfort of "position sense" consistency and "thermal sense" is reduced.

In the suggested system, the communication methods are adjusted to be close to those in real life, in terms of body size, hand-contact position, and body temperature. Our system consists of a touch panel display that can project half of a person's life-size image and a transparent heater that conveys the body's warmth, as shown in Figure 3.

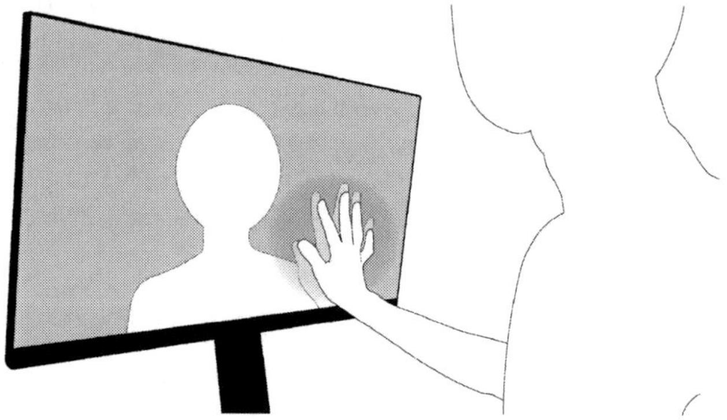

Figure 3. "Unity-Warmth" concept image.

The noveloty of our system is to emphasize existence by presenting the warmth of interlocutor's body temperature while maintaining consistency between visual and position sense.

The system is named "Unity-Warmth", meaning "connecting and uniting the warmth of remote areas".

A. System Structure

Figure 4 shows the system structure of Unity-Warmth.

Unity-Warmth consists of a computer, an Arduino Pro Micro as a micro-controller, a display(27 inches) that shows the user, an ultra-wide-angle web camera (ELP USBFHD06H-BL170), and an IR touch frame to detect hand touch position. The Arduino is connected to a circuit for presenting a warm sensation. In addition, a webcam (Logitech C270n) is connected for use as the camera in the general video meeting for comparison in the experiment. It is also used as a microphone. The two computers for communication are connected by a network. The video and audio are transmitted using the web conferencing application "Zoom Meetings" (Zoom Video Communications, Inc.) [24].

By adjusting the user's size ratio using a large display, the user's size can be projected as a person's life-size image. When

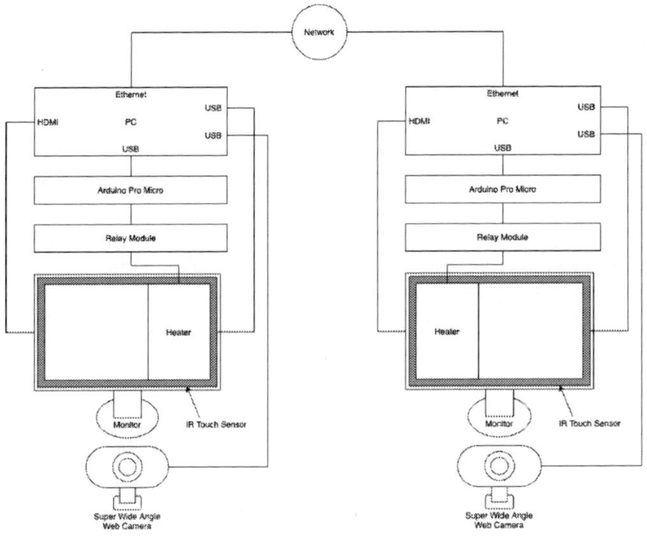

Figure 4. Unity-Warmth structure diagram.

one user touches the display, the touch location is transmitted to the other device through the network. A warm sensation is presented at the corresponding point on the communications partner's device to provide a sense of contact from a remote location.

An IR touch frame for contact detection and a heater for warmth presentation are attached to an acrylic panel as the warmth presentation unit. The heater is attached to the right edge of the screen on one device and to the left edge of the screen on the other device. Accordingly, the system can reproduce the warmth of face-to-face and hand-to-hand contact. The warmth presentation unit was placed at a 250 mm distance from the display. The black cloth covers the display and warmth presentation unit to disguise the insertion of light and display gap.

To capture both the human upper body and the hand touching the warmth presentation unit using one camera, an ultra-wide-angle camera is attached to the bottom of the display, capturing images as if looking up from below. Trapezoidal correction is performed on the captured images to make it appear as if they were shot from the front. Therefore, the system enables the capture of the hand and the user's upper body touching the warmth presentation unit in a form close to the actual size. Figure 5 shows a side-view schematic of the system.

Figure 6 provides the developed device.

Figure 7 shows the circuit diagram.

When one user contacts the warmth presentation unit, the transmission program sends the contact state to the partner's computer. When the receiving program receives the contact state, it sends it to the Arduino. When the Arduino receives the contact state via serial communication, it turns on the LEDs connected to the GPIO pin to indicate the operation status and outputs a voltage to the pins connected to the relay module. The output voltage from the GPIO pin is input to an 8-channel

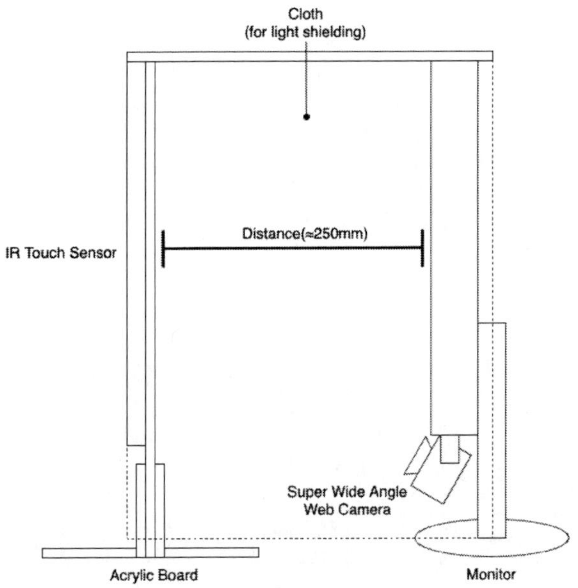

Figure 5. Side-view system schematic.

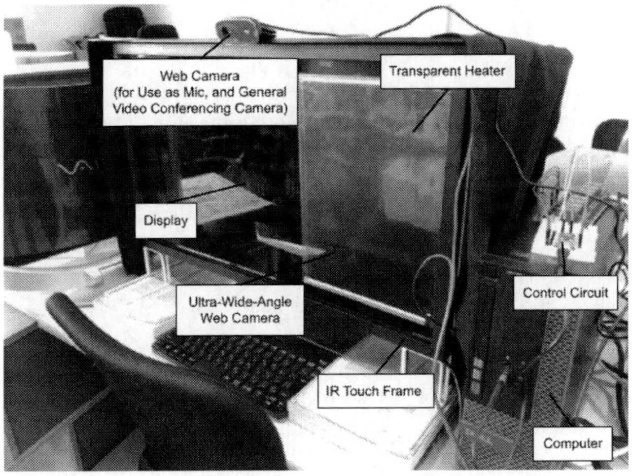

Figure 6. Picture of the developed device.

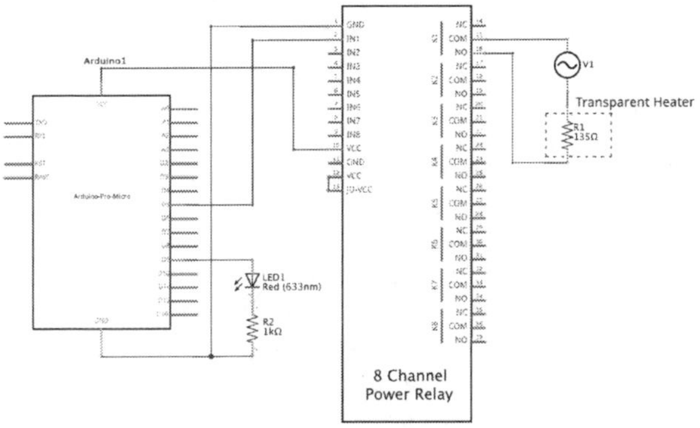

Figure 7. Circuit diagram.

relay module. A transparent heater (Mirai Tech (now: Heat Lab. Corporation) high-transparency flexible heater, A4 size) was connected to the output of the relay module to provide a warm sensation. An AC 100 V output from a household outlet is used to operate the transparent heater. Heating was controlled to activate heating when a hand touched the device and stopped when the hand is removed. Therefore, the heating of this system was not controlled by the temperature at this time.

Figure 8 shows the developed control circuit.

Figure 8. Control circuit.

The relay module is on the left, and the Arduino on the right. Only 1ch of the relay is used at this time.

IV. EXPERIMENT

The effectiveness of Unity-Warmth was verified by comparing a conventional computer-mediated communication method (web meeting application: Zoom Meetings) with the suggested method (Unity-Warmth). Specifically, a questionnaire survey was conducted to determine whether the user's perception changes by changing the "visual size ratio of the user presented" and "presence of a thermal sensation through the display", and the results were then analysed.

A. Experimental Methods

The analysis was conducted from three viewpoints: "subjective evaluation", "user's emotional change", and "existence". This experiments used a within-subjects design. The questionnaire was administered using the Visual Analog Scale (VAS). Each questionnaire item was compared by a t-test between the conventional and suggested method.

Assuming power = 0.80, effect size (delta) = 0.60, and significance level = 0.05, the optimal number of samples was n = 23.8. Therefore, 24 samples were collected for this experiment.

B. Tasks

To conduct a controlled experiment, the degree of attention directed to the displays and the conversations conducted through the displays should remain the same. Participants were asked to perform the following three tasks to satisfy this condition. The first task is a chat, including greetings and introductions, to build a relationship with the interlocutor and check the conversation's spontaneity. The second task is to check the color of their partner's eyes or the state of their partner's fingernails to make the participants aware of their partner by paying attention to their partner's appearance. The third task is to compare the hand sizes to confirm the consistency difference of the "positional sense" and "thermal sense" between the conventional and suggested methods.

These three tasks help the interlocutors deepen their relationship with the first and second tasks, and then simulate skin-to-skin contact through the system to check for changes in emotion with the third task.

The tasks were the same for both the conventional and suggested methods, and the only difference is whether the touching, hand-to-hand action was performed through the suggested method during the third task.

C. Experiment Environment

A device was placed in two rooms, and participants communicate while seated in chairs.

Figure 9 shows participants participating in the experiment.

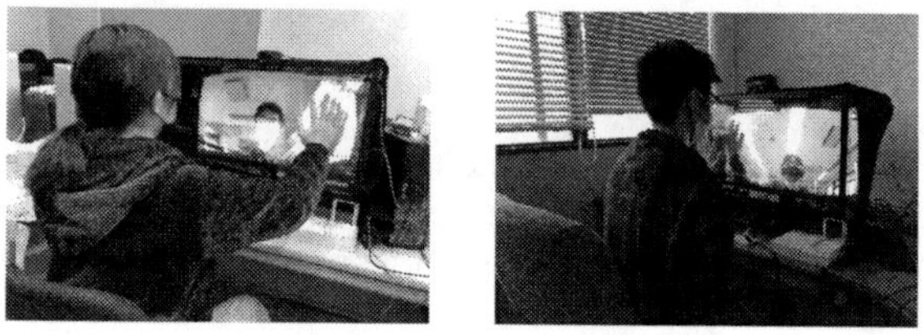

(a) Room 1 (b) Room 2

Figure 9. Experimental landscapes.

Participants sit at a certain distance such that their entire face can be seen on the display when communicating with the conventional method and as close as possible to the warmth presentation unit when communicating with the suggested method, because of the camera's viewing angle .

D. Questionnaire

1) Subjective Evaluation: The questionnaire was designed to assess discomfort in computer-mediated communication subjectively. The questions were the five items listed in Table II.

TABLE II. QUESTIONNAIRE ITEMS RELATED TO SUBJECTIVE EVALUATION

Q1	The person speaking in remote may not be human (Discomfort regarding human existence)
Q2	The person speaking in remote may not be the person himself (Discomfort regarding personal existence)
Q3	The person speaking in remote may not be spending the same amount of time together (Discomfort regarding real-time progression)
Q4	The person speaking in remote may not be listening to me (Discomfort regarding attention)
Q5	The person speaking in remote may not be having me favor (Discomfort regarding favoritism)

This questionnaire aims to investigate the degree of reduction concerning the discomfort that occurs compared with real-world communication between the conventional method (web meeting) and suggested method (Unity-Warmth). Five discomforts were targeted: human existence, personal existence, real-time progression, attention, and favoritism.

2) Emotional Change: SAM (Self-Assessment Manikin): SAM was used to evaluate emotions [25]. SAM consists of emotional valence and arousal levels and can evaluate pleasant/displeased and excited/relaxed states on 9 levels, respectively. The participants were instructed to answer the questionnaire for emotional valence with the center as the normal state and the questionnaire for arousal level with the rightmost state as the normal state.

3) Existence: IPQ (Igroup Presence Questionnaire): IPQ was used to evaluate existence [26]. IPQ consists of four factors: an overall presence, presence of the virtual space, awareness of the outside world, and sense of reality. It scores the presence, immersion, and sense of presence of each content. This experiment used the six questions listed in Table III.

TABLE III. QUESTIONNAIRE ITEMS RELATED TO EXISTENCE

Q1	I had a sense that the interlocutor projected on the computer was "being there".
Q2	I did not feel that I was present beside the interlocutor
Q3	I had a sense of participating with the interlocutor
Q4	I felt present in the same space as the interlocutor
Q5	How real did the interlocutor seem to you?
Q6	How much did your experience of computer-medicated communication seem consistent with your real-world communication experiences?

Items that were unsuitable for the experiment or that were synonymous with other questions when converted into Japanese were excluded, and only items regarding existence were selected from these.

E. Participants

Participants were students between the ages of 21 and 23. Each questionnaire answered by the participant in one experiment was treated as one sample. Different combinations of participants were treated as separate samples.

V. Results

The results are presented in three viewpoints: "subject evaluation", "emotional change", and "existence". Assuming power = 0.80, effect size (delta) = 0.60, and significance level = 0.05, the optimal number of samples was n = 23.8. Therefore, 24 samples were collected for this experiment.

A. Subjective Evaluation

Table IV lists the results of the t-test and average values of the subjective discomfort evaluation.

TABLE IV. T-TEST RESULTS OF SUBJECTIVE DISCOMFORT EVALUATION

Questions	Result(t-value)	Average Value	
		Web Meeting	Unity-Warmth
Q1	n.s.	85.21	88.29
Q2	n.s.	83.50	88.13
Q3	n.s.	75.58	82.25
Q4	n.s.	76.04	78.38
Q5	n.s.	31.63	31.04

Significant differences were not observed from this evaluation.

B. Emotional Change

Table V lists the results of the t-test and average values for the emotional change. Q1 is the result of the emotional valence, and Q2 of the arousal level.

TABLE V. T-TEST RESULTS OF SUBJECTIVE EMOTIONAL CHANGE EVALUATION

Questions	Result(t-value)	Average Value	
		Web Meeting	Unity-Warmth
Q1	n.s.	60.96	64.96
Q2	n.s.	49.96	59.00

Significant differences were not observed from this evaluation.

C. Existence

Table VI lists the results of the t-test and average values for existence.

TABLE VI. T-TEST RESULTS OF SUBJECTIVE EXISTENCE EVALUATION

Questions	Result(t-value)	Average Value	
		Web Meeting	Unity-Warmth
Q1	p<.001	30.29	53.83
Q2	n.s	37.83	44.67
Q3	p=.009	53.21	69.25
Q4	p=.009	48.50	64.58
Q5	p=.002	56.25	39.71
Q6	p=.005	51.42	66.88

This evaluation obtained significant differences in five out of six questions.

Figure 10 shows a radar chart of the average values of the five items for which a significant difference was obtained.

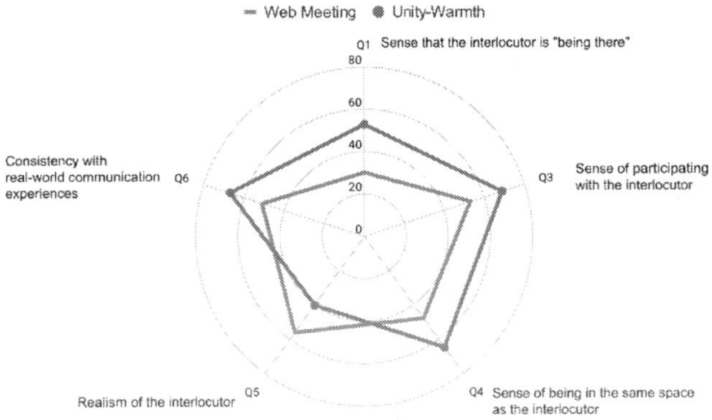

Figure 10. Radar chart of the significant differences observed from existence items.

Figure 11 shows the results of the five "existence" questions in which significant differences were obtained.

This graph is a box plot. The thick line at the center of the box plot represents the median of the data. The top of the box represents the third quartile, and the bottom of the box represents the first quartile. The upper and lower whiskers refer to the largest and smallest data points, respectively, in the range between (first quartile - 1.5*(third quartile - first quartile))

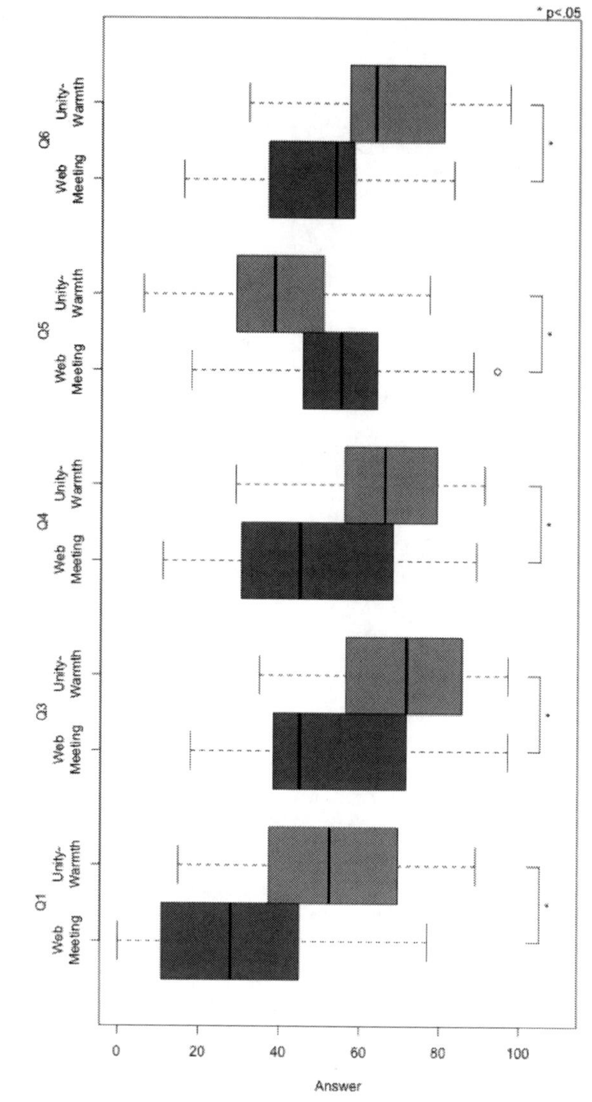

Figure 11. Box plot of the significant differences observed from existence items.

and (third quartile + 1.5*(third quartile - first quartile)). The circles represent data points that are larger or smaller than the whiskers, i.e., outliers.

VI. Discussion

In this section, clarification of the reason why significant differences were obtained for "existence" but not for "subjective evaluation" and "emotional change". Each of the questions about the three viewpoints is discussed.

A. Subjective Evaluation

A paired t-test was performed on the questionnaire results of Q1 "The person speaking in remote location may not be a human (discomfort regarding the sense of human presence)". Significant differences were not observed between the conventional method (web meeting) and suggested method (Unity-Warmth) on this question. The answers showed that many samples were obtained without significant differences between the conventional and the suggested methods. This result may be because the participants were university students, who are accustomed to video meeting, and therefore, minimally discomforted regarding the existence of the interlocutor. This may also be related to all participants knowing each other, having met face-to-face just before the experiment.

A paired t-test was performed on the questionnaire results of Q2 "The person speaking in remote may not be the person himself (Discomfort regarding personal existence)". Significant differences were not observed between the conventional method (web meeting) and suggested method (Unity-Warmth) on this question. The answer showed that many samples were obtained without significant differences between the conventional and suggested methods. This result seems to be caused by problems of participant combination, as in Q1.

A paired t-test was performed on the questionnaire result of Q3 "The person speaking in remote may not be spending the same amount of time together (Discomfort regarding real-time progression)". Significant differences were not observed between the conventional method (web meeting) and suggested method (Unity-Warmth) on this question. This result seems to be caused by problems of participant combination, as in Q1 and Q2.

A paired t-test was performed on the questionnaire result of Q4 "The person speaking in remote may not be listening to me (Discomfort regarding attention)". Significant differences were not observed between the conventional method (web meeting) and suggested method (Unity-Warmth) on this question. In this item, some answers show improvement in the suggested method (Unity-Warmth) compared to the conventional method (web meeting). However, some answers show deterioration in the suggested method compared to the conventional method. This result may be because of the unnaturalness of the line of sight and images, as Unity-Warmth uses an ultra-wide-angle web camera and performs a Trapezoidal correction.

A paired t-test was performed on the questionnaire result of Q5 "The person speaking in remote may not be having me favor (Discomfort regarding favoritism)". Significant differences were not observed between the conventional method (web meeting) and suggested method (Unity-Warmth) on this question. Many of the experiments were conducted with male participants who were not romantically involved with each other. This result may be because the participants were less likely to feel affection for each other, and thus, significant differences were not obtained.

B. Emotional Change

A paired t-test on the questionnaire results of the emotional valence (Q1) did not show significant difference between the conventional and suggested methods. Similarly, the corresponding t-test on the questionnaire results of the arousal level (Q2) did not show significant difference between the conventional and suggested methods.

These results may indicate that the number of experiments conducted with male participants who were not romantically involved with each other was too large to obtain significant differences in emotional change. After the experiment, some male participants who were romantically attracted to women said, "I think I would be more excited and happy to use this system with a woman". This opinion suggests that the emotional change is more significant when the partipants are romantic partners.

C. Existence

A paired t-test was performed on Q1 "I had a sense that the interlocutor projected on the computer was 'being there'". Significant differences were obtained between the conventional method (web meeting) and suggested method (Unity-Warmth) on this question. The average VAS value of the suggested method (Unity-Warmth) was 53.83 mm, and that of the conventional method (web meeting) was 30.29 mm. In this question, a VAS value of 0 mm means "not at all", and 100 mm means "very much". Therefore, the suggested method (Unity-Warmth) provides "the sense that the interlocutor is 'being there'" more significantly than the conventional method (web meeting).

A paired t-test was performed on Q2 "I did not feel that I was present next to the interlocutor". Significant differences were not obtained between the conventional method (web meeting) and suggested method (Unity-Warmth) on this question.

A paired t-test was performed on Q3 "I had a sense of acting with the interlocutor". Significant differences were obtained between the conventional method (web meeting) and suggested method (Unity-Warmth) on this question. The average VAS value of the suggested method (Unity-Warmth) was 69.25 mm, and that of the conventional method (web meeting) was 53.21 mm. In this question, a VAS value of 0 mm means "fully disagree", and 100 mm means "fully agree". Therefore, the suggested method (Unity-Warmth) provides "the sense of participating with the interlocutor" more significantly than the conventional method (web meeting).

A paired t-test was performed on Q4 "I felt present in the same space with the interlocutor". Significant differences were obtained between the conventional method (web meeting) and suggested method (Unity-Warmth) on this question. The average VAS value of the suggested method (Unity-Warmth) was 64.58 mm, and that of the conventional method (web meeting) was 48.50 mm. In this question, a VAS value of 0 mm means "fully disagree", and 100 mm means "fully agree". Therefore, the suggested method (Unity-Warmth) provides "the sense of being in the same space as the interlocutor" more significantly than the conventional method (web meeting).

A paired t-test was performed on Q5 "How real did the interlocutor seem to you?". Significant differences were obtained between the conventional method (web meeting) and suggested method (Unity-Warmth) on this question. The average VAS value of the suggested method (Unity-Warmth) was 39.71 mm, and that of the conventional method (web meeting) was 56.25 mm. In this question, a VAS value of 0 mm means "not real at all", and 100 mm means "completely real". Therefore, the suggested method (Unity-Warmth) provides "the realism of the interlocutor" more significantly than the conventional method (web meeting).

A paired t-test was performed on Q6 "How much did your experience of computer-medicated communication seem consistent with your real-world communication experience?". Significant differences were obtained between the conventional method (web meeting) and suggested method (Unity-Warmth) on this question. The average VAS value of the suggested method (Unity-Warmth) was 66.88 mm, and that of the conventional method (web meeting) was 51.42 mm. In this question, a VAS value of 0 mm means "not consistent", and 100 mm means "very consistent". Therefore, the suggested method (Unity-Warmth) gives "consistency with real-world communication experience" more significantly than the conventional method (web meeting).

Significant differences were obtained for five of the six items, indicating an improved existence. That is, this system can provide communication with an existence significantly more effective than web meeting.

Another reason for the lack of significant differences in Q2 may have been the difficulty understanding the questionnaire. For the question "I did not feel that I was present beside the interlocutor", a VAS value of 0 mm meant "not at all", and 100 mm meant "very much". Therefore, several participants asked, "Which is 'I felt that I was present next to the interlocutor'?" about the interpretation of the question. It may have been necessary to explain the interpretation of the questions and response scales to all participants in advance.

VII. Conclusion and Future Work

This study shows that Unity-Warmth provide better communication with existence even in remote areas. In the future, Unity-Warmth can be applied to communication between people who struggle to meet in person and express physical intimacy, such as "grandparents and grandchildren" and "celebrities and their fans". The following section introduces the conclusion and future works in detail.

A. Conclusion

This study aims to emphasize the existence (of the distant partner) by reducing two discomforts "visual" and "somatosensory" of computer-medicated communication.

In the suggested system, Unity-Warmth, the communication methods are adjusted to be close to those in real life, in terms of body size, hand-contact position, and body temperature. Unity-Warmth consists of a touch panel display that can project half of a person's life-size image and a transparent heater that conveys the body's warmth.

An experiment verified the effectiveness of Unity-Warmth by comparing the conventional system (Zoom Meetings) with Unity-Warmth. Consequently, significant differences were not obtained for "subjective evaluation" and "emotional change".

However, the "existence" questionnaire obtained significant differences in five of the six questions. The suggested method (Unity-Warmth) was more effective than the conventional method (web meeting) in terms of the sense that the interlocutor is "being there", sense of participating with the interlocutor, sense of being in the same space as the interlocutor, realism of the interlocutor, and consistency with real-world communication experience. That is the suggested method (Unity-Warmth) can provide better "communication with existence even in remote areas", which is the goal of this research, compared with the conventional method (web meeting).

However, because significant differences were not identified in the questionnaires of the "subjective evaluation of discomfort" and "emotional change", questions remain concerning the discomfort changes of "visual" and "somatosensory". A possible reason for the absent significant differences in this survey can be the combination of participants. In addition, the suggested method (Unity-Warmth) requires some visual improvements, such as "video distortion and line of sight improvement", "internal reflection reduction", and "quality of transmitted video and audio". Addressing these improvements is expected to provide existence further.

B. Future Work

The participants in this experiment were only niche students who knew each other and were not romantically involved with each other. The results shows that there is no significant difference was in the subjective evaluation of discomfort.

In the future, we would like to conduct experiments with a wider range of age groups and participants with romantic or friendship relationships and compare the results.

Investigating whether the suggested method helps resolve the sense of discomfort in long-distance communication is expected.

Conducting the survey again by collecting a sample that considers whether the respondents are in romantic interest involved is expected.

Furthermore, Unity-Warmth will be tested with couples in long-distance relationships, which is the long-term background of this study to investigate the degree to which the suggested system enriches long-distance communication. Moreover, Unity-Warmth can be applied to communication between people who struggle meeting directly and expressing physical intimacy, such as "grandparents and grandchildren" and "celebrities and their fans".

In evaluating communication involving remote contact, the 9-item questionnaire exists to measure the "Social Disfordance" of Mediated Social Touch, with three scales that focus on Social Discomfort, Communicational Expressiveness, and Need for Additional Consideration [27]. Conducting more suitable questionnaires for evaluating communication involving remote contact is expected.

The following four points can be identified as areas of improvement for suggested device. First, the images captured by the ultra-wide-angle camera are distorted. Second, adjust the camera position to make the line of sight natural. Third, the content displayed on display is reflected in the captured image owing to the internal reflection of the acrylic plate of the warm sensation unit placed in front of the display. Fourth, is the quality of the transmitted video and audio. These improvements will produce better results. In addition, the heating of the present device was not controlled by the temperature. Therefore, verifying the difference in effect depending on the temperature provided by the device is expected.

References

[1] C. Neustaedter and S. Greenberg, "Intimacy in long-distance relationships over video chat," *Proceedings of the SIGCHI Conference on Human Factors in Computing Systems*, pp. 753–762, Association for Computing Machinery, 2012.

[2] A. P. N. Aguila, "Living long-distance relationships through computer-mediated communication," *Social Science Diliman*, vol. 5, pp. 83–106, 2011.

[3] S. Greenberg and C. Neustaedter, "Shared living, experiences, and intimacy over video chat in long distance relationships," *Connecting Families: The Impact of New Communication Technologies on Domestic Life*, pp. 37–53, Springer London, 2013.

[4] L. Kusisto, "The impact of video chatting on idealization and disillusionment for long distance dating couples," *Theses and Dissertations–Family Sciences*, vol. 31, University of Kentucky Libraries, 2015.

[5] E. Tamaki, "[Method of presenting somatosensory stimuli in a VR environment] VR kankyou ni okeru taiseikannkaku sigeki no teizi houhou (in japanese)," *Journal of the Society of Biomechanisms*, vol. 43, no. 1, pp. 3–9, 2019.

[6] H. Tsujita, K. Tsukada, and I. Siio, "Syncdecor: Communication appliances for couples separated by distance," *2008 The Second International Conference on Mobile Ubiquitous Computing, Systems, Services and Technologies*, pp. 279–286, 2008.

[7] Y. Itoh, A. Miyajima, and T. Watanabe, "'tsunagari' communication: fostering a feeling of connection between family members," *CHI '02 Extended Abstracts on Human Factors in Computing Systems*, pp. 810–811, 2002.

[8] H. Chung, C. J. Lee, and T. Selker, "Lover's cups: Drinking interfaces as new communication channels," *CHI '06 Extended Abstracts on Human Factors in Computing Systems*, CHI EA '06, pp. 375–380, Association for Computing Machinery, 2006.

[9] H. Tsujita, K. Tsukada, and I. Siio, "Inphase: Evaluation of a communication system focused on "happy coincidences" of daily behaviors," *Proceedings of the SIGCHI Conference on Human Factors in Computing Systems*, CHI '10, pp. 2481–2490, Association for Computing Machinery, 2010.

[10] C. Chen, J. Forlizzi, and P. L. Jennings, "Comslipper: An expressive design to support awareness and availability," *CHI '06 Extended Abstracts on Human Factors in Computing Systems*, CHI EA '06, pp. 369–374, Association for Computing Machinery, 2006.

[11] K. Suzuki and S. Hashimoto, "Feellight: A communication device for distant nonverbal exchange," *Proceedings of the ACM SIGMM 2004 Workshop on Effective Telepresence - ETP 2004*, pp. 40–44, 2004.

[12] J. Häkkilä, H. Li, S. Koskinen, and A. Colley, "Connected candles as peripheral emotional user interface," *Proceedings of the 17th International Conference on Mobile and Ubiquitous Multimedia*, pp. 327–333, Association for Computing Machinery, 2018.

[13] I. Siio, J. H. Rowan, and E. D. Mynatt, "Peek-a-drawer: Communication by furniture," *CHI '02 Extended Abstracts on Human Factors in Computing Systems*, pp. 582–583, Association for Computing Machinery, 2002.

[14] K. Suhonen, K. Väänänen, and K. Mäkelä, "User experiences and expectations of vibrotactile, thermal and squeeze feedback in interpersonal communication," *Proceedings of the 26th Annual BCS Interaction Specialist Group Conference on People and Computers*, pp. 205–214, BCS Learning & Development Ltd., 2012.

[15] R. Wang, F. K. H. Quek, D. G. Tatar, J. K. S. Teh, and A. D. Cheok, "Keep in touch: Channel, expectation and experience," *Proceedings of the SIGCHI Conference on Human Factors in Computing Systems*, pp. 139–148, Association for Computing Machinery, 2012.

[16] H. Nakanishi, K. Tanaka, and Y. Wada, "Remote handshaking: Touch enhances video-mediated social telepresence," *Proceedings of the SIGCHI Conference on Human Factors in Computing Systems*, CHI '14, (New York, NY, USA), pp. 2143–2152, Association for Computing Machinery, 2014.

[17] F. Mueller, F. Vetere, M. R. Gibbs, J. Kjeldskov, S. Pedell, and S. Howard, "Hug over a distance," *CHI '05 Extended Abstracts on Human Factors in Computing Systems*, pp. 1673–1676, Association for Computing Machinery, 2005.

[18] J. Nakanishi, H. Sumioka, and H. Ishiguro, "Virtual hug induces modulated impression on hearsay information," *Proceedings of the 6th International Conference on Human-Agent Interaction*, pp. 199–204, Association for Computing Machinery, 2018.

[19] D. Gooch and L. A. Watts, "Communicating social presence through thermal hugs," *Proc. Ubicomp 2010 SISSE Workshop*, pp. 11–20, 2010.

[20] H. A. Samani, R. Parsani, L. T. Rodriguez, E. Saadatian, K. H. Dissanayake, and A. D. Cheok, "Kissenger: Design of a kiss transmission device," *Proceedings of the Designing Interactive Systems Conference*, pp. 48–57, Association for Computing Machinery, 2012.

[21] H. A. Samani, J. K. S. Teh, E. Saadatian, and R. Nakatsu, "Xoxo: Haptic interface for mediated intimacy," *2013 International Symposium on Next-Generation Electronics*, pp. 256–259, 2013.

[22] "CAPCOM: Toraware no palm official site." https://www.capcom.co.jp/palm/. [retrieved: May, 2022].

[23] R. Pan, S. Singhal, B. E. Riecke, E. S. Cramer, and C. Neustaedter, ""myeyes": The design and evaluation of first person view video streaming for long-distance couples," *Proceedings of the 2017 Conference on Designing Interactive Systems*, pp. 135–146, Association for Computing Machinery, 2017.

[24] "Zoom meetings | zoom." https://explore.zoom.us/en/products/meetings/. [retrieved: May, 2022].

[25] M. M. Bradley and P. J. Lang, "Measuring emotion: the self-assessment manikin and the semantic differential," *Journal of behavior therapy and experimental psychiatry*, vol. 25, no. 1, pp. 49–59, 1994.

[26] "igroup presence questionnaire (IPQ) overview | igroup.org – project consortium." http://www.igroup.org/pq/ipq/index.php. [retrieved: May, 2022].

[27] K. Mejia and S. Yarosh, "A nine-item questionnaire for measuring the social disfordance of mediated social touch technologies," *Proc. ACM Hum.-Comput. Interact.*, vol. 1, no. CSCW, pp. 1–17, 2017.

Subliminal Warnings – A New Approach to Change Users' Behavior

Mini Zeng
mzeng@ju.edu
Computer Science Department
Jacksonville University
Jacksonville, USA

Feng Zhu
fzhu@uah.edu
Computer Science Department
University of Alabama in Huntsville
Huntsville, USA

Sandra Carpenter
carpens@uah.edu
Psychology Department
University of Alabama in Huntsville
Huntsville, USA

Abstract— **People use web applications and services every day. They encounter many cyber-attacks in their daily lives. Cybersecurity warnings remind users to be cautious but often they are not effective because users ignore them. Existing warnings often compete for the limited resource – conscious attention. Cognitive psychology indicates that human behavior can be affected by non-conscious processing. The goal of this paper is to explore the effectiveness of subliminal warnings. We propose a subliminal warning design that directly suggests users behave cautiously. We used a pilot study to guide our design. We conducted a lab experiment to evaluate the subliminal warning strategy in the context of privacy protection. We implemented an integrated hardware and software environment to evaluate our warning design, study users' behavior, and to validate and verify the proper display of subliminal warning messages. Our experimental results showed that subliminal warnings effectively reduced identity disclosure. Warning designs based on cognitive psychology and human factors may better protect people's privacy.**

Keywords - Subliminal Messages; Non-conscious Processing; Warnings.

I. INTRODUCTION

People use web applications and services every day. They encounter many cyber-attacks in their daily lives (e.g., phishing and Domain Name System spoofing attacks). Websites or apps may send numerous spam emails. Many users have connected to legitimate websites with erroneous or self-signed certificates [1]. They often unnecessarily disclose identity information, thus putting their privacy at risk. The identity information may be collected, sold, and even maliciously used. Computer warnings protect users from exploits, but many people still fall into attackers' traps. Humans are not very good at mitigating cyber-attacks. They are considered the weakest component in security systems [2].

Warnings are used as one of the last lines of defense in computer security and are fundamental to users' security interactions with technology. When people see computer warnings, however, most of the time, they ignore them [3]. Moreover, some people do not even pay attention to security warnings [4]. On the other hand, when individuals were asked about their concerns about their private information, they claimed that they had been careful about their personal information [5]. This contradiction may be explained by the ineffectiveness of warnings [8]. The effectiveness of warnings depends on the fact that they attract users' attention, communicate clearly about the risks, and provide straightforward instructions for avoiding the hazards[6].

Researchers believe one of the fundamental problems is the lack of attention paid to warnings [7] So, recent warning designs try to grab users' attention by discontinuing their primary tasks [9]. Other researchers claimed that too much exposure to warnings and interruptions would make users quickly habituate to warnings [7] and feel "warning fatigue" [8].

Current warning theories and practices occur only at the conscious level and require attention [9]. However, researchers found that a great deal of information processing happens at noncouscious level. In addition, human behaviors are affected by non-conscious stimuli [10].

We utilize the non-conscious processing ability for warnings instead of competing for conscious attention. The last 50 years of cognitive psychology research indicate that non-conscious processing can be nudged by human perception and behavior[11]. We want to evaluate the impact of cybersecurity warnings via non-conscious processing, specifically using subliminal messages. Our previous work showed that subliminal warnings can remind users about their security and privacy attitudes [12].

In this paper, we further evaluate subliminal warnings that directly suggest cautious behavior. Our subliminal warning designs require no active attention and do not interfere with a user's primary task. The warning messages pop up just in time when the user clicks the text entry for identity information. These messages are only displayed for dozens of milliseconds. The nature of our very brief warning stimuli in non-conscious processing may even reduce habituation (warning fatigue) [13].

We use our warnings to help people avoid unnecessary identity exposure and more cautiously share their personal information online. This is an important area because there are 17 million identity theft victims every year in the U.S [17]. Unfortunately, while people are very concerned about their privacy, they do not protect their personal information well and unnecessarily expose their information online [15].

The experiment for the subliminal warning is conducted in a context of a restaurant table reservation app. We developed an experiment environment that includes eye-tracking and a scene camera. The eye tracker was used to study participants' gaze behavior, whereas the scene camera verified the proper display of the warning messages. Our experiment results indicate that our subliminal warning messages can effectively reduce disclosure.

II. Background and Related Work

A. Computer Warning Framework

Warnings encourage safe behaviors. Researchers have been working on warning designs for decades. They find that users frequently ignore warnings and focus, instead, on their tasks [6]. To understand how people process warning, several models were developed, such as the Communication-Human Information Processing (C-HIP) Model [6][19], the sequential model [17], and the levels of performance model [18]. The C-HIP model separates the warning process into two aspects of the warning (i.e., source, channel) and six stages of human information processing: delivery, attention switch, comprehension, attitudes and beliefs, motivation, and behavior [6]. To increase the effectiveness of warnings, researchers and warning designers have developed many approaches to attract users' attention, to communicate clearly about the risks, and to provide straightforward instructions for avoiding the hazard [22][23].

B. Cybersecurity Warnings

Due to the reality that the human is the weakest link of the cybersecurity chain, researchers have been trying to enhance the security of this weakest link by developing and improving the security warnings for decades [24]–[26]. Researchers found that there are two common issues of ineffective security warnings. One is the lack of attention [24]. The other one is habituation [25]. Researchers have used eye tracking, mouse tracking, functional magnetic resonance imaging [29], and galvanic skin response [27] to study user behavior.

For the lack of attention, a critical approach is the warning designs with required actions, called active warnings. Such as forcing users to click the URL in the SSL warning [28], making users click through several buttons or sub-pages with multi-level warnings [29], and a pop-up warning with required buttons or links to continue current workflow [30]. These successful warning designs make warnings hard to ignore [24][34], or totally interrupt users' workflows [25][35]. But other researchers [19] argue that it is rational for users to ignore warnings because of the amount of conscious attention needed. Warnings can interrupt users' workflow, leading to "warning fatigue."

More effective approaches were therefore developed. One of the common approaches includes appropriate icons, symbols, and physical security metaphors. For example, police offer symbols were widely used [33]. Firewall warnings were designed with a physical security metaphor (using a figure dressed in a prisoner's uniform, carrying a knife and a thief's bag) [33]. Also, an SSL warning with a red background and a "Stop sign officer" security metaphor [29] has been effective.

To make the transition of attention switch and maintenance smoothly, passive warnings without forcing users to take actions were designed. For example, a windows action center sends notification massage in a "pop-up balloon" shows up and fades out after a few minutes [34]. A red open lock designed as a SSL warning indicator [31][33]. An eye-gaze controlled security warning is displayed when eye gaze moves to the hazard area and fades out when users do not need it [35].

C. Subliminal Stimulation and Applications

Contemporary research in cognitive psychology reveals that part of our information processing is at the conscious level, whereas other perception efforts may take place beneath a threshold that thus we are not consciously aware of (known as subliminal) [36]. Non-conscious level priming has not yet been considered an approach to improving computer warnings. But it has been used in other areas for years, such as advertising and education [40][41]. Many research has been done on the effect of non-conscious level priming on human behavior [39][42].

To what extent can non-conscious perception affect our behaviors? This has been one of the most controversial issues in psychology for decades. Researchers addressed this issue through experiments that use subliminal stimulation methods [40]. A subliminal stimulus is presented below a subjective threshold for conscious perception. Subliminal perception is inferred when a stimulus is demonstrated not to be consciously perceived while still influencing thoughts, feelings, actions, learning, or memory [41]. Three models could be applied for subliminal priming: subliminal priming mapping with response [42], priming by spatial attention [43] and priming by strategies [39].

Studies showed that arbitrary stimulus-response mappings could apply to subliminal stimuli [39][47]. The stimulus-response mapping is a strategy to generate a connection between a response and a stimulus. The goal of stimulus-response mapping is to encourage a response when a stimulus is displayed. Stimuli presented below the threshold of awareness can systematically influence choice responses determined by the instructed stimulus–response (S–R) mapping. Researchers also investigated whether such stimuli influence a free choice between two response alternatives under conditions in which the choice subjectively appears to be internally generated and free. This is relevant for our research because our goal is for people to choose cautious rather than risky disclosure behavior. For example, the primes were left- and right-pointing double arrows (<< and >>). The choices provided were either left- and right-pointing double arrows or outward-pointing double arrows (< >). The experimental results demonstrated that apparently "free" choices are not immune to not consciously triggered biases [44]. In our research, we apply S-R mapping in subliminal messages and icon design.

Subliminal messages have been used in advertising for decades to influence purchasing behavior. Subliminal advertising became notorious in 1957 through the publicity. James Vicary, a private market researcher tried to increase sales of Coca Cola and popcorn in a movie theatre by secretly

TABLE 1 PILOT STUDY CONDITIONS

Condition	Subliminal Prime	Duration for each display	Number of Displays	Display
1	Text message “Fake it”	50 ms	Five Times	At the top of Address textbox
2	Text Message “Fake it”	50 ms	Once	At the top of Address textbox
3	Icon: Yellow Triangle	50 ms	Five Times	At the right of “Next” button
4	Icon: Yellow Triangle	50 ms	Five Times	At the right of Address textbox

and subliminally flashing the message "Drink Coca Cola" and "Eat popcorn" [37]. After that, other researchers demonstrated that subliminal priming of a brand name of drink positively affected participants' choice and their intention, the primed brand, but only for participants who were thirsty [40][47]. This led some people to claim that subliminal advertising was unethical [48]. It should be used only for non-profit and beneficial purposes, such as stopping smoking or improving academic performance. For example, subliminal words were randomly displayed in different locations on slides presented to students [38]and enhanced their later performance.

In our previous work, we designed a subliminal warning message to remind users of their security and privacy attitudes based on C-HIP model. The warning was using a yellow background message "Privacy" to strengthen user's access to their own security attitudes and beliefs [12]. The approach emphasizes the effect of warning on attitudes and beliefs level of C-HIP model. In this paper, we bypass the other stages of C-HIP model and directly use the stimulus-response mapping to trigger the safe behavior.

D. *Privacy and Identity Exposure*

Personal privacy has been emphasized for decades. People often claim that they care about their privacy when discussing their privacy attitudes and concerns. However, they still provide sensitive information such as their income, investments, and home addresses on the Internet without a good reason [46]. People's identity disclosure behavior often does not match their privacy attitudes, privacy concerns, and actions that they claimed to take to protect their identities [47]. They often lack adequate information about protecting their identity information and tend to have a sense of personal immunity to common hazards [48].

III. SUBLIMINAL WARNING STRATEGY AND PILOT STUDY

Subliminal stimuli are defined as occurring below the threshold of conscious awareness [49]. The threshold is defined by whether less than half of people can consciously perceive the stimuli. We conducted a set of pilot studies to guide us on the duration of the subliminal stimuli in our restaurant reservation context and how many times we should display the subliminal prime. The pilot study helped us choose the key design factors to maximize the success rate of presenting a warning message. We tested two types of subliminal stimuli - text messages and icons. The subliminal warnings were presented just in time. For example, after a user clicks the input textbox and right before disclosing information, a subliminal stimulus is shown. In Table 1, we represent the conditions tested in the pilot studies.

Condition one tested subliminal mitigation - the message "Fake it" was used as a subliminal warning message. The message is displayed between a pre-mask image and a post-mask image. The pre-mask was a food image (from the restaurant being viewed) displayed 2000ms before the subliminal prime. The post-mask was a food image displayed 2000ms after the subliminal prime. The subliminal message is displayed five times before the identity input page. The message was shown again on the identity input page when a user clicked the address input box. Subliminal messages were shown for 50ms.

Condition two tested the message "Fake it" only once for 50ms.

Condition three tested the effectiveness of an icon - a yellow triangle (pointed to the left). We used the same pre-mask and post-mask strategy. It is displayed 5 times before an identity input page. The duration was set to 50ms. The icon appeared on the right side of the "Next" button on the identity input page.

Condition four tested the same icon as condition three but the icon displayed at the right side of the address input textbox.

We recruited 22 participants for our pilot study from computing science students and psychology students. Participants were randomly assigned to one of the four conditions. We tested 7 participants in condition one, and 5 participants for each other conditions. Institutional Review Board (IRB) approved the pilot study.

Participants navigated through a restaurant reservation application that requests identity information. The subliminal stimuli automatically appeared in pages or when identity elements were requested.

The percentage of participants who disclosed their identity information is shown in Table 2. From the results of the pilot studies, we can see that a warning design with the subliminal message that shows up once was more effective than other subliminal warning designs. This finding aligns with those of other research projects that focused on semantic processing – that short messages are one of the most effective stimuli [50]among all effective subliminal message forms (i.e., photos, words, signs, and shapes/polygons).

Because the subliminal warnings were displayed during a very short period of time, a concise message is needed to suggest safe behavior. When an app or a website collects a large amount of identity information, we can suggest users to

TABLE 2 PILOT STUDY RESULT: PERCENTAGE OF PARTICIPANTS DISCLOSING PERSONAL INFORMATION

Subliminal Prime	Condition	First name	Last name	Email	Phone Number	Address	Zip code
Message	1	71%	57%	43%	29%	43%	57%
	2	80%	80%	20%	20%	25%	20%
	3	100%	100%	80%	80%	80%	80%
Icon	4	100%	100%	100%	80%	100%	100%

"fake it" or "skip it." Warning words need to be congruent with users' attitudes, beliefs, motivations, and behavior. Research has shown that congruity between a subliminally presented word and a user's goal has a significant influence on behavior [39]. Most people want to keep their information private [51], so there should be congruency between the suggested cautious behavior and attitudes.

More than one strategy may be used to warn users. For example we may suggest the user to "fake it" or "skip it." Considering some of the web applications set most of the personal information fields as required, users can not skip them. In this paper, we decided to present the subliminal warning message "fake it" with a 50 ms display duration, one time, above the requested identity information field.

IV. Experimental Design

We conducted an experiment to evaluate the effectiveness of the subliminal warnings. We used an eye-gaze based verification system with an eye tracker and a scene camera and a post-experiment questionnaire for evaluation.

The design of this experiment has two conditions: the control condition (with no warning) and the subliminal warning condition (with the subliminal message to "fake it", display 50ms on top of the address line one). We target the street address for not disclosure based on an assumption that the street address would be more sensitive than another field (zip code, state, etc) for a table reservation app. We conducted our study to achieve the following goals.

- Ascertain that subliminal warnings are effective.
- Verify and validate that subliminal warnings can be displayed at the right time, right place, and for the proper duration.
- Gain an understanding of participants' identity disclosure behavior under the subliminal warning condition. We wanted to document participants' behavior (e.g., eye gaze, personal information disclosure) when the warning was shown for milliseconds.

A. Participants

We recruited 58 participants on campus for the experiment. 40 were women, and 18 were men. Their ages ranged from forty-eight to seventeen, with a median of twenty one. We list this experiment on a psychology department's website. We prepared a cover story for the experiment as a user evaluation for a restaurant reservation app. Students received activity points as an option toward a course assignment.

B. The Hardware and Software

Because of the short display duration of the subliminal message, we require high-frequency sampling rate for the eye tracking system. The sampling frequency of the scene camera was 120Hz. The sampling frequency of the eye tracker was 250Hz. We ran all software (Eyetracking, scene camera recording, the restaurant scheduling application, and eyetracking analysis) on one machine in the first demo. The high rates of data sampling caused performance degradation (i.e., the sampling intervals were prolonged). Thus, we moved to two PCs that were connected via a wired LAN that was dedicated to the experiment. We executed eye tracking and the restaurant scheduling application on the SMI Server and the scene camera on another laptop computer to guarantee the performance of eye tracking sampling frequency. We also developed new software, which collected and analyzed eye tracking data and synchronized events and eye tracking. Figure 1 shows an integrated software environment that synchronized the eye tracking system, the ReserveME app, the scene camera, and the respective event logs.

Based on this setting, the eye tracking system consistently sampled at 4ms, but the scene camera could not reach the speed of its specification. We sampled 1000 frames each for 6 participants (3 in the control condition and 3 in the subliminal condition) in our pilot study. We generated timestamps for the scene camera videos. Theoretically, the scene camera samples at every 8.3ms (120Hz). The actual sampling rate was on average at 11.24ms (89Hz). Thus, we used the 11.24ms as our frame duration for our analysis of the scene camera videos.

C. The Warning Design

In the restaurant scheduling application, ReserveME, we implemented a subliminal warning that suggested participants

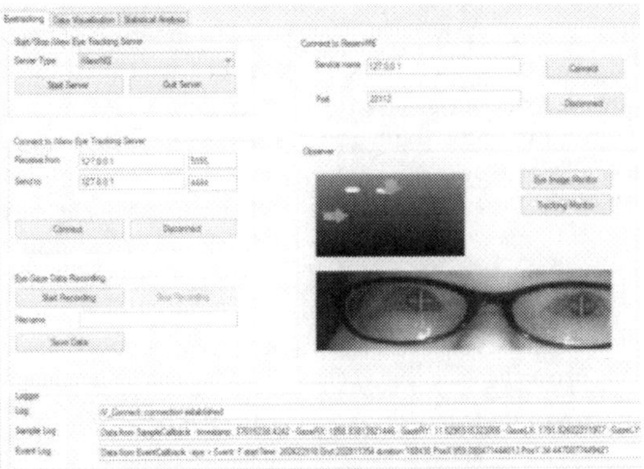

Figure 1. Integrated software environment for the experiment

provide a piece of fake identity information. In our experiment, we used "FAKE IT" as shown in Figure 2. We wanted to display the message just-in-time. That is, when a user clicked on the street address textbox and right before they input their information, a subliminal text message was shown. The subliminal message was set to display for 50ms right above the input textbox, where participants' eye gazes were most likely to be located.

We were specifically interested in six pieces of information: street address, city, state, zip code, email address, and phone number. When zip code, phone number, and email address were requested, the warning message was not shown. (Phone number and email address were requested on the following page of the app.) We wanted to find the impact of subliminal warnings for the targeted behavior – disclosure of street address – as well as for disclosure of the other information.

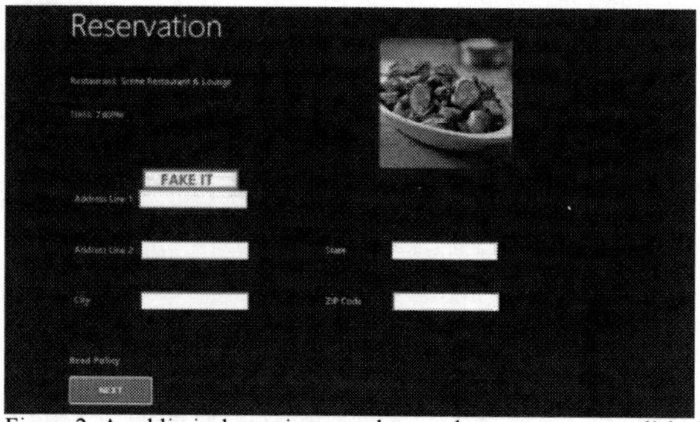

Figure 2. A subliminal warning was shown when a user mouse-clicked the input textbox.

D. Procedure

The participant signed the consent form and disclaimer first. The disclaimer stated that the restaurant reservation app was developed by a third-party software company and the purpose of this study is to evaluate the useability of the software. In the disclaimer, we informed that participants' information would be shared with the software company. This mock disclaimer was used to reduce the university environment bias so that the university researchers would be cautious with participants' information. We did not share their information with any third-party company. A short introduction to the experimental procedure was provided to participants. Participants were told to use the ReserveME app without communication with the researcher unless they had technical questions. A post-experiment survey was given after they reached the last page of the ReserveME app. The entire procedure for each participant took about 30 minutes. Durations varied somewhat for different participants because of eye-tracking calibration or other technical issues. Our university's Institutional Review Board (IRB) approved the experiment procedure.

In the experiment, we did not directly record their identity information. We recorded whether they provided a certain piece of information. In our database of the restaurant reservation app, we coded "1" for participants who provided accurate information and "0" for those not provided accurate information. (The accuracy of the information was obtained from responses participants gave on the post-experiment survey; see below.) Their input of the identity information was discarded as they were typing the information, but participants were not aware of this during the experiment. The eye tracker collects the X, Y coordinates of eye fixation and movement. The scene camera record the change of pages and the pop-up and fade out of the subliminal warning. In our after-experiment debriefing, we told participants that none of their actual information had been saved in the database or would be shared with a third party. We also told them the subliminal warning message was displayed on the address page and the real purpose of the experiment.

E. Post-Experiment Survey

The first part of the post-experiment survey asked questions about participants' experience with the ReserveME app.

In the second part of the survey, we asked participants whether or not they provided accurate information on the identity entry questions in the ReserveME app. We also asked why they provided accurate or inaccurate information. In the third part of the survey, we asked whether they saw anything on the page on a specific spot. We provided a screenshot of the application page to remind them. If they reported yes, we asked them to describe the message they saw.

Then, the focus of the questionnaire shifted to privacy attitudes in the fourth part. We asked participants to rate four pieces of identity elements and whether it was important to keep the identity elements private. We also asked about their concerns related to spam, identify theft, and the like.

Last, we asked participants about their demographic information.

V. EXPERIMENTAL RESULTS

A total of fifty-eight participants were in our two experimental conditions – thirty in the control condition and twenty-eight in the subliminal warning condition.

A. The Display of the Subliminal Warnings

Verified by the data collected by scene camera, the subliminal warning message was displayed in all cases in the subliminal condition. The average display duration of the warning message was 84ms, although we set the display duration for 50ms (see Section 4.2 for how we measured the durations). For twenty-seven participants, the warning message lasted 56ms (5 frames) to 101ms (9 frames). For one participant, the message lasted much longer 135ms (12 frames). This was an unusually long display of the message. The long display was consistent with the event logs of ReserveME and eye tracking data. (The participant did not report seeing the message.) Therefore, the display durations of subliminal warning message may have variations in different runs.

B. Were Participants Consciously Aware of the Warning Message?

Six out of twenty-eight participants in the subliminal warning condition could report the subliminal warning

TABLE 3. SUBLIMINAL WARNING EXPERIMENT RESULTS

	Did not input information				Faked information				Exposed real information			
	Con -trol	Sub-liminal	P-value	Odds ratio	Con-trol	Sub-liminal	P-value	Odds ratio	Con-trol	Sub-liminal	P-value	Odds ratio
Address	1	5	**0.035**	6.30	5 (29)	10 (23)	**0.048**	2.78	24	13	**0.004**	0.22 (4.62)
City	0	2	0.068	∞	3 (30)	7 (26)	**0.065**	3.00	27	19	**0.017**	0.23 (4.26)
State	0	2	0.068	∞	3 (30)	5 (26)	0.192	1.95	27	21	0.065	0.33 (3.00)
Zip code	0	2	0.068	∞	3 (30)	9 (26)	**0.019**	4.26	27	17	**0.004**	0.17 (5.82)
Email	0	4	**0.016**	∞	2 (30)	10 (24)	**0.003**	7.78	28	14	**<0.001**	0.07 (12.1)
Phone	2	5	0.095	3.04	3 (28)	9 (23)	**0.019**	4.26	25	14	**0.003**	0.20 (5.00)

message in one way or another. Three of them recalled the exact action suggested, "FAKE IT;" two remembered the message "falsify" which was semantically correct, and the other one ("red boarder") seemed not to have processed the warning message at the semantic level. Unlike the other five, this participant provided accurate information for all identity elements.

The average display duration of the subliminal warning message for this small group who recalled the warning message was 90ms (8 frames). Next, we ran a t-test to evaluate whether the mean of the number of frames displayed for this group was different from the rest of the participants in the subliminal condition. Those participants who recalled the subliminal warning messages were shown 8.0 frames on average, and those who did not recall the message were shown 7.36 frames on average. Having the p-value of 0.333, we believe there was no difference between the two groups. In addition, we ran six one-way analysis of variance (ANOVA) tests to determine whether the number of frames of the prime impacted its effectiveness on identity exposure of the six elements. None of the tests turned out to be significant.

C. *Identity Disclosure Behavior*

We analyze participants' behavior between the control and subliminal conditions from three aspects: (a) the number of participants who did not input their information; (b) the number of participants who faked their identity elements when they input; and (c) the number of participants who provided accurate identity information. The sums of the numbers in all three aspects equal the total number of participants. We ran the two proportion Z-tests (left-tailed) to determine whether participants in the subliminal warning condition group behaved statistically differently from the control group in all three aspects and for all six identity elements. Table 3 shows subliminal warning experiment results for the two experimental conditions. Probability values (p-values) less than 5% (bold) indicate statistically significant differences between the control and subliminal message conditions. The numbers in parentheses indicate the number of participants who input information. The numbers in parentheses indicate the odds ratios when we compare the control condition to the subliminal condition (i.e., reciprocals of the odds ratios that compared the subliminal condition to the control condition).

More participants in the subliminal warning condition did not input their information for all six identity elements than those in the control condition. Note that the subliminal warning message was triggered by the mouse click event on the street address field. This indicated that participants in the subliminal condition wanted to input information for the first identity element, but they did not. Two proportion Z-tests show that for street address and email, participants in the subliminal condition behaved statistically different from the control group. For the address field, for example, participants in the subliminal condition were about 6.3 times (i.e., odds ratio) more likely to skip their input in the field.

For participants who input their information, those in the subliminal condition were much more likely to fake their identity elements than those in the control condition. Except for the state, all other five identity elements were statistically different for the subliminal and control conditions. Participants were two to eight times (1.95 – 7.78) more likely to fake their identity information for the subliminal group than the control group.

When we combine the first two aspects (a and b), we have the total effect of the subliminal warning message – the reduction of the real identity disclosure. For instance, thirteen participants provided real street address information in the subliminal condition compared to twenty-four of them in the control condition. The two proportion Z-tests show that the difference was statistically significant. Participants in the subliminal condition had a 22% chance (i.e., odds ratio) to provide their street address when compared to those in the control group. That is, those in the control group were 4.6 times (the reciprocal of 0.22) more likely to provide their real street addresses than those in the subliminal condition. The results (Table 3) show that participants were much less likely to provide their real information in the subliminal condition for all elements except for their state information.

The scale of identity exposure and behavior was very different between the two groups, as shown in Table 3. For example, all except one participant did not provide the street address; all others typed in information in the control group. For the subliminal group, two persons did not type in anything in all four fields and went to the next page. Another three skipped the street address part and moved on to the following fields (city, state, and zip code).

Emails and phone numbers were requested on a subsequent page of the ReserveME app. Participants in the subliminal condition, however, were still much more likely to not provide or to fake the information than those in the control condition. Thus, we have an interesting and important observation: even though "FAKE IT" was suggested once for the street address, it may have impacted the disclosure of identity elements after that.

D. What the Eye Tracking Data Show

We were interested in the eye gaze fixation and the time period when the subliminal warnings were shown. We acquired quality eye tracking data in twenty-four cases in the subliminal condition and did not have quality data for the other four due to the eye tracker's loss of the participants' eye gazes during the display of the subliminal message and by an automated system update which negatively impacted the eye-tracking sampling rates.

In twenty out of twenty-four cases, participants' eye gazes were near the subliminal warning message as shown in the white rectangle area (up to 50 pixels away in X or Y coordinates from the "FAKE IT" message) as shown in Figure 3. This was the most reasonable place for participants' gazes to be located because when a participant needed to click on the textbox, they would look at the textbox. Therefore, we displayed the subliminal warning message at that location and at the moment of input as one of the best bets to be successful. Eye-tracking data confirmed that most participants were looking at or near that location. Figure 3 shows a participant's eye gaze during the display of the subliminal warning message. The colored dots represent eye-gaze locations with 4ms intervals that overlay on top of each (the lighter the color, the more recent the eye gaze location).

Participants behaved differently from the rest in the subliminal condition in three cases. First, their eye gaze locations were not on or near the street address textbox. It seemed that they looked at the textbox and moved their mice over the textbox a few seconds prior. They looked elsewhere and then clicked on the field. Thus, they missed the warning message. Two of them provided real identity elements for all the six pieces requested. One of the participants perhaps noticed a message; about 80ms after the subliminal message, his/her eye gaze moved right to the location where the subliminal message was displayed and looked at the area for about 300ms.

In the other case, there seemed to be a significant delay (about 120ms) between the time when the participant clicked the street address textbox and the display of the subliminal message. When the subliminal message was displayed, the participant had already been looking at the keyboard and typing. This participant provided real information for all identity elements.

Learning from these cases, we may display the warning when the mouse is over the street address textbox. Such an approach needs to solve the issues that a user is not looking at the field but the mouse happens to move over or stop on the specific location. Further research and experiments are needed to improve these mechanisms. In addition, we will evaluate the display of the subliminal message within the input textbox in future experiments.

E. How Participants Explained their Disclosure Behavior

In the questionnaire, we asked participants why they provided truthful or false identity information during their interaction with the app. Their 72 responses were classified into one or more of nine categories of explanations shown in Table 4. We use thematic analysis for the classification of this qualitative data. We took the bodies of the data and then groups them according to similarities.

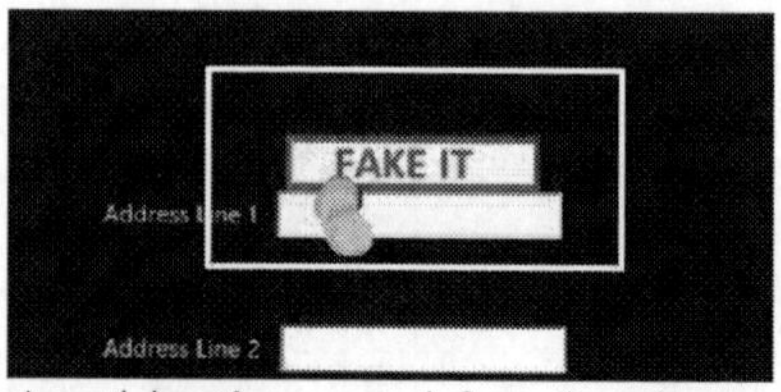

Figure 3. A participant's eye gaze information when a subliminal warning shows up

TABLE 4. PARTICIPANTS' EXPLANATIONS OF WHY THEY DID OR DID NOT PROVIDE THEIR PERSONAL INFORMATION.

Reasons for Providing Truthful Information		
	Control	**Subliminal**
Information is not sensitive or it is not risky to disclose.	7	11
Trust in the app or experimental context.	12	6
Information is needed by the app or experiment.	4	2
Information is already known.	2	2
Habit.	4	0
Reasons for Falsifying Personal Information		
	Control	**Subliminal**
Information is sensitive or risky to disclose.	4	11
Distrust the app/experimental context.	1	1
Information is not needed by the app/experiment.	1	1
Told to "fake it."	0	3

Some participants gave explanations fitting into more than one category. The most frequently occurring categories (n = 33 responses; 7 + 11 giving being truthful; 4 + 11 falsifying) used to explain disclosure (or non-disclosure) were related to the sensitivity (i.e., riskiness) or lack of sensitivity of the information. For example, "I feel uncomfortable sharing this information" or "this information is safe to give." The second most frequent reason for disclosure was related to trust/distrust of the app or the experimental context (n = 20 responses), such as "I trust apps like this." Note that only half as many participants in the warning condition, compared to the control condition, indicated that they trusted the app/ experiment. Eight participants indicated that they thought the information was (or was not) needed by the app or experimenter. Four participants indicated that they disclosed out of habit. Another four explained that they thought the information was already (or readily) available to the researcher or app. Three participants said they falsified information because the app told them to "fake it."

F. The Relationships among Behavior, Privacy Attitudes, Concerns, and the Subliminal Warning

People's privacy attitudes, concerns, and other unknown factors may all affect their privacy disclosure behavior. Having the data of participants' privacy attitudes and concerns from the questionnaire and our experimental data, we analyzed the relationships between these factors and participants' behavior.

We created indices from the data in the following way: a) a disclosure index that combined participants' disclosure behavior by giving weights of 1 to a street address, email, and phone number, and weights of 0.5, 0.3, and 0.2 to zip code, city, and state, respectively; The weights were assigned based on the sensitivity of different field. (state is much less risky to be disclose than street address) b) an attitude index that combined participants' ratings of four attitude questions; c) a concern index that combined participants' ratings of six related questions; and d) dummy coded 1 for eye gaze at or near the subliminal message, and 2 for other cases including for participants in the control condition. These indices were used in multiple regression models for the relations between the predictors and the disclosure behavior.

In the full linear regression model that included all variables, the eye gaze location had very strong correlations with experiment conditions (-0.861) and the number of frames of the warning message (-0.886). Due to this high collinearity, we ran a reduced model with just eye gaze location, experiment condition, or the number of frames. The models

Model Summary

Model	R	R Square	Adjusted R Square	Std. Error of the Estimate
1	.581[a]	.338	.298	1.33455

ANOVA

Model		Sum of Squares	df	Mean Square	F	Sig.
1	Regression	45.393	3	15.131	8.496	.000[b]
	Residual	89.051	50	1.781		
	Total	134.444	53			

Coefficients

Model		Unstandardized Coefficients		Standardized Coefficients		
		B	Std. Error	Beta	t	Sig.
1	(Constant)	2.406	1.295		1.858	.069
	DistanceToSubliminalMsg	1.543	.386	.475	4.003	.000
	Attitudes	-.091	.065	-.175	-1.403	.167
	Concerns	-.042	.039	-.132	-1.086	.283

Figure 4. Liner regression results. The relationships between behavior, privacy attitudes, concerns, and eye gaze locations.

respective R squares were 0.338, 0.286, and 0.263. Thus, we used eye gaze location for the reduced linear regression model as shown below.

$$Disclosure = \beta_0 + \beta_1 x_1 + \beta_2 x_2 + \beta_x x_3$$

where $x1$ = "Eye gaze location"

$x2$ = "Attitudes"

$x3$ = "Concerns"

The linear regression results are shown in Figure 4. Compared to the full model, the adjusted R squares for this reduced model increased from 0.275 to 0.298. The eye gaze location was a statistically significant factor in predicting participants' behavior, but attitudes and concerns were not significant factors in predicting disclosure in this context.

VI. LIMITATIONS

Like any other experimental study, our experiment has its limitations. First, we used a lab environment to study whether subliminal warnings reduce identity disclosure. We are keenly aware of the questions raised regarding the realism of the method and the generalizability of experiments. Experiments, however, provide the best control over factors that might influence disclosure. They are the most effective way to test our hypotheses by studying participants' behavior directly when warning messages are shown for dozens of milliseconds. They allow us to measure the duration of the subliminal messages and participants' eye gazes.

Second, our ReserveME app collects identity information and also displays warnings. This does not seem logical in a real-world application, but the approach avoids further complication of our software and does not affect the proof of concept of subliminal warnings. In a commercial implementation, the functionality of subliminal warnings may be realized by operating systems or as a web browser plug-in (similar to the autofill function in browsers to identify form fields).

Third, our experiment was run in a university lab setting. Often, participants trust researchers in this type of setting, thus challenging privacy research. People may believe that researchers will not put them at risk. It was the case for our experiment, as shown in Table 2. Given the trusting nature of our research participants, however, warnings that do decrease disclosure of private information will likely be effective in a lower trust real-world environment.

Last, our participants were college students (most of them were between eighteen and twenty-two). Thus, our results might have limited generalizability. This age group, however, may be one of the most representative age groups who use apps to make reservations and purchases online. In our future work, we plan to study participants with more diverse backgrounds and age groups.

VII. CONCLUSION AND FUTURE WORK

Instead of reminding users of their privacy and security attitudes as we did in a previous study using the word "privacy" [15], our primary goal and contribution of this research were to design a subliminal warning by suggesting safe behavior using stimulus–response mapping model. When an app or a website collects a large amount of identity information, we can suggest users to "fake it." This design bypassed the upper stages and emphasized the last level of C-HIP model. Cognitively more straightforward to trigger the safe behavior (not provide personal information). We conducted a pilot study and tested two categories of warnings (message and icon) to guide the design of the subliminal warning. We used eye tracking and scene camera recording to verify the display duration of the subliminal warning and users' attention during the experiment. The result of the experiment showed that the subliminal warning with the suggested response could effectively reduced disclosure of identity information.

This paper proposed the basic idea by focusing on scientific theory and evaluations. The subliminal warnings could be implemented as an application solution to motivate safety behavior. Part of our future work is to implement the application solution of the subliminal warning. We envision that an application implementation of subliminal warning could be developed as a third-party application or as a web browser plug-in.

We learned several lessons and limitations of our study. The application of the strategy that uses mouse click events to trigger the warning display may not work for all types of user behavior. System delays might also have an impact on the warning effectiveness. In this experiment, we evaluated only one display duration. We will study the warning effectiveness with regard to different display durations of the subliminal messages. Moreover, future experiments may examine different warning words and their locations.

It is also quite interesting that, in the pilot study, condition two obtained better results than condition one. The warning was presented five times in condition one, while the warning was only displayed once in condition two. It could be because of the pre-mask and post-mask in condition one. We added them to make sure the warning satisfies the subliminal threshold. In our future work, we plan to extend the experimental study with multiple times displays of subliminal warnings, different warning words, duration, colors, and background of the message. We will also apply other statistical analyses such as the omnibus test to test different parameters and Bonferroni correction to mitigate family-wise errors.

Our ongoing research is to develop a framework for non-conscious security warnings. We want to discover other effective subliminal warning strategies. We want to investigate how these strategies facilitate users' memory access, remind them of their security and privacy attitudes, and motivate them to take safe actions. Another goal is to compare the effectiveness of the different strategies and to find their limitations.

REFERENCES

[1] J. Sobey, R. Biddle, P. C. van Oorschot, and A. S. Patrick, "Exploring user reactions to new browser cues for extended validation certificates," in *European Symposium on Research in Computer Security*, 2008, pp. 411–427.

[2] A. Wiesmann, A. Stock, M. Curphey, and R. Stirbei, "A guide to building secure web applications and web services," *The Open Web Application Security Project*, 2005. http://www.i-pi.com/Training/BSS/OWASPGuide2.0.1.pdf (accessed May 19, 2022).

[3] K. Krol, M. Moroz, and M. A. Sasse, "Don't Work. Can't Work? Why It's Time to Rethink Security Warnings," *Risk and security of internet and systems (CRiSIS), 2012 7th International conference*, pp. 1–8, 2012.

[4] A. Vance, D. Eargle, J. L. Jenkins, C. B. Kirwan, and B. B. Anderson, "The fog of warnings: how non-essential notifications blur with security warnings," in *Fifteenth Symposium on Usable Privacy and Security (SOUPS 2019)*, 2019, pp. 407–420.

[5] S. Carpenter, F. Zhu, M. Zeng, and M. Shreeves, "Expert sources in warnings may reduce the extent of identity disclosure in cyber contexts," *International Journal of Human--Computer Interaction*, vol. 33, no. 3, pp. 215–228, 2017.

[6] M. S. Wogalter, "Communication-Human Information Processing(C-HIP)Model," in *Handbook of Warnings*, M. Wogalter, Ed. Mahwah,NJ, USA, 2006, pp. 51–62.

[7] B. Anderson, T. Vance, B. Kirwan, D. Eargle, and S. Howard, "Users aren't (necessarily) lazy: using NeuroIS to explain habituation to security warnings," *Thirty Fifth International Conference on Information Systems*, pp. 1–15, 2014.

[8] D. Akhawe and A. P. Felt, "Alice in warningland: a large-scale field study of browser security warning effectiveness," *Proceedings of the 22nd USENIX Security Symposium*, pp. 257–272, 2013.

[9] C. Bravo-Lillo, L. F. Cranor, J. Downs, and S. Komanduri, "Bridging the gap in computer security warnings: A mental model approach," *IEEE Security and Privacy*, vol. 9, no. 2, pp. 18–26, 2011, doi: 10.1109/MSP.2010.198.

[10] S. Dehaene, J. P. Changeux, L. Naccache, J. Sackur, and C. Sergent, "Conscious, preconscious, and subliminal processing: a testable taxonomy," *Trends in Cognitive Sciences*, vol. 10, no. 5, pp. 204–211, 2006, doi: 10.1016/j.tics.2006.03.007.

[11] J. Kihlstrom, "The Congnitive Unconscious," *Science (1979)*, vol. 237, pp. 1445–1452, 1987.

[12] F. Zhu, S. Carpenter, and M. Zeng, "Subliminal Warnings: Utilizing the High Bandwidth of Nonconscious Visual Perception," in *17th International Conference PERSUASIVE*, , Mar. 2022, pp. 255–271.

[13] R. M. Montoya, R. S. Horton, J. L. Vevea, M. Citkowicz, and E. A. Lauber, "A re-examination of the mere exposure effect: The influence of repeated exposure on recognition, familiarity, and liking.," *Psychological Bulletin*, vol. 143, no. 5, pp. 459–498, 2017, doi: 10.1037/bul0000085.

[14] E. Harrell and L. Langton, "Victims of identity theft, 2014," *U.S. Department of Justice*, no. December, p. 27, 2015.

[15] S. Spiekermann, J. Grossklags, and B. Berendt, "E-privacy in 2nd generation E-commerce: privacy preferences versus actual behavior," in *Proceedings of the 3rd ACM conference on Electronic Commerce*, 2001, pp. 38–47.

[16] V. C. Conzola and M. S. Wogalter, "A Communication – Human Information Processing (C – HIP) approach to warning effectiveness in the workplace," *Journal of Risk Research*, vol. 4, no. 4, pp. 309–322, 2001, doi: 10.1080/1366987011006271.

[17] M. Lehto and J. Miller, "Warning volume I: Fundamentals, design, and evaluation methodologies," *Ann Arbor MI: Fuller Technical Publications*, vol. I, no. Warning, 1986.

[18] M. R. Lehto, "A proposed conceptual model of human behavior and its implications for design of warnings.," *Percept Mot Skills*, vol. 73, pp. 595–611, 1991.

[19] C. Bravo-Lillo, L. F. Cranor, J. Downs, and S. Komanduri, "Bridging the gap in computer security warnings: A mental model approach," *IEEE Security and Privacy*, vol. 9, no. April, pp. 18–26, 2011, doi: 10.1109/MSP.2010.198.

[20] M. S. Wogalter, R. J. Sojourner, and J. W. Brelsford, "Comprehension and retention of safety pictorials," *Ergonomics*, vol. 40, no. 5, pp. 531–542, 1997.

[21] D. Holender, "Semantic activation without conscious identification in dichotic listening, parafoveal vision, and visual masking: A survey and appraisal," *Behavioral and brain Sciences*, vol. 9, no. 01, pp. 1–23, 1986.

[22] D. H. Nguyen, A. Kobsa, and G. R. Hayes, "An empirical investigation of concerns of everyday tracking and recording technologies," in *Proceedings of the 10th International*

Conference on Ubiquitous Computing, 2008, pp. 182–191. doi: 10.1145/1409635.1409661.

[23] B. Schneier, *Secrets and lies: digital security in a networked world.* John Wiley & Sons, 2011.

[24] P. Sumner, P.-C. Tsai, K. Yu, and P. Nachev, "Attentional modulation of sensorimotor processes in the absence of perceptual awareness.," *Proc Natl Acad Sci U S A*, vol. 103, no. 27, pp. 10520–10525, 2006, doi: 10.1073/pnas.0601974103.

[25] A. Amran, Z. F. Zaaba, and M. K. Mahinderjit Singh, "Habituation effects in computer security warning," *Information Security Journal: A Global Perspective*, vol. 27, no. 2, pp. 119–131, 2018.

[26] C. Bravo-lillo and et al., "Your attention please: Designing security-decision UIs to make genuine risks harder to ignore," in *SOUPS '13 Proceedings of the Ninth Symposium on Usable Privacy and Security*, 2013, pp. 1–18. doi: 10.1145/2501604.2501610.

[27] M. R. Lehto, "Human Factors Models," in *Handbook of Warnings*, M. S. Wogalter, Ed. Mahwah, NJ, USA: Lawrence Erlbaum Associates, 2006, pp. 63–88.

[28] A. P. Felt, R. W. Reeder, H. Almuhimedi, and S. Consolvo, "Experimenting at scale with google chrome's SSL warning," *Proceedings of the 32nd annual ACM conference on Human factors in computing systems - CHI '14*, pp. 2667–2670, 2014, doi: 10.1145/2556288.2557292.

[29] J. Sunshine, S. Egelman, H. Almuhimedi, N. Atri, and L. F. Cranor, "Crying wolf: An empirical study of SSL warning effectiveness," in *18th USENIX Security Symposium*, 2009, pp. 399–432. doi: 10.1016/S1353-4858(01)00916-3.

[30] A. P. Felt *et al.*, "Improving SSL warnings: Comprehension and adherence," in *Conference on Human Factors in Computing Systems - Proceedings*, Apr. 2015, vol. 2015-April, pp. 2893–2902. doi: 10.1145/2702123.2702442.

[31] D. Akhawe and A. P. Felt, "Alice in warningland: a large-scale field study of browser security warning effectiveness," in *Proceedings of the 22nd USENIX Security Symposium*, 2013, pp. 257–272.

[32] S. Egelman and S. Schechter, "The importance of being earnest [in security warnings]," in *International Conference on Financial Cryptography and Data Security*, 2013, pp. 52–59.

[33] F. Raja, K. Hawkey, S. Hsu, K.-L. Wang, and K. Beznosov, "A brick wall, a locked door, and a bandit: a physical security metaphor for firewall warnings," 2011. doi: http://doi.acm.org/10.1145/2078827.2078829.

[34] P. Domingues, L. Andrade, and M. Frade, "A Digital Forensic View of Windows 10 Notifications," *Forensic Sciences*, vol. 2, no. 1, pp. 88–106, Jan. 2022, doi: 10.3390/forensicsci2010007.

[35] M. Zeng, F. Zhu, and S. Carpenter, "Eye Gaze Based Dynamic Warnings," *9th International Conference on Advances in Computer-Human Interactions (ACHI)*, vol. i, no. c, pp. 204–211, 2016.

[36] E. K. Cressman, M. Y. Lam, I. M. Franks, J. T. Enns, and R. Chua, "Unconscious and out of control: Subliminal priming is insensitive to observer expectations," *Consciousness and Cognition*, vol. 22, no. 3, pp. 716–728, 2013, doi: 10.1016/j.concog.2013.04.011.

[37] L. Smarandescu and T. A. Shimp, "Drink coca-cola, eat popcorn, and choose powerade: testing the limits of subliminal persuasion," *Marketing Letters*, vol. 26, no. 4, pp. 715–726, 2015, doi: 10.1007/s11002-014-9294-1.

[38] R. Radel, P. Sarrazin, P. Legrain, and L. Gobancé, "Subliminal priming of motivational orientation in educational settings: Effect on academic performance moderated by mindfulness," *Journal of Research in Personality*, vol. 43, no. 4, pp. 695–698, 2009.

[39] E. J. Strahan, S. J. Spencer, and M. P. Zanna, "Subliminal priming and persuasion: Striking while the iron is hot," *Journal of Experimental Social Psychology*, vol. 38, no. 6, pp. 556–568, 2002, doi: 10.1016/S0022-1031(02)00502-4.

[40] P. M. Merikle and M. Daneman, "Psychological investigations of unconscious perception," *Journal of consciousness studies*, vol. 5, no. 1, pp. 5–18, 1998.

[41] S. Kouider and S. Dehaene, "Levels of processing during non-conscious perception: a critical review of visual masking.," *Philos Trans R Soc Lond B Biol Sci*, vol. 362, no. 1481, pp. 857–75, 2007, doi: 10.1098/rstb.2007.2093.

[42] H. F. Sperdin, L. Spierer, R. Becker, C. M. Michel, and T. Landis, "Submillisecond unmasked subliminal visual stimuli evoke electrical brain responses," *Human Brain Mapping*, vol. 36, no. 4, pp. 1470–1483, 2015, doi: 10.1002/hbm.22716.

[43] H. Reuss, A. Kiesel, W. Kunde, and P. Wühr, "A cue from the unconscious - masked symbols prompt: Spatial anticipation," *Frontiers in Psychology*, vol. 3, no. OCT, pp. 1–10, 2012, doi: 10.3389/fpsyg.2012.00397.

[44] F. Schlaghecken and M. Eimer, "Masked prime stimuli can bias 'free' choices between response alternatives.," *Psychon Bull Rev*, vol. 11, no. 3, pp. 463–468, 2004, doi: 10.3758/BF03196596.

[45] M. Rogers and K. H. Smith, "Public perceptions of subliminal advertising: Why practitioners shouldn't ignore this issue," *Journal of Advertising Research*, vol. 33, no. 2, pp. 10–19, 1993.

[46] S. Spiekermann, J. Grossklags, and B. Berendt, "E-privacy in 2nd Generation E-Commerce: Privacy Preferences versus actual Behavior," 2001.

[47] F. Zhu, S. Carpenter, and A. Kulkarni, "Understanding Identity Exposure in Pervasive Computing Environments," *Pervasive and Mobile Computing*, vol. 8, no. 5, pp. 777–794, 2012.

[48] J. R. Bettman, J. W. Payne, and R. Staelin, "Cognitive considerations in presenting risk information," *Learning about Risk–consumer and worker responses to hazard information*, pp. 13–41, 1987.

[49] M. Bar and I. Biederman, "Subliminal Visual Priming," *Psychological Science*, vol. 9, no. 6, pp. 464–468, 1998, doi: 10.1111/1467-9280.00086.

[50] R. M. Montoya, R. S. Horton, J. L. Vevea, and E. A. Lauber, "A Re-Examination of the Mere Exposure Effect : The Influence of Repeated Exposure on Recognition , Familiarity , and Liking," vol. 143, no. 5, pp. 459–498, 2017.

[51] M. S. Ackerman, L. F. Cranor, and J. Reagle, "Privacy in e-commerce: examining user scenarios and privacy preferences," in *Proceedings of the 1st ACM conference on Electronic commerce*, 1999, pp. 1–8.

Automated Visual Verification of Avionics Cockpit Displays

Muhammed Onur Güngör*†, Gökhan İnce†
*MGEO Test and Verification Directorate, ASELSAN Inc., Ankara, Turkey
mogungor@aselsan.com.tr
†Faculty of Computer and Informatics Engineering, Istanbul Technical University, İstanbul, Turkey
{mogungor, gokhan.ince}@itu.edu.tr

Abstract—**The purpose of the study is to design a system to automate the visual verification of avionics cockpit displays using digital cameras. The proposed system captures images from avionics cockpit display systems, and registers to the model of the cockpit display system, while being compliant with international standards, such as DO-178C. In this system, we included three visual verification tasks which are text verification, symbology verification, and color verification. We proposed to use Region Of Interest (ROI) generator, ground truth generator, camera calibration tool, image capture service, image registration service, comparison services, and test execution tool. As a consequence, visual verification test cases have been automated and executed without human intervention. We measured the accuracy of the system using F1 score while detecting text, colors, and objects. We also verified the effectiveness of the proposed system using System Usability Scale (SUS). Experiments show that this system is an effective method for using in automated visual verification.**

Index Terms—**Automated Test, Avionics HMI Test, Cockpit Display Systems Test**

I. Introduction

Failure of the avionics systems can be vital for the safe operation of aircraft, therefore avionics systems are designed with strict rules. One of the main regulations is European Aviation Safety Agency (EASA) Certification Specification (CS) CS-25. Various standards have been developed to comply with these regulations, such as DO-178C [1] and DO-254 [2]. Testing activities must be performed to comply with these standards. Some of the testing activities constitute the verification of the values in the cockpit display systems. Visual verification test cases are usually performed by manually comparing the values on the cockpit screen. For this reason, it is not only desirable to automate the test cases to eliminate human error, but also desirable to minimize the testing cost [3].

Nguyen et al. group testing frameworks in 4 different categories according to the test case development technique. They are script-based method, capture and replay, random-walk, and automated model-based method [4]. Dyachenko et al. state that it is possible to implement Human-Machine Interface (HMI) verification using computer processing methods, especially image and sound recognition algorithms. Their proposed architecture sets up the test environment and specifies the expected result. Test cases are executed to generate expected values on target screen. Actual values are recorded with a camera and microphone. The software takes the streams and compares them with expected values and generates a test result report [5].

Sartaj et al. provide a model-based technique for automating Cockpit Display Systems (CDS) testing. They proposed a Unified Model Language (UML) profile that is compatible with modern CDS design tools. The offered model is used to generate test cases automatically. They use state-of-the-art automated visual inspection techniques for evaluation on a simulator [6]. Sartaj et al. provide a tool for generating, executing, and evaluating test cases [7]. Tom et al. developed an automation system using GUI screenshots. They developed an editor to write visual scripts. User can select any image for a condition and also user can define an action for this condition [8].

In our study, a hybrid method, which is a mixture of script-based and capture and replay, is proposed. Test cases are not generated automatically as in automated model-based, but suggestions have been made for rapid development of test cases. Automated visual verification is referred in the Dyachenko et al. study, but details about the design are not given. There is no explanation and experimental results about finding ROI, generating expected values, and evaluating them. Unlike the Sartaj et al. approach, the outputs of the CDS design tools are not used to generate test cases automatically in this work. Instead, they are used to generate ground truth images for comparison within the scope of this study. The method we propose enables requirement-based testing instead of model-based testing. Sartaj et al. do not offer a solution for taking the image from target instead of a simulator. In our proposed system, taking the image from the target is discussed in detail.

The image on the CDS was captured with a digital camera and registered according to the given model of the CDS. The ROI on the image is determined after the screenshot is captured. These determined regions store information about the absolute position of the expected value in the coordinate plane. Test cases are developed using this information. There are four types of verification, which are text verification, foreground and background color verification, font size verification, and symbology verification. Optical Character Recognition (OCR) procedures are used to read the text in an ROI for text verification. The challenge is that the test developer should be able to supply the absolute position of the relevant word(s) for each test case in a simple and fast manner. Color classification is used for color verification. The difficulty is that due to anti-aliasing, the color of pixels on the edges of characters and objects will be lighter. Color calibration should also be done if the image was captured with a digital camera. Template matching is used for symbology verification. The generation of ground truth symbols is needed for comparison. The main challenge for symbology verification is producing the ground truth symbologies quickly and easily to use in a test case.

Taking into account all of the issues mentioned above, a systematic research should be conducted to accomplish automated visual verification in avionics systems. Architecture and used methods are detailed in Section II. Experimental results are given in Section III. Final words are given in Section IV.

II. Automated Visual Verification System

In this chapter information about proposed system for automated visual verification will be given. An automated visual verification architecture for pages of cockpit display systems is suggested.

A. Architecture

The automated visual verification system environment is shown in Fig. 1.

1) **PC:** PC is used for test execution, ground truth image generation, and ROI definition.
2) **Test Execution Tool:** It runs the test cases and controls the interface cards to create interface messages based on the demands in the test cases.
3) **Ground Truth Image Generator:** It generates ground truth images on a simulator or target hardware for each ROI.
4) **Ground Truth Image Database:** It stores the ground truth images to use in test cases as expected image.
5) **ROI Manager:** It is used to determine ROIs on the cockpit display screens.
6) **ROI Database:** It stores ROIs to use in test cases for defining the exact position of the expected image or text in the coordinate plane.
7) **Web Browser:** A simple web browser for initializing image registration service.
8) **Interface Cards:** Test execution tool uses interface cards to send necessary messages to the cockpit display system to drive screens. These interfaces can be MIL-STD-1553, Serial Port, CAN Bus, Ethernet, ARINC-429 etc.
9) **Comparator:** It processes the comparison request from the test execution tool (2). An image is requested from the image registration server and sent to the submodules according to the comparison type.
    a) **Text Comparison:** Optical Character Recognition (OCR) is used to process the raw image. The expected value is compared with the OCR text output.
    b) **Color Comparison:** The foreground or background color of the ROI in the captured image is compared with the expected color.
    c) **Object Comparison:** The captured symbol in the ROI is compared with the ground truth symbol.
10) **Image Registration:** The comparator accepts the images which have the same perspective to be able to compare them. The image registration module transforms the perspective of the captured images to the perspective of the ground truth image. It not only transforms perspective but also crops out of the screen. Image Registration uses calibration data to register the captured image.
11) **Calibration Tool:** The image registration data, also known as homography, is generated using the calibration tool. Homography is produced by analyzing at least three points on the reference and sensed images. These points and the matching of these points are prompted by the user.
12) **Screen Capture API:** It provides an application program interface to capture the image of the cockpit display system using a digital camera.
13) **Camera:** It is a Digital Single Lens Reflex (DSLR) camera whose AV, TV, and ISO values can be adjusted using its API.
14) **Cockpit Display System:** It is the target device which has the flight screens to be verified.

B. Screen Capturing

There are two ways to get screenshot of the cockpit display system. The first one is taking the screenshots directly through the screen buffer of the graphics card. Exporting this buffer at the software level is a destructive method while considering a real-time system. On the other hand, exporting this buffer at the hardware level is not time and cost efficient while considering different hardware architectures. It is possible to take a screenshot of the cockpit display system using a digital camera. An image equivalent to the image taken from the screen buffer of the graphic card can be captured by calibrating the position and color of the digital camera. Image registration and consequent image processing techniques allow getting the image from the same perspective. The idea of using image registration, which is a technique for matching two distinct images in image processing, as position calibration of the camera is one of the main contributions of this study.

One of the images in image registration is considered as a reference image, and the other is a sensed image that is used to register to the reference image [9]. Image registration performs 2-dimensional transformation on the sensed image with respect to reference image. This transformation operates on homogeneous coordinates and it is calculated using (1).

$$\tilde{x}_0 = \tilde{H}\ \tilde{x}, \tag{1}$$

where $\tilde{H}$ is an arbitrary 3x3 matrix used to calculate $\tilde{x}_0$ which is transformed image matrix and $\tilde{x}$ is the original image matrix.

In this study, it is aimed to find $\tilde{H}$ matrix. In order to calculate this matrix, the common features on the ref-

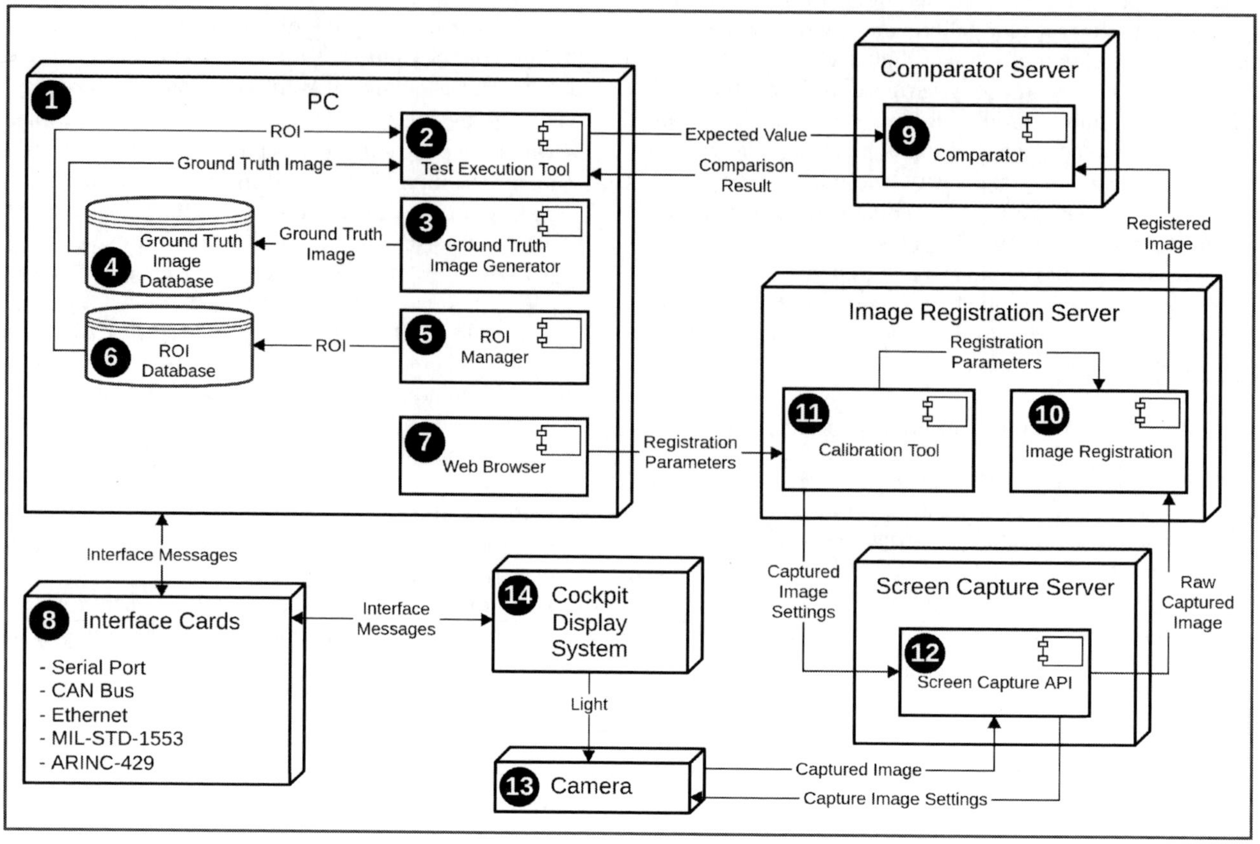

Fig. 1. Automated Visual Verification System

erence image (CAD models of the cockpit display system) and sensed image must be found and matched. Common features can be found automatically using feature detection algorithms [10], [11], [12]. Since these methods, which automatically find features, do not work in a deterministic way, manual determination of these points will be preferred while considering safety-critical systems.

C. Test Case Development and Execution

The data on the cockpit display system should be partitioned since verification activity involves a specific partition on the screen. Each of these partitions is called the ROI. It can be generated manually or automatically. The exported data from graphical modeling tools such as Presagis VAPS XT or Ansys SCADE can be used to create automatically. To create the ROIs manually, the existing pages in the cockpit display system are partitioned according to the software requirements using an ROI manager tool. Manual partitioning provides a more flexible structure and will eliminate the dependency on graphics modeling tools. The positions of the ROI are determined using at least three points. The verification type for an ROI, such as background color verification, text, font verification, etc. should be provided. A previously created ground truth is also provided if an object is to be verified.

Ground truth image is used as an expected image while comparing objects in the test cases. Generating ground truth images is a time-consuming and difficult task to run the entire system, giving all the required inputs and obtaining the expected value as a ground truth image. Instead of utilizing the Operational Flight Program (OFP), a cockpit display design template developed with VAPS XT or SCADE may easily be modified to obtain data using injected codes. In this way, ground truth values can be produced quickly.

ROI and expected value (a text, a color or ground truth image) are sent to the comparator module. The expected value and the actual value are compared by the comparator module.

D. Comparison Methods and Verification

Comparison is a complex task for the machines to automatically perform. It is a simple process for humans, but it is slow and error-prone. There are three types of comparisons which are text comparison, object (image) comparison, and color comparison. Flow diagram for comparison is shown in Fig. 2.

Text comparison is made by reading the ROI field using OCR techniques. ROI given in the test case is cropped from

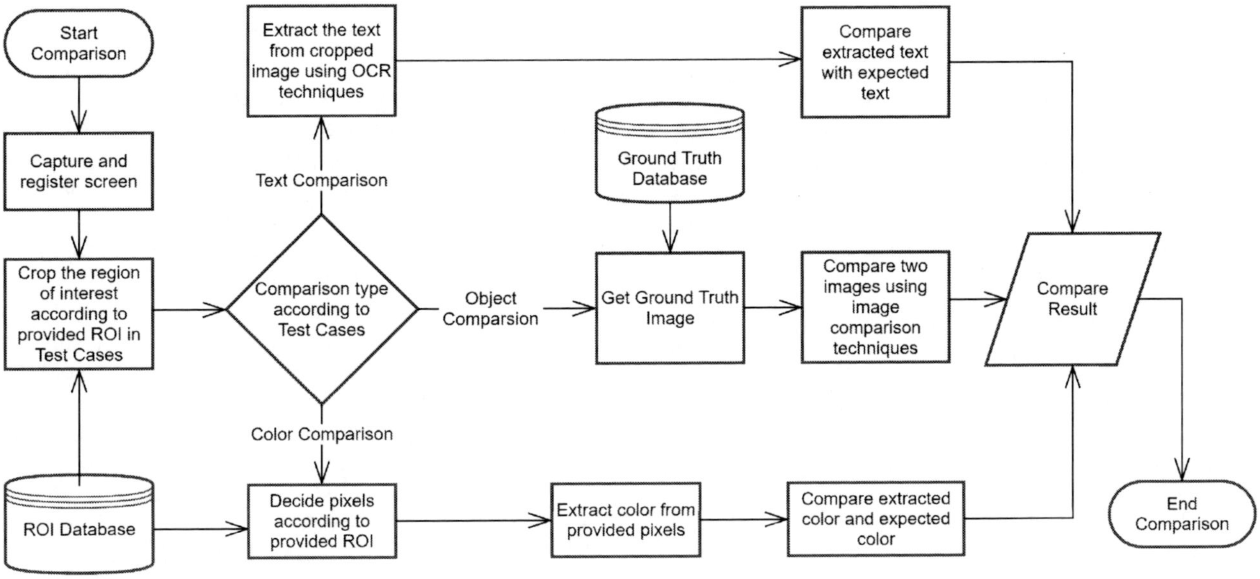

Fig. 2. Comparison Flow Diagram

the registered screenshot. This cropped image is given to the OCR framework. The text output from the OCR framework is compared with the expected value and the result is returned. State-of-the-art OCR techniques are used to extract text from an image to compare with expected text. Tesseract [13], which is also supported by Google, offers an advanced framework. Some parameters can be provided to show improved performance. These parameters are the number of lines, language, white list characters, etc.

Object in the ROI field is compared with ground truth image by using several image comparison techniques. The ROI given in the test case is first cropped from the registered screenshot. This cropped image and ground truth image are given to the image comparison framework. The output from the image comparison framework is returned. Template matching algorithm is used to compare symbologies.

Color comparison is needed when verifying the background or foreground color of the text or color of the object in the ROI. The ROI given in the test case is first cropped from the registered screenshot. The foreground and background pixels of a text must be identified if their colors are to be verified. The pixels of the object must be identified if the color of an object is to be verified. These pixels are given to the color comparison framework. The output from the color comparison framework is returned. Support Vector Machine (SVM) is used for color classification. There are 16 colors to identify in the scope of this study. The fixed-size rectangles formed with these colors are positioned randomly on the screen to train the SVM model. These rectangles are partitioned and labeled. In this way, 786432 pixels and the label of these pixels are determined. Model accuracy on test set is found to be 1.0.

III. Experiments and Results

In this chapter information about the experiments and their results will be given. Experiments were carried out for assessing the performance and usability of the system. How successfully text recognition, color recognition and object comparison can be made has been demonstrated by $F1$ scores with the performance tests. Effectiveness and satisfaction of the designed system are measured with System Usability Scale (SUS) [14].

A. Experiments

In order to measure the performance of the proposed system, two different test datasets are prepared using Primary Flight Display (PFD) page of the Cockpit Display System by simulating flight. Dataset 1 (DS1) is prepared for verification of text, text size, and foreground and background color of the text and Dataset 2 (DS2) is prepared for symbology verification. DS1 consists of 208 ROIs which have text with different foreground and background colors and text sizes. DS2 is a data set consisting of 30 images belonging to 6 different objects in CDS. It consists of 5 images of each object taken with different AV, TV, and ISO configuration. The configuration list is given Table I.

TABLE I
Image Configuration

Configuration	AV	TV	ISO
Config1	3.5	30	100
Config2	3.5	30	200
Config3	3.5	50	200
Config4	4.0	25	100
Config5	4.5	25	100

B. Results on the Recognition Performance

The texts of 200 out of 208 ROIs were correctly recognized and the text sizes of 190 out of 208 ROIs were correctly recognized as a result of the experiment using DS1. The table of confusion obtained for the foreground and background color recognition as a result of the experiment using DS1 is given in Table II and Table III. Foreground color recognition accuracy is 0.40865. Although the color recognition accuracy of the SVM model is 1.0, it does not have sufficient $F1$ score because of anti-aliasing algorithm on the text. Studies in this area are still ongoing. Background color recognition accuracy is 0.81731. The results are better than foreground color recognition since the background color has no anti-aliasing effect. $F1$ score of all colors could not be calculated because not all colors are used in the data set, they are shown in the table as N/A.

TABLE II
FOREGROUND COLOR RECOGNITION

Color	TP	TN	FP	FN	F_1
Amber	0	177	0	31	0
Black	0	199	2	9	0
Brown	0	170	38	0	0
Cloud	0	146	62	0	0
Cyan	0	206	0	2	0
Gray	0	177	2	31	0
Green	0	193	0	15	0
Light Blue	0	207	1	0	0
Magenta	0	207	0	1	0
Red	2	169	4	33	0.10
White	83	106	18	1	0.90

TABLE III
BACKGROUND COLOR RECOGNITION

Color	TP	TN	FP	FN	F_1
Amber	5	208	0	0	1
Black	45	126	7	30	0.71
Dark Gray	116	54	30	8	0.80
Red	2	206	0	0	1
White	2	206	0	0	1

The normalized cross-correlation for the object recognition as a result of the experiment using DS2 is given in Table IV. C_n stands for calculated normalized cross-correlation between ground truth image and captured image for image configuration $\mathrm{Config_n}$ in the table.

TABLE IV
OBJECT RECOGNITION

Object	C_1	C_2	C_3	C_4	C_5
Plane	0.86	0.86	0.93	0.84	0.84
Arrow	0.94	0.93	0.93	0.94	0.94
Stop	0.98	0.98	0.98	0.98	0.98
Compass	0.96	0.95	0.96	0.96	0.96
Plane	0.96	0.96	0.96	0.96	0.96
Target	0.97	0.92	0.96	0.97	0.96

C. Results on the Usability Performance

The usability of the system was measured with the SUS questions directed to 13 testers at different experience levels. The average age of the participants was 29.69±3.62. 46.15 percent of the participants were female and 53.85 percent were male. Participants were comprised of those with bachelor's degree in Computer Engineering, bachelor's degree in Electrical and Electronics, and bachelor's in Statistics, and their percentages were 38.46, 46.15, and 15.39, respectively. The average work experience of the participants was 6.77±4.04 years. The average test experience of the participants was 5.85±3.67 years. All participants used at least one test tool for one year in their working life.

First of all, a 1-hour training on how the system and tools work was given to the participants. The participants were given 3 different types of tasks to perform using all the test tools in the system. These tasks are; 1) Camera Calibration, 2) ROI Identification and Ground Truth Generation, and 3) Developing and Executing a Test Case with Defined ROIs and Ground Truths. After each task, 3 questions were asked about the difficulty of the task, the adequacy of time and the adequacy of the technical support they received. The averages of the answers for each task are given in Fig. 3.

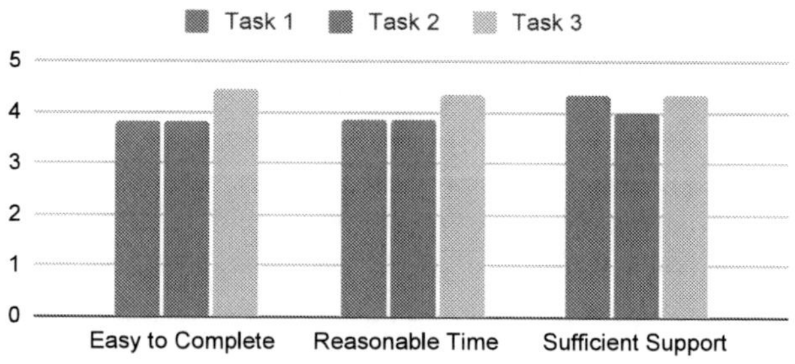

Fig. 3. The Average of the Answers for Tasks

At the end of these tasks, the SUS questionnaire was applied to the participants. The SUS score of our proposed system is 71.92. A SUS score of 70 and above is considered acceptable for the usability of a designed system [14]. Participants thought that it is easy to develop tests with the proposed system but they thought that the preparations made before test case development are more difficult.

IV. CONCLUSION

It is aimed to perform automated visual verification for cockpit display systems on images captured with a professional camera within the scope of this study. The captured images have been transformed to the same perspective as the cockpit screen using the image registration technique. In this way, it is ensured that the position of each ROI is fixed regardless of the perspective of the captured image. The cockpit screen has been successfully partitioned into regions and labeled with the developed ROI Manager tool. ROIs, generated using ROI Manager, were used in the Test

Case Development tool for defining the ROI. Ground Truth Generator tool is used to generate ground truth image for an ROI that needs symbology verification. Text and color values are given directly through the Test Case Development Tool when text or color verification will be performed. State-of-the-art OCR techniques, Tesseract, are used for text recognition. The text verification was performed flawlessly. A simple SVM model was created for color recognition by training 786432 pixels produced within the scope of this study. Template matching was used for object recognition.

In the future, color recognition, especially text foreground color recognition, should be improved with various image processing techniques. The SUS score can be increased by developing more user-friendly methods for camera calibration and ROI creation.

REFERENCES

[1] *RTCA DO-178C, Software Considerations in Airborne Systems and Equipment Certification.* RTCA Incorporated, 2011.

[2] *RTCA DO-254 Design Assurance Guidance for Airborne Electronic Hardware.* RTCA Incorporated, 2000.

[3] E. Dustin, T. Garrett, and B. Gauf, *Implementing automated software testing: How to save time and lower costs while raising quality.* Pearson Education, 2009.

[4] B. N. Nguyen, B. Robbins, I. Banerjee, and A. Memon, "Guitar: an innovative tool for automated testing of gui-driven software," *Automated software engineering*, vol. 21, no. 1, pp. 65–105, 2014.

[5] S. Dyachenko, D. Ilyashenko, and E. Neretin, "Overview of automation tools for avionics verification," in *Journal of Physics: Conference Series*, vol. 1958, no. 1. IOP Publishing, 2021, p. 012012.

[6] H. Sartaj, M. Z. Iqbal, and M. U. Khan, "Testing cockpit display systems of aircraft using a model-based approach," *Software and Systems Modeling*, pp. 1–26, 2021.

[7] ——, "Cdst: A toolkit for testing cockpit display systems of avionics," *arXiv preprint arXiv:2001.07869*, 2020.

[8] T. Yeh, T.-H. Chang, and R. C. Miller, "Sikuli: using gui screenshots for search and automation," in *Proceedings of the 22nd annual ACM symposium on User interface software and technology*, 2009, pp. 183–192.

[9] S. S. Bisht, B. Gupta, and P. Rahi, "Image registration concept and techniques: a review," *J Eng Res App*, vol. 4, pp. 30–5, 2014.

[10] D. G. Lowe, "Object recognition from local scale-invariant features," in *Proceedings of the seventh IEEE international conference on computer vision*, vol. 2. Ieee, 1999, pp. 1150–1157.

[11] H. Bay, T. Tuytelaars, and L. Van Gool, "Surf: Speeded up robust features," in *European conference on computer vision.* Springer, 2006, pp. 404–417.

[12] E. Rublee, V. Rabaud, K. Konolige, and G. Bradski, "Orb: An efficient alternative to sift or surf," in *2011 International conference on computer vision.* Ieee, 2011, pp. 2564–2571.

[13] R. W. Smith, "An overview of the tesseract ocr engine," in *Ninth international conference on document analysis and recognition (ICDAR 2007)*, vol. 2. IEEE, 2007, pp. 629–633.

[14] J. Brooke, "Sus: a retrospective," *Journal of usability studies*, vol. 8, no. 2, pp. 29–40, 2013.

PoseToCode: Exploring Design Considerations toward a Usable Block-Based Programming and Embodied Learning System

Nisha Chatwani*
Viterbi School of Engineering
Dept. of Computer Science
University of Southern California
Los Angeles, USA
email: nchatwan@usc.edu

Chloe Kuo*
Viterbi School of Engineering
Dept. of Computer Science
University of Southern California
Los Angeles, USA
email: cmkuo@usc.edu

Thomas R. Groechel*
Viterbi School of Engineering
Dept. of Computer Science
University of Southern California
Los Angeles, USA
email: groechel@usc.edu

Maja J Matarić
Viterbi School of Engineering
Dept. of Computer Science
University of Southern California
Los Angeles, USA
email: mataric@usc.edu

***Abstract*—As interest and need for computer science skills continue to grow, educators have been teaching block-based programming languages to young students. Such languages are intuitive and widely available, but have not as yet explored** *embodied (i.e., kinesthetic)* **learning techniques. To explore the use of embodied learning for teaching programming, we created PoseToCode (P2C), a web-based embodied learning programming activity in which students perform physical poses with their arms to create code blocks that control an on-screen robot. We first conducted a pilot study to identify key P2C design considerations. We used those insights to finalize P2C and then deployed it in a local 5th grade class (*n*=24, 10 students completed all surveys) to measure P2C usability, compare it to a seated block-based programming activity (Code.org), identify new design considerations, and explore if P2C increased student curiosity in learning coding. Our results support P2C as a usable system design, show no difference in student curiosity when compared to a traditional block-based programming language, and identify potential improvements to our design considerations for future activities that integrate embodied learning with block-based programming. This work aims to inform the process of creating usable and effective systems for block-based programming and embodied learning activities.**

Keywords*—*embodied learning; block-based programming; education; human-computer interaction

I. Introduction

Computer programming is a challenging subject to learn; educators have been exploring ways to make it more accessible to students [1]. With computer programming skills (i.e., coding skills) becoming increasingly more desirable for students interested in pursuing science, technology, engineering, and math (STEM), block-based coding activities are often used to introduce basic coding concepts through a simple interface. Block-based programming exercises have become widespread in recent years as programming is being taught to even younger students [2]. *Block-based programming* is the use of dragging and dropping code blocks that snap together in order to make a program or series of instructions in a natural language [3]. Code blocks can have slots allowing for other blocks to be inserted, and code blocks can also represent higher level coding structures, such as loops, conditional statements, and functions. Past research has compared block-programming to text-programming activities in classrooms [4] and identified properties of block-based coding activities that contribute to the activity's convenience [5], such as the plug-and-play functionality and the ability to clearly see what each code block accomplishes, making the learning activity more intuitive than text-based programming activities.

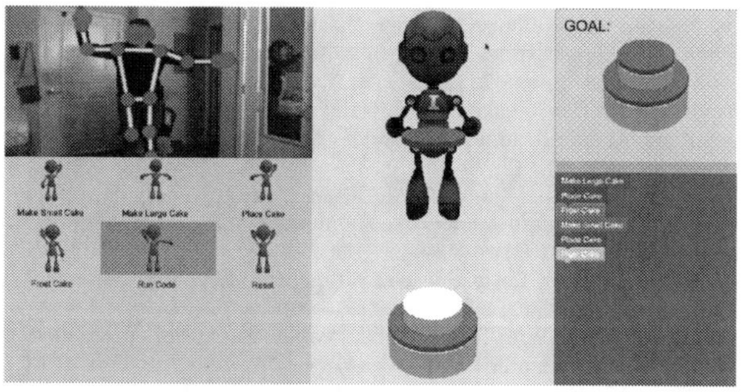

Figure 1: PoseToCode Exercise 3: Build a Cake. The user (top left) must physically perform poses (bottom left) to create a sequence of codeblocks (bottom right), which, when executed, instruct the virtual robot (middle) to construct a cake (top right). The robot is displayed near the top of the screen because the following exercise involves programming objects underneath it.

Block-based programming languages are focused on mentalistic (i.e., non-kinesthetic) learning. As the COVID-19 pandemic has demonstrated, mentalistic learning can become difficult and tiresome for many students [6]. *Embodied learning*, on the other hand, integrates the body with the mind through movement based-learning. Research in embodied learning has shown the general approach to have a positive effect on children's learning outcomes [7]. Inspired by this literature, we aimed to develop a block-based programming environment that supports embodied learning, since, to the best of our knowledge, no such kinesthetic block-based programming environment exists.

To address this gap, we created PoseToCode (P2C), which combines embodied learning with block-based programming to create a usable system with the end goal of increasing student curiosity and understanding of programming. P2C (Figure 1) is an embodied learning block-based coding activity where students perform poses to create code blocks that guide a virtual robot through a series of exercises. We created a set of design considerations for P2C discovered in informal pilot testing. To validate P2C design, we deployed it in a local 5th grade classroom of 24 students. We measured usability and performed a comparison to a traditional block-based programming activity, and analyzed the study results to develop future design considerations for making P2C more intuitive and easier to use. The results of the study support P2C as a usable design and identify improvements for future coding languages that integrate embodied learning and block-based programming. We have made P2C open-source and have posted a publicly accessible repository [8] and demonstration [9].

II. Background

This research builds on past work relating to block-based programming and embodied (i.e., kinesthetic) learning.

A. Block-Based Programming

Block-based programming exercises have become very popular because coding blocks are usually easier to interpret than text-based code [5]. With interest in STEM education dropping off in middle and high school [10], block-based programming provides a way to introduce coding to students at a young age in order to nurture curiosity about computer science. Block-based programming exercises allow novice programmers to develop quickly because they use *component-based programming*, wherein code instructions are partitioned into distinct functionalities [11]. This approach promotes reusability of software components, as well as flexibility in replacing components with code that has the same functionality [12], making it easier for students without extensive programming experience to put components together and build more complex programs.

The most popular block programming environments like Scratch [13] (Figure 2) and Code.org [14] provide users with the opportunity to explore different parts of programming such as loops and conditional statements, allowing users to make games and create artwork with ease [5]. The plug-and-play nature of block-based programming makes it more appealing to students compared to text-based programming.

Recent work has compared student perceptions of block-based programming and traditional programming. A 5-week study in a high school computer science class revealed that the students using a block-based coding environment retained more programming knowledge and showed greater interest in

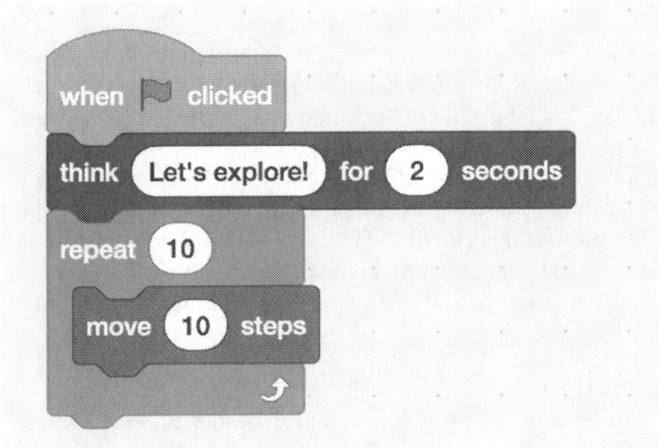

Figure 2: Scratch: A popular block-based programming environment that allows users to program virtual characters to execute sequences of actions [13].

learning coding than the students using a text-based programming environment [4]. Studies have also been conducted to explore what students find beneficial and effective in block-based programming environments [5]. The results showed that students recognized the individual block colors, natural language block labels, and drag-and-drop functionality of block programming environments made them visually more clear [5]. Our work aims to utilize these known positive aspects of block-based programming and integrate them with embodied learning.

B. Embodied Learning

Embodied learning has been recognized as an alternative to traditional mentalistic (i.e., non-kinesthetic) learning [7]. Embodied learning (i.e., kinesthetic learning) is the set of "pedagogical approaches that focus on the non-mental factors involved in learning, and that signal the importance of the body and feelings [15]."

Embodied learning has been shown to promote engagement by increasing student curiosity about topics they are learning. Past work has explored teaching methods that promote engagement through embodied learning in the classroom [16]. A study on gesture-based learning used a Microsoft Kinect sensor and application to create an interactive learning environment in which students moved their body to learn about the solar system [17]. The study results showed that gesture-based learning resulted in students wanting to learn more, and they felt more engaged in the learning process. The positive outcomes of gesture-based learning–increased student engagement and curiosity about the topic–inspired our work.

Embodied learning has also been shown to be beneficial in improving youth cognition and academic performance. A study conducted in elementary school classrooms used motion-based educational games to implement embodied learning, and demonstrated positive impacts on the students' cognitive skills, including their short-term memory, and their linguistic academic performance [16].

Given its potential, embodied learning has been explored in computer science education. One study examined the effects of teaching middle and high school students introductory programming concepts through a gesture-based interface. While the results were not significant, the results validated the promise of engaging students in programming through embodied learning activities [18]. Our work further expands on the potential benefits of embodied learning in early computer science education since the act of programming is kinesthetic in P2C.

III. PoseToCode Design

This section outlines the technical design of PoseToCode and pilot study insights leading to design considerations.

A. *Technical Design*

PoseToCode (P2C) enables users to create and execute code by posing with their body. The P2C interface (Figure 3) has the user's **video feed (A)** in the top left corner where the Mediapipe pose detection library [19] draws lines showing landmarks on the user's body. Directly below the video feed, a grid shows a set of **progress bars (B)**, with images depicting the virtual robot performing a pose; each pose image is labelled to indicate what code block it will create. The **virtual robot (C)** is in the middle of the screen, and in the top right corner, there is an image of the **goal state (D)** indicating what the code blocks should produce to complete the exercise. Lastly, the Blockly workspace with the **code blocks (E)** created so far is on the right of the visual interface.

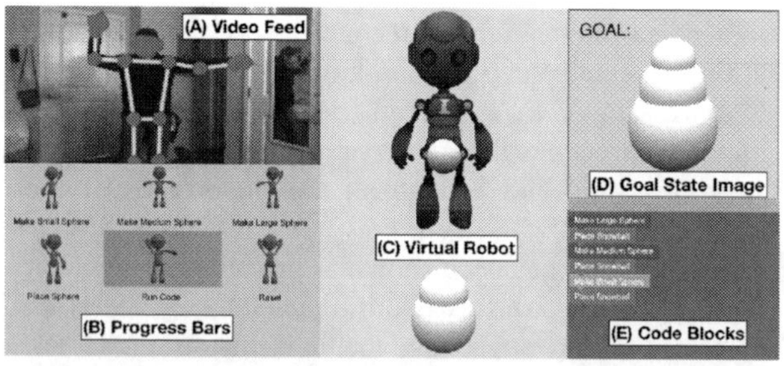

Figure 3: PoseToCode Exercise (Level 2): Student (top left) posing to create code blocks (bottom right) that guide the virtual robot to build a snowman. A) Flipped video feed with the MediaPipe detected pose drawn. B) Grid of pose images and progress bars for each pose. C) Virtual robot that performs instructions from code blocks. D) Goal state image. E) Blockly workspace with crated code blocks.

In P2C, the user's poses are recognized with Google Mediapipe pose detection software [19] executing at 60Hz. At time t, the pose key points are run through a deep neural network to map each arm to $\{$HIGH, MED, LOW, NONE$\}$. Based on the arm mappings, the corresponding pose progress bar (e.g., $\{$Left: HIGH, Right: MED$\}$ $\rightarrow$ "Run Code") fills at a rate of $1.2 * \Delta(t, t-1)$ while all other progress bars decay at the rate of $0.8 * \Delta(t, t-1)$. When the user holds a pose for 4 seconds, a custom Blockly [20] code block that corresponds to that pose is created. Code blocks are instructions that control a virtual robot on the screen; they can be created, erased, and executed. If the user's executing code reaches the goal state, they are moved to the next exercise. Alternatively, if the code fails to reach the goal state, the user must continue attempting the same challenge until they succeed or their time spent on the activity reaches the 10-minute limit. We chose that time limit based on pilot testing the activity and ensuring that it fit into the available classroom time.

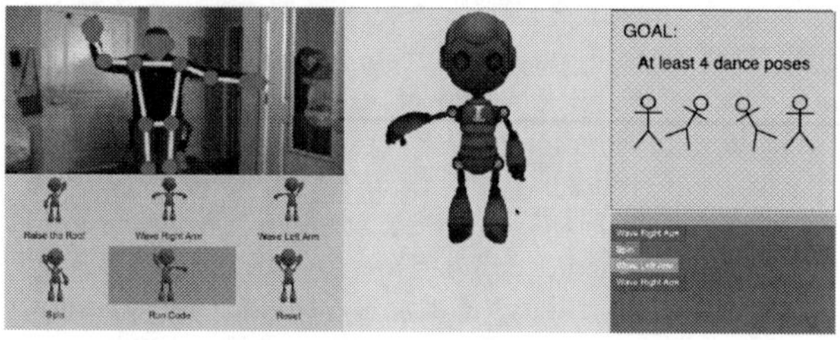

Figure 4: PoseToCode Exercise 1: Choreographing a dance routine for the virtual robot

A full P2C activity is composed of a series of three challenges for the user to complete within 10 minutes. The process consists of creating code blocks by posing and then executing all of the created code blocks. To complete the first challenge (Figure 4), the user must instruct the virtual robot to perform a dance routine of four or more dance moves. To complete the second challenge (Figure 3), the user must instruct the robot to build a snowman. To complete the third challenge (Figure 1), the user must instruct the robot to construct a frosted three-tiered cake. After all three challenges are completed, the user moves on to a freeplay mode challenge until the time limit is reached.

B. *Pilot Study Insights About Design Considerations*

We performed an informal pilot test of P2C with two engineering students at our university, using the snowman building exercise. We gained the following insights about P2C design considerations:

- *Accessibility across low-end computers*: Schools use a variety of laptops with a wide range of processing power and operating systems. Therefore, we created PoseToCode to be operating-system agnostic, executing via the web at 60Hz on the currently most popular Chromebook with a webcam.
- *Accessibility at a distance*: Multiple interface elements are needed to accommodate students who stood away from the computer while completing the programming exercises.
  - *Visibility*: Code blocks must have clear visibility, requiring them to be large, and therefore also enforcing having fewer on-screen components.
  - *Webcam as the only input source*: We piloted different interfaces (e.g., space bar pressing) but participants did not wish to step to and away from the computer, preferring to only use their body pose as input.

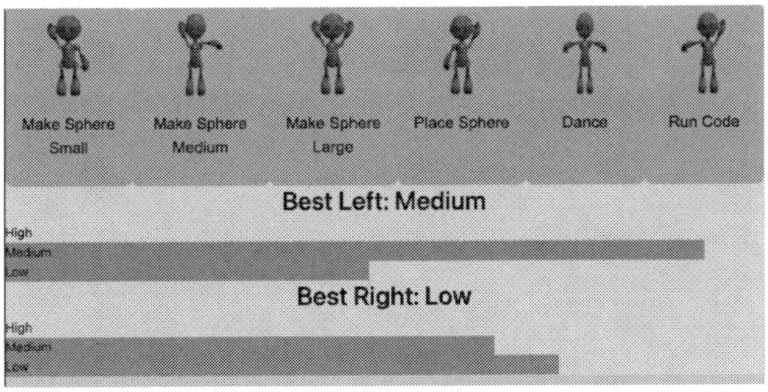

(a) Original pose key with individual bars for each arm.

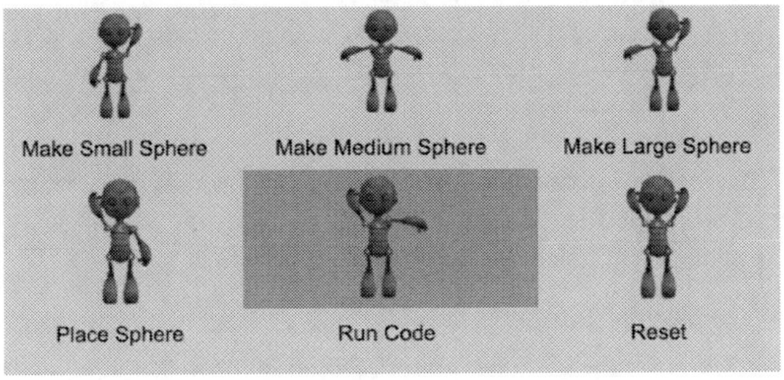

(b) Updated pose key where pose bars fill up directly.

Figure 5: Original (a) and updated (b) pose key designs. The original design showed each individual arm state and a pose map. Participants found this difficult to map the arm states to each pose. The updated design directly filled up each respective pose.

- *Real time input and feedback*: The webcam continually collects input from the user at 60Hz, resulting in the following considerations:
  - *Direct pose key* The original pose key (Figure 5a) consisted of left and right arm states ({HIGH,MED,LOW,NONE}) with only the accumulated states shown to the user, not the state of the best current pose. When the progress bar corresponding to the state from each arm reached 100% completion, the mapped pose produced the corresponding code block. Many pilot users cited this as complicated as they needed to read the arm states and then the respective texted-based pose map. To address this, we developed an updated direct pose key (Figure 5b) that combines the state of the arms into one pose state that corresponds directly to a progress bar.
  - *Reactive and persistent pose bars*: To increase reactivity, the best pose progress bar at time t increases at the rate of $1.2 * \Delta(t, t-1)\%$ while all other bars decay at the rate of $0.8 * \Delta(t, t-1)\%$. The slower decay rate (0.8) compared to the growth rate (1.2) allows for a semi-persistent pose meter, because the progress bars grow faster than they shrink. For example, when a user is doing run code pose, if their left arm goes out of frame, the run code meter decays more slowly than it grows. Thus when the user brings their arm back into the frame, the progress of the run code pose is easily recovered.
  - *Both arms down not used as input*: Users need to take time to think about their input. The most common pose while thinking was leaving both arms at their sides, leading to a {L=LOW, R=LOW} classification.

IV. Methods

We used the insights from the pilot study to design the following full user study.

A. Hypotheses

Hypothesis 1 (H1): *Users will evaluate PoseToCode to be a usable system.*

B. Procedure

A single-session within-subject study was conducted virtually over Zoom with a local 5th grade class in the context of a K-12 STEM outreach event. The study was approved by the University's Institutional Review Board (IRB #UP-20-01171).

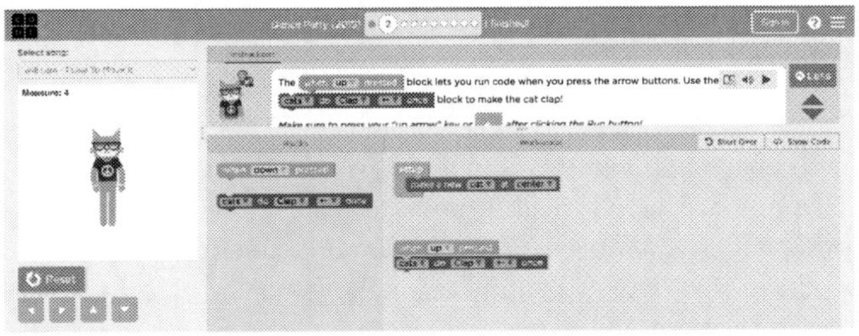

Figure 6: Code.org: Dance Party 2019 block programming activity that aims to teach basic coding concepts by guiding users to code a dance routine for a virtual character [14].

The student participants were randomly assigned to one of two conditions: 1) PoseToCode programming activity first; and 2) Code.org [14] Dance Party 2019 activity (Figure 6) first, a drag-and-drop block programming exercise giving students instructions to create a dance routine for a virtual character. We chose Code.org's Dance Party 2019 Activity because, similarly to PoseToCode, it teaches sequential code logic, and code blocks are used as instructions for a virtual character. Each student participant used a Chromebook to complete the activities.

Student participants first completed a demographic survey. They then engaged in their first coding activity for up to 10 minutes, followed by a post-activity survey. The student participants then moved to their second activity, followed by a second post-activity survey. Finally, the student participants were given a final survey comparing the two activities. The student participants were allowed to end an activity early at any point, in which case they were automatically directed to the next step in the study procedure. A diagram of the study procedure is shown in Figure 7.

This study was conducted virtually, given the COVID-19 pandemic. The virtual format of the study constrained the ability to provide clarifications and assistance to the student participants to only the Zoom chat function, where the students

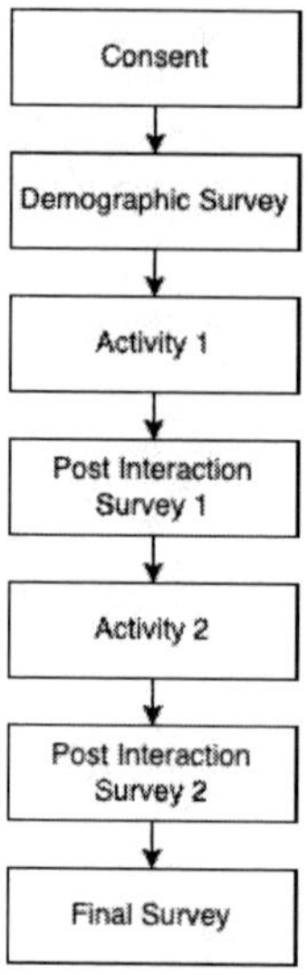

Figure 7: Diagram of the study procedure: pre-study survey, two coding activities, post-activity surveys after each activity, and an activity preference survey.

asked questions via this function. A single teacher in the classroom had to physically move to each individual student participant to answer their questions. Conducting the study in person has the potential to make student participants' experience more enjoyable.

C. Participants

A local Los Angeles 5th grade class of 24 students (7 male, 16 female) was recruited. All student participants were volunteers and were given no form of compensation. Prior to the study, formal consent was obtained from each students' legal guardian and child assent was obtained from each student participant. A total of 10 participants (5 male, 5 female) completed all surveys and both programming activities. This paper reports on the data and analyses from those 10 participants. We recognize this could lead to survivorship bias, but this was chosen to reduce possible ordering effects and to use all pairwise data.

In the pre-survey, we asked student participants what programming education platforms, if any, they had used in the past. All 10 indicated that they had previous technical experience with Scratch and two indicated that they also had past experience with Code.org. Additionally, we asked student participants to indicate their level of agreement with the statement "I want to learn more about computer programming." Of the 10 participants, 5 strongly agreed with the statement, and the other 5 agreed with the statement.

D. Data Collection

The pre-study surveys collected data on the students' prior exposure to programming. The post-activity surveys obtained system usability scores (SUS) [21], aiming to assess the perceived activity difficulty for PoseToCode and Code.org, and to capture the student participants' attitudes towards programming after each activity. The final post-study survey obtained each student's preferred activity between PoseToCode and Code.org, as well as qualitative data via a write-in form on why they preferred one activity over the other.

P2C behavioral data were automatically collected in order to 1) find behavioral data correlations for usability; and 2) create a dataset to compare future iterations of P2C to. As the student participants performed the PoseToCode activity, behavioral data were collected consisting of the time each student took to complete the activity, the number of exercises each student successfully completed within the time limit, and the number of code blocks created throughout the activity.

V. Results

This work evaluates the usability of P2C through participant surveys outlined in Section IV-D. Participant interviews were also analyzed for details about their experience.

A. Quantitative Results

To explore design considerations about PoseToCode, we adapted the System Usability Scale (SUS) [21] questionnaire for young students in order to compare usability compared to the Code.org activity. PoseToCode yielded a median SUS score of 63.75, slightly below the SUS average of 68, and Code.org yielded a median of 75, above average. A SUS score between 68 and 89 indicates that the system has "good" or above average usability, and PoseToCode's SUS score is within the 35-40th percentile [22]. The statistical power of the SUS scores generated are low since there are only 10 responses. Thus, this supports hypothesis 1 but leaves room for improvement. Figure 8 shows the difference in SUS scores between Code.org and P2C. Mann-Whitney tests indicated that PoseToCode (*Mdn* = 4) is more difficult than Code.org (*Mdn* = 5) with conditions (U = 20, p = .020).

A Pearson's r correlation indicated no significant relationship between total time spent on the PoseToCode activity and SUS score (rs(10) = -0.367). Similarly, Pearson's r correlation

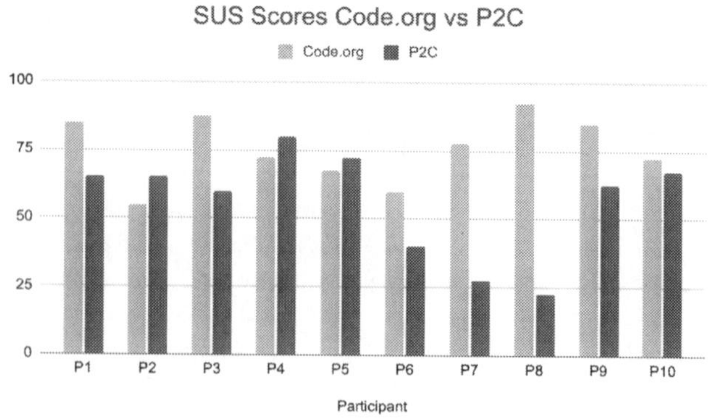

Figure 8: Bar graph comparing SUS scores for Code.org and P2C for all 10 student participants (Ok = 25-59, Good = 60-89, Excellent = 90-100 [22]).

did not yield statistical significance between the number of code blocks created by a student participant during the PoseToCode activity and SUS score (rs(10) = -0.252). Both post-activity surveys asked participants how much they agree with the statement "I want to learn more about computer programming." Mann-Whitney tests revealed an insignificant difference between the responses for PoseToCode (*Mdn* = 4 (Agree)) and Code.org (*Mdn* = 5 (Strongly Agree)) conditions ($U = 41$, $p = .480$).

B. Qualitative Results

The qualitative results from the post-study survey showed that 5 of 10 student participants preferred PoseToCode over Code.org. For the participants who started with PoseToCode, 4 of 5 preferred PoseToCode, and for the participants who started with Code.org, 4 out of 5 preferred Code.org. Two themes emerged from analyzing the free responses, as follows.

1) PoseToCode is more active than than Code.org: Participants who preferred PoseToCode found PoseToCode to be a more active and engaging activity than Code.org. Three of five participants who preferred PoseToCode over Code.org used the word *fun* to describe PoseToCode in their reasoning for choosing their preference. Only one student out of five who preferred the Code.org activity over PoseToCode described Code.org as *fun.* P3 indicated that they preferred PoseToCode because they *get to be active and move around,* and similarly, another participant noted that with PoseToCode, *you do more activity and more exercise* than Code.org.

2) Code.org is easier to use: Student participants who preferred Code.org found Code.org easier to use than PoseToCode because it had fewer software bugs when compared to PoseToCode. For example, P1 wrote about Code.org, *It's much more easy to use. (I like coding this way)* while P2 wrote, *in Code.org it's simple and fun and it's a good way to pass the time but PoseToCode is super frustrating and got me annoyed because of glitched like when it highlights your screen green and then kicks you out.* Three participants wrote in the final survey that PoseToCode was *frustrating* because it *glitched* often, making Code.org more desirable. Additionally, two participants wrote that Code.org gave *more instruction* than PoseToCode and provided more guidance on how to be successful in the activity.

VI. Discussion

This work explored design considerations and validated the usability of PoseToCode (P2C), an embodied learning block-based programming language. Half of the 5th grade student participants who completed all of the surveys preferred P2C over Code.org but this may be linked to an ordering effect. Students who preferred P2C referred to it as being more *fun* and *engaging* while those who preferred Code.org found it easier to use and *less buggy.* While some students reported a *buggy* P2C, we still see moderate to high usability scores of many of the students (Figure 8). We believe this indicates the high potential of P2C as an engaging activity with straightforward room for technical improvement.

We observed some student participants helping one another with PoseToCode. This is worth exploring toward developing collaborative programming activities. The trend of student participants who preferred PoseToCode stating that it was more engaging and active than Code.org indicates a positive feature about PoseToCode and the way its embodied learning focus distinguishes it from standard mentalistic programming activities like Code.org. On the other hand, a potential reason why more participants preferred Code.org is that students are generally more familiar with Code.org's teaching style of programming, therefore making it more intuitive and easier to use than PoseToCode.

A. Limitations and Future Work

The most cited issues during the study were the technical glitches that occurred as students interacted with PoseToCode. One participant described being "kicked out" of the activity after performing the run code pose stopped recognizing their poses from their video feed. A set of unit tests and integration tests need to be designed to interact with the system. Another flawed design consideration noted by a student was that the PoseToCode instructions were unclear. This problem should be addressed with a video tutorial before the main activity that shows students how to create code blocks, execute the code, reset the code, and indicate that they have completed a task.

Some students stayed seated during PoseToCode and some performed the activity while standing. Because PoseToCode was designed to be a standing activity, those who stayed seated may not have been able to have the same range of motion and movement experience as those who interacted while standing, as intended. Study instructions should make it clear that the interaction should be done while standing.

The surveys we used were potentially too long and tedious for the student participants; while 24 students participated in the exercises, only 10 completed all the surveys and are included in the analysis. A future study should take the student age into account when selecting the survey tools. Additionally, when data are collected in person, individual interviews with students could yield additional insights not easily gathered via Zoom.

VII. Conclusion

This work explored introducing embodied learning capabilities into block-based programming toward encouraging student curiosity for coding. We explored how to design a usable system. Through a pilot study and a full study with 5th graders, we learned about key design considerations and needed improvements forming a basis for designing web-accessible embodied (kinesthetic) activities like PoseToCode. P2C is open-sourced and shown in a publicly accessible repository [8] and demonstration [9].

Acknowledgments

Authors denoted with * provided equal contribution.

This work was supported by the National Science Foundation (NSF) under award IIS-1925083 and University of Southern California's Viterbi School of Engineering under the Merit Research Award and Viterbi Fellowship Award.

Citation Diversity Statement – Recent work in several fields of science has identified a bias in citation practices such that papers from women and other minority scholars are undercited relative to the number of papers in the field [23]–[27]. We recognize this bias and have worked diligently to ensure that we are referencing appropriate papers with fair gender and racial author inclusion. First, we predicted the gender of the first and last author of each citation using images of authors. By this measure, our references contain 27% woman(first)/woman(last), 15% man/woman, 12% woman/man, and 46% man/man. This method has limitations since images and names used to predict genders may not be entirely accurate and this method does not account for non-binary, transgender, and intersex people.

REFERENCES

[1] J. Schilling and R. Klamma, "The difficult bridge between university and industry: a case study in computer science teaching," *Assessment & Evaluation in Higher Education*, vol. 35, no. 4, pp. 367–380, 2010.

[2] N. Zamin *et al.*, "Learning block programming using scratch among school children in malaysia and australia: An exploratory study," in *2018 4th International Conference on Computer and Information Sciences (ICCOINS)*, pp. 1–6, 2018.

[3] T. W. Price and T. Barnes, "Comparing textual and block interfaces in a novice programming environment," in *Proceedings of the Eleventh Annual International Conference on International Computing Education Research*, ICER '15, (New York, NY, USA), pp. 91—-99, Association for Computing Machinery, 2015.

[4] D. Weintrop and U. Wilensky, "Comparing block-based and text-based programming in high school computer science classrooms," *ACM Trans. Comput. Educ.*, vol. 18, oct 2017.

[5] D. Weintrop and U. Wilensky, "To block or not to block, that is the question: Students' perceptions of blocks-based programming," in *Proceedings of the 14th International Conference on Interaction Design and Children*, IDC '15, (New York, NY, USA), pp. 199—208, Association for Computing Machinery, 2015.

[6] E. Eika, "Learning in higher education under the covid-19 pandemic: Were students more engaged or less?," *International Journal of English Linguistics*, vol. 11, no. 3, pp. 96–97, 2021.

[7] M. Macedonia, "Embodied learning: why at school the mind needs the body," *Frontiers in psychology*, pp. 2098–2099, 2019.

[8] N. Chatwani, C. Kuo, G. Thomas, J. Cordero, and R. Agrawal, "PoseToCode." https://github.com/interaction-lab/PoseToCode, June 14, 2022.

[9] "PoseToCode demonstration." https://posetocode.web.app/tutorial.html, June 14, 2022.

[10] T. L. Pittinsky and N. Diamante, "Going beyond fun in stem," *Phi Delta Kappan*, vol. 97, no. 2, pp. 47–51, 2015.

[11] S. N. H. Mohamad, A. Patel, Y. Tew, R. Latih, and Q. Qassim, "Principles and dynamics of block-based programming approach," in *2011 IEEE Symposium on Computers Informatics*, pp. 340–345, 2011.

[12] A. Seyfi and A. Patel, "Briefly introduced and comparatively analysed: Agile sd, component-based se, aspect-oriented sd and mashups," in *2010 International Symposium on Information Technology*, vol. 2, pp. 977–982, 2010.

[13] M. Resnick *et al.*, "Scratch: programming for all," *Communications of the ACM*, vol. 52, no. 11, pp. 60–67, 2009.

[14] F. Kalelioğlu, "A new way of teaching programming skills to k-12 students: Code. org," *Computers in Human Behavior*, vol. 52, pp. 200–210, 2015.

[15] A. Paniagua and D. Istance, *Teachers as Designers of Learning Environments: The Importance of Innovative Pedagogies. Educational Research and Innovation.* ERIC, 2018.

[16] P. Kosmas, A. Ioannou, and P. Zaphiris, "Implementing embodied learning in the classroom: effects on children's memory and language skills," *Educational Media International*, vol. 56, no. 1, pp. 59–74, 2019.

[17] M. A. Shakroum, K. W. Wong, and C. Fung, "The effectiveness of the gesture-based learning system (gbls) and its impact on learning experience," *Journal of Information Technology Education: Research*, vol. 15, pp. 191–210, 2016.

[18] L. Streeter and J. Gauch, "Teaching introductory programming concepts through a gesture-based interface," in *International Conference on Human-Computer Interaction*, pp. 116–123, Springer, 2018.

[19] C. Lugaresi *et al.*, "Mediapipe: A framework for building perception pipelines," *arXiv preprint arXiv:1906.08172*, 2019.

[20] E. Pasternak, R. Fenichel, and A. N. Marshall, "Tips for creating a block language with blockly," in *2017 IEEE blocks and beyond workshop (B&B)*, pp. 21–24, IEEE, 2017.

[21] A. Bangor, P. Kortum, and J. Miller, "Determining what individual sus scores mean: Adding an adjective rating scale," *Journal of usability studies*, vol. 4, no. 3, pp. 114–123, 2009.

[22] B. Klug, "An overview of the system usability scale in library website and system usability testing," *Weave: Journal of Library User Experience*, vol. 1, no. 6, 2017.

[23] N. Caplar, S. Tacchella, and S. Birrer, "Quantitative evaluation of gender bias in astronomical publications from citation counts," *Nature Astronomy*, vol. 1, no. 6, pp. 1–5, 2017.

[24] M. L. Dion, J. L. Sumner, and S. M. Mitchell, "Gendered citation patterns across political science and social science methodology fields," *Political analysis*, vol. 26, no. 3, pp. 312–327, 2018.

[25] J. D. Dworkin, K. A. Linn, E. G. Teich, P. Zurn, R. T. Shinohara, and D. S. Bassett, "The extent and drivers of gender imbalance in neuroscience reference lists," *Nature neuroscience*, vol. 23, no. 8, pp. 918–926, 2020.

[26] D. Maliniak, R. Powers, and B. F. Walter, "The gender citation gap in international relations," *International Organization*, vol. 67, no. 4, pp. 889–922, 2013.

[27] S. M. Mitchell, S. Lange, and H. Brus, "Gendered citation patterns in international relations journals," *International Studies Perspectives*, vol. 14, no. 4, pp. 485–492, 2013.

Analysis of Personal Data Visualisation Reviews on Mobile Health Apps

1st Yasmeen Anjeer Alshehhi
School of Information Technology
Deakin University
Burwood, Australia
yanjeeralshehhi@deakin.edu.au

2nd Mohamed Abdelrazek
School of Information Technology
Deakin University
Burwood, Australia
mohamed.abdelrazek@deakin.edu.au

3rd Alessio Bonti
School of Information Technology
Deakin University
Burwood, Australia
a.bonti@deakin.edu.au

***Abstract*—Mobile health apps give end-users tools to track and improve their health and well-being. The amount of data collected and managed by these apps grows massively over time, emphasising the need for user-friendly mobile data visualisations that make it easy for end-users to understand and make better decisions on their health and well-being. However, there are no clear guidelines or best practices for developing quality and user-friendly mobile data visualisations. App reviews offer an indirect anchor for researchers to examine how non-expert users perceive and interact with data visualisations and identify the key challenges and recommendations to develop mobile data visualisations. This paper introduces an analysis of app reviews on data visualisations reported on a data set of 217 mobile health apps on the Google Play Store. We identified 8,406 comments related to data visualisations. We then reviewed these comments and labelled them as neutral (919 comments), negative (1,557 comments) and positive (5,930 comments). We then manually clustered these comments into groups of concerning issues, including missing functionality, wrong charts, look and feel, etc. From analysing the user reviews, functional requirements turned out to be the most common problem across these app reviews, followed by the look and feel and then data problems. A complete set of data visualisations seem to be the most well-received capability of mobile health apps. We also introduce a set of mobile data visualisation guidelines based on these user reviews. We are currently working on an evaluation experiment to measure the impact of these guidelines on the quality of the produced mobile data visualisations.**

Keywords*—*smartphones; mHealth tracking apps; user experience; data visualisation assessment

I. Introduction

The easy access to mobile devices made data visualisations widely adopted by non-experts for several personal needs. For example, tracking health data is one of the most common personal tracking aspects [1] in which end-users use the provided data visualisation as a communication tool [2], decision-making [3] and tracking tool [4]. Personal data visualisations rely on mobile devices as the primary platform for user interactions [5]. However, mobile data visualisations introduce new display size, resolution, computing power, storage, and interaction modality challenges. Consequently, the field of visualisation interface design needs improvement to achieve users' satisfaction and cope with the challenges of the unique environment [6].

Graphs, charts, and icons are the main components of health tracking apps that help users track their goals, habits, and achievements [5]. Commendable efforts have been conducted in data visualisation related to diabetes, but apparent gaps in designing and understanding visualised data in the personal tracking apps are still present [7]. The main two reasons for these gaps are the diversity of data visualisation audiences [8] and the lack of generic guidelines that suit non-expert users and mobile devices (smartphones). Furthermore, although research studies have been comprehensive and continuously evolving to provide better user experiences for mobile data visualisation, users still report issues and challenges with their data [6] [7]. Thus, there is a need to examine users' perspectives toward data visualisation in mobile apps and understand the usage context to achieve better data visualisation on mobile devices [5].

User surveys and app reviews are great tools to understand user needs and challenges. User surveys are useful to answer specific questions but usually are limited in terms of the number of participants and generic instead of reflecting on experience on a specific app. On the other hand, app reviews are beneficial for understanding the common challenges and gaps [14] across a range of apps, and a broad group of audience/users [10]. App reviews have also been used to source and inform app improvements and new features [11], [12], [13]. Thus, this paper focuses on app reviews to identify key challenges and problems that end-users face with regard to mobile data visualisations for mHealth apps as our specific application domain. The paper addresses the following research questions:

- RQ1: What are the common visualisation tasks and charts that have been adopted in mHealth apps?
- RQ2: What are the top data visualisation issues in health tracking apps?
- RQ3: What are critical user concerns on mobile data visualisations in mHealth apps?

The rest of the paper is organised as follows: Section 2 presents the related work and Section 3 presents the research method. Section 4 presents the results and analysis. Section 5 presents the analysis discussion related to the found gaps and introduces suggestions for better developing and designing data visualisation in the mobile health (m-health) apps and presents threats to validity. Finally, Section 6 concludes the paper with a summary of the paper's findings and discussions.

II. Related Work

This section presents reviews on the importance and purposes of using app reviews. Then, it elaborates on the studies related to self-tracking and mobile health apps. In conclusion, examining users' reviews of m-health apps regarding data visualisation has not been studied yet.

A. User Reviews

Users feedback is currently applied to seek users' opinions, and satisfaction with a specific service or product [15]. For example, the industrial sector applied this communication method to evaluate the quality of products and services based on user experiences to improve their services. The same concept applied to app reviews in which users give either positive or negative comments [15].

In 2008, Gebauer et al. [16] investigated the required factors of 4 mobile devices from users' point of view. These devices included a cell phone, 2 PDAs, and an ultra-light laptop. The data was collected from www.cnet.com, an online website that allows users to write their technology-related comments. The authors followed automated and non-automated processes to evaluate 144 comments as a sample size. After evaluating the results of each process, the authors decided that these two methods had their advantages and disadvantage. However, they concluded their study that both processes are the basis for continued analysis of highly dynamic technological development and proved that user reviews aid in delivering user requirements.

In 2014, Khalid. H [18] studied the impact of app reviews on user preferences when selecting apps from the app store. In addition, he investigated how to use app reviews to source new features and issues that need to be addressed by the development teams to achieve user satisfaction and solve problems reported in the comments. The author investigated the apple store's user reviews by reviewing 6390 comments across the most popular 20 apps. He collected the 1 and 2 stars comments using a web crawler and applied an iterative process to classify the comments. Finally, he classified the issues into 3 groups, developer issues, strategic issues, and content issues. He concluded his study that low rating comments negatively impact the quality of the apps, which affects the app's popularity and revenue.

In 2018, Caldeira et al. [17] published a review of 32 mood tracking apps and deeply analysed 1,000 reviews. One of their primary findings was that data visualisation needed to be varied to match multiple people's preferences. As patient share their mental state with health providers, the authors claimed that the used data visualisation might be suitable for patients or the general population but not for the health providers. Thus, possible audiences of health data visualisation need to be considered through developing m-health apps.

B. Self-tracking and mobile health apps

The widespread of mobile devices has helped increase the number of end-users interested in tracking their data. These include tracking sports activities, nutrition, health conditions, memories tracking [21], mood tracking [22] and other tracking activities. As a result, significant efforts have been made mainly in 2 areas. The first is related to user interaction with their data. The latter is related to developing and evaluating apps that help users track health data.

We found that heroic efforts have been made to understand quantified selfers and their interaction with tracking apps [23]. In this study, users have been requested to record videos and answer 3 questions: "what you did", "how you did it", and "what you learned" [23]. After analysing 52 videos, the authors reported that health condition was the main tracked data. However, they also stated that the presented data was too much, making users give up tracking and analysing their data. By answering the question "how you did it?" participants reported a spreadsheet as the primary tool to analyse their data and commercial hardware for data collection. However, users wanted to have their tool. They also complained about the complexity of reading their charts due to a lack of scientific knowledge. Thus, developing simple m-health apps is needed to serve this group of people to understand their data.

In 2018, Lee et al. [24] published a workshop proposal to investigate mobile devices' opportunities as data visualisation platform. They named multiple apps that have been developed for self-tracking. Examples of these apps are sleep tight which visualises sleep patterns by showing sleep duration and quality. Another application is ConCap which shows diabetes patients their data over a timeline. Finally, OmniTrack included a dashboard of charts presenting different data types that the app collected. However, the authors claimed the lack of methods to evaluate data visualisation on mobile apps.

These apps take us to a new mobile health app (m-health) terminology. We found that research efforts have been made in this area, focusing on providing a specific framework to develop a well-defined contextual m-health app [25], and another study focused on m-health designing based on customers' experiences [26]. In addition, further investigations in the health area are related to providing a security framework for m-health apps in terms of data analysis and visualisation [26].

There is a noticeable development in mobile data visualisation apps. Nevertheless, a set of best practices to develop and evaluate these mobile data visualisations has not been studied yet [24], specifically in developing guidelines that include targeted audiences, data visualisation components (charts, data and tasks), and smartphone capabilities.

III. Research Method

This section presents our process of extracting data visualisation related reviews from the Google Play Store and assigning these reviews to different clusters of issues related to data visualisations. Figure 1 shows these processes highlighting the sub-tasks in each step.

Step1:Query Google App Store for mHealth Apps: The first step was to identify the relevant apps to consider in this study. We decided to focus on apps on Google Play Store, given that there are available APIs that we can use to get

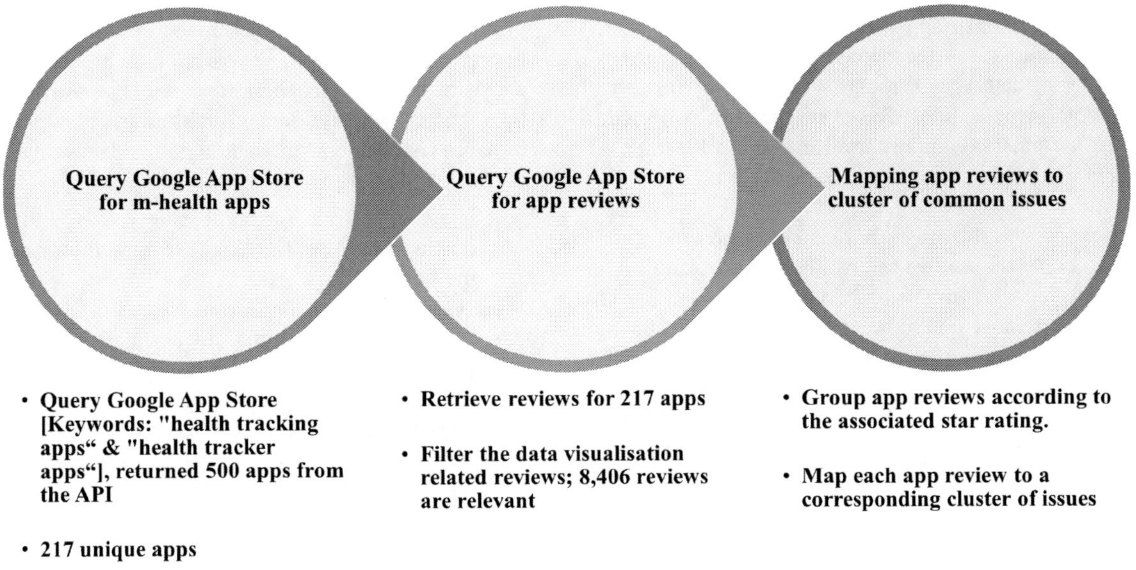

Figure 1. Apps and comments collecting, filtering and mapping process.

details about the apps on the store. These APIs expect to pass in a list of keywords (here, we used "health tracking app" and "health tracker apps"). Additionally, these APIs are limited to only the top 250 apps per query. Although this sounds to be a limited number of apps compared to the number of mHealth apps on the Google App Store (hundreds of thousands), we used these apps to represent the issues even on the top apps under this category. Ideally, with the highest number of downloads and higher potential for user feedback. We ran the query twice and got 500 apps with some duplicates that we removed and ended up with 217 unique mobile health applications (mHealth) apps. The list of apps included step tracker, food tracker, sleep tracker, fertility tracker, water drinking tracker, sport and activity, mood tracker, pet training, body measurement and weight loss tracker, pill reminder, chronic diseases, blood pressure and heart rate tracker, baby feeding tracker Stress and Anxiety. The query results are in the following format:

App metadata: app ID, URL, icon, version, score

Step2: Query Google App Store for App Reviews: The second step was to identify and filter the returned comments. We had 2,750,000 app reviews for the 217 apps. After removing duplicate and undefined rows, the remaining rows have decreased to 10,601. First, we manually analysed 200 comments as sample (Tables II, III, IV and V example comments) to identify the data visualisation related terms (graph, chart, visual). Then, we filtered the reviews associated with these visualisation terms (graph, chart, visual) and ended with 8,406 rows (reviews) related to data visualisation in the following format:

App review: rating, review, reviewer, user image, date, score, reply text, reply date

Step3: Mapping App Reviews to Cluster of Common Issues: The third step was mapping the reviews to a cluster of common issues. We first separated reviews based on their star ratings (minimising and organising the investigation process). Then, two of the team manually reviewed the app review and assigned two labels to each review: 1) sentiment label (positive, negative and neutral) regardless of the review star rating; and 2) common issue cluster/type. The number of clusters (issues) grow organically as we go through the reviews - i.e. every time we find a new type of concern, we created a new cluster and revised the previous labels to make sure there is no wrong labels or overlaps. The final list of reviews, sentiment and cluster is available (here).

IV. Results and Analysis

This section presents the results and key findings of our study mapped to the research questions in Section I (Introduction).

A. RQ (1) What are the common visualisation tasks and charts that have been adopted in these mHealth apps?

We analysed the screenshots included in the app description looking for data visualisation screens. 93% of the returned apps included data visualisations. We identified 12 common visualisation charts across these apps including: Waterfall, stock, table, timeline, scatter, map, line chart, calendar, area chart, bar chart, pie chart, maps and Iconography. The maximum number of charts found in each app was 5.

Figure 2 summarises the percentage of each chart in the total number of data visualisations we found in 203 apps that included data visualisations. Based on the data collected, five charts are the most commonly used in the top best apps: line chart, area chart, pie chart, calendar, and bar chart.

Iconography was the most used visualisation type (found in 141 apps) as it was used in indicating statues using numbers or texts with related symbols and colours. Line and bar charts are the second most common visualisation type (83 apps). Calendar as a visualisation type has been found in 32 apps. It is mainly used to track mood, period, pregnancy, and medication reminders. The map was used in 21 apps as data visualisation to help users track their walking, running, and cycling activities. It shows the number of steps and starting and endpoint information. Another visualisation type found is colours. They indicate high and low moods for monthly or yearly tracking and create patterns and trends. Stock, waterfall, and scatter plot visualisation types were the least (1 app).

Fourteen mHealth tracking apps in our dataset (7% of the 217 apps) did not include any charts. It was interesting to find out that these apps were all rated either 1 or 2 stars. Additionally, user reviews reflected these highlighting that charts are essential to track their progress and goals. Four apps had the maximum number of charts (5) (Anxiety Tracker - Stress and Anxiety Log, Blood Pressure Diary, Heart Rate Monitor, morePro), three are rated with more than four stars, and one app is rated with 2.5, which turned to have other issues. Therefore, this shows that including data visualisations can lead to positive impact on app adoption and rating.

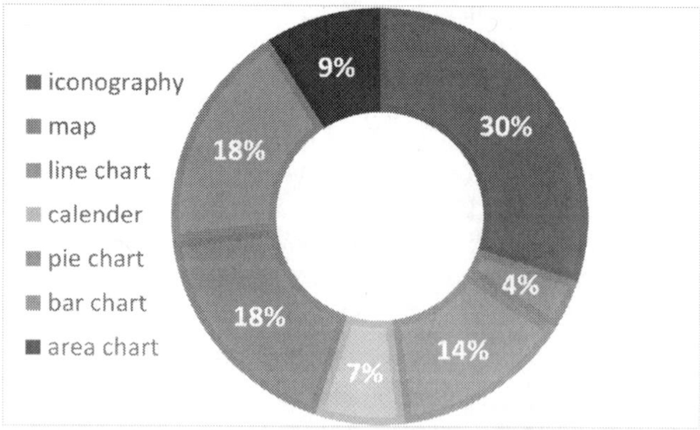

Figure 2. The most adopted charts in 203 apps.

In terms of visualisation tasks, we used Saket et al. [19] list of 10 essential data visualisation tasks including finding Anomalies, finding clusters, finding correlations, derived values, characterise distributions, filter, order, range, min-max, and retrieve value. In the apps in our dataset, developers focused primarily on one primary task: tracking progress. The purpose of this task varied based on the tracked activity. For example, in weight loss apps, the main functions were to track progress and achieve goals, and in mood tracking, the primary process was to track mood and find a monthly mood pattern. A comparison task was adopted in 2 apps (Fasting app and K health — Telehealth app). All apps provided read-only interactions with the data visualisations. However, app users have requested to consider adding other data visualisation tasks of these essential ten tasks:

- "..,but is terrible for comparing your results to previous results, everyone wants to see how they progress on all the fields."
- "you can't view plots from X date to Y date"
- "There is no continuity in calculation between months (maybe other timespans as well when you zoom out or in). If I weigh x at the end of a month, x-2 on the first measurement of the next month and x-2.1 on the next measurement, 2kg will be unaccounted for in the monthly totals shown above the graph. That's just useless."

B. RQ (2) What are the Top Data Visualisation Issues?

We manually reviewed the comments reported by app users to extract the common data visualisation issues. We grouped issues based on the following categories: functional requirement - related to user needs, data – related to data used to create the visualisations, look and feel – related to usability and types of charts, interactivity and device compatibility - related to screen and platform related issues. For each category we considered three attributes: completeness, correctness, and consistency. After reviewing the app reviews, we ended up having 18 issues, as shown in Table 1. Missing functional requirements were the most frequent negative reviews. For example, 50 % of the functional requirements issues are related to missing some needed graphs such as weekly or monthly charts, progress charts and charts to track aspects such as blood pressure, heart pulse, and baby feeding. Other complaints were about the functionality and display of the chart. Additionally, there are four main issues related to data visualisation design (look and feel):

- Chart scaling issues (40%)
- Graph styling (font size, chart ranges, and colours do not indicate meaningful information, including grid lines in the charts and axis titles)
- Interactivity (scrolling, zooming, landscape, choose graphs options)
- The chart type is not appropriate (bar chart, pie chart and bar chart)

Data is another primary aspect that users criticised. Data related issues included issues related to insufficient and incorrect data presented in the graph. In contrast, there are more general positive reviews than negative reviews that are related to users' satisfaction, which includes "love this graph" and "like this chart" without specifying any unique feature of the chart or graph (single and app visualisation). The other aspect that users rarely mention is device capabilities and adaptability including: 1) being able to rotate the device to see the graph

TABLE I
SUMMARY OF APP REVIEWS' ISSUES

Issues	Count	Percentage
1: Missing graphs and functionalities	948	34 %
2: Displaying the wrong charts	22	0.7%
3: Charts are mixed up	60	2%
4: Missing the chart type	224	8%
5: Chart scaling, layout and font size	404	14%
6: Zooming problem and graphs lines are mixed	128	4%
7: Missing graph information	202	7%
8: Not accurate info charts units	98	3%
9:Not showing information correctly	32	11%
10: Missing the ability of phone rotating	10	0.3%
11: Scale is not suiting screen size	4	0.1%
12: Different OS & different functionalities	36	1.2%
13: Two colour menus confusing	154	5.5%
14: Visualisation is meaningless	74	2.6%
15: Low quality of graphs charts	94	3.3%
16: Missing Tooltips	20	0.7%
17: Screen size problems	36	1.2%
18:No consistency in showing graphs	4	0.1%

in landscape mode and visualisation consistency between the two operating systems, android and IOS; and 2) Chart fitting with screen size.

C. *RQ (3) What are critical user concerns on mobile data visualisations in mHealth apps?*

In this research question, we reviewed the comments of the five best and worst apps to key issues that could affect app rating, as shown in Figure 3.

Figure 3 (left side) showed the top 5 apps: These are non-free apps rated with more than 4.5 stars and had the highest number of positive reviews related to data visualisation compared with negative reviews. **Functional requirement:** These 5 best apps were the highest-rated apps in terms of data visualisation among 217 apps. However, there were still some missing graphs that could be added according to the collected comments (C) in table 2, such as weight blood pressure(C1 - Table 2), A1C (a simple blood test that measures your average blood sugar levels over the past three months) (C2 - Table 2) [20], blood sugar results (C3 - Table 2). In contrast, users were satisfied with the other functions provided in the app related to data visualisation, such as charting entries (C4 - Table 2) and (C5 - Table 2). **Data:** Users commented that they felt happy as they could understand their progress through the charts: (C6 - Table 2), (C7 - Table 2) and (C8 - Table 2). **Look and feel styling and interactivity:** are the most important aspects that users' mentioned in their positive reviews, such as (C9 - Table 2) comment. However, some users were not satisfied with the colour selection (C10 - Table 2) **platform and device:** There were no comments mentioned related to this dimension in any of these apps.

Figure 3 (right side) shows the top 5 worst apps in terms of the total number of negative reviews. As displayed, 2 apps were in the best 5 apps due to the number of positive reviews, and appeared in this graph as 5 of the worst apps (Blood Glucose and Baby tracker). Withings health mate is the worst app used to track various aspects such as weight, activities and sport, sleep analysis and blood pressure. However, it is a free app that has been downloaded by nearly 100,000 times. The 1- and 2-stars rating reviews were about look and feel, presented data, and adaptability to devices' screens. In terms of look and feel, users complained that the trend line is missed in the charts, so they cannot do any comparison tasks. User comments related to this aspect are shown in Table 3. The issues related to the adaptability of devices are about the screen size, touch interaction and rotating devices to get landscape mode (Table 4).

In terms of the lowest negative reviews, carb manager is a non-free app downloaded by more than 103,000 users. The biggest issue that users complained about was missing functional requirements. Examples of these issues were blank charts, and missing graphs are shown in Table 5.

V. DISCUSSION

This section discusses the findings and implications of developing and designing data visualisation for mHelath tracking apps.

We found that mhealth tracking apps covered different health aspects related to users' interests, such as sports activities, diet activities, and health conditions monitoring. However, the analysis revealed a lack of support for the data visualisation component in these apps. By analysing the app reviews, we found that users complained about issues related to data visualisation components such as functional requirement, data presented, chart styling, and suitability of the chart functions with the smartphones.

Users raised multiple concerns about missing charts. For example, some apps did not include charts like "map my fitness", "WhatsUp mental health app" and "pregnancy and baby tracker". Further issue related to missing charts, was about charting the correlated data in one app, such as heart monitoring and blood pressure. For example, "A chart shows the heart beating, but no chart shows blood pressure". Therefore, there is a lack of complete and correct functional requirements.

Furthermore, users wrote negative reviews about the chart's interactivity and styling. Approximately 90% of the 217 apps provided read-only charts. In the app comments, users complained about the difficulty of doing some tasks such as: comparing between two variables, enlarging font size, setting the preferred colour theme, getting details of the presented data, and rotating the device to landscape mode to get a detailed chart. This, in turn, leads to a sense of the incomplete look and feels and interactivity.

The presented data was another issue that users repeated in their reviews. Insufficient and uncomprehending data were the two main reported issues. Thus, many users highlighted the difficulty of making conclusions from the presented data as the presented data is not detailed and included miss leading labels. Device compatibility was a minor issue reported in user reviews. However, all the issues reported occurred due

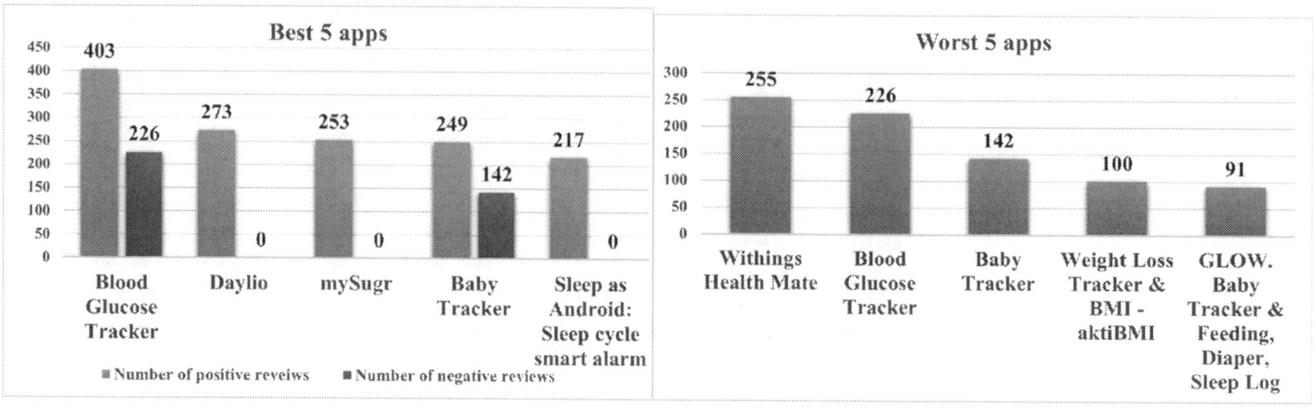

Figure 3. Best and worst 5 mHealth apps according to data visualisation reviews.

TABLE II
EXAMPLES OF POSITIVE AND NEGATIVE USERS' REVIEWS

C1: A lot of info you can put on here. It would be nice to see multiple graphs for weight blood pressure as well. Even an option to send info as an attachment to emails for our doctors– negative
C2: As a glucose tracking log it is easy to use and the chart is handy.Would like a similar chart for A1C results. If it linked to my meter, it would be awesome –negative
C3: An excellent app. Wish it graphically displayed blood pressure the way it does blood sugar but it's still the best blood sugar app I've found –negative
C4: Charts and graphs your blood sugar and tracks–positive
C5: Does just what I needed it to Gives you the average and plots a graph so it shows your entries easily. Thanks – positive
C6: love it brilliant at visually showing me how I've been and can predict my moods even bought the full app – positive
C7: Being newly diabetic this app has been extremely helpful in keeping things logged. It's also given me some comfort as I am able to see the effort I put in as clear to read results through their graphs and whatnot. I would recommend this app to anyone.–positive
C8: Has helped me visualise and control my blood glucose levels –positive
C9: The easy-to-read graphs show when I am in the red or in the green and ultimately show my blood sugar trending down. –positive
C10: For the feeding graph the colours blend too much and hard to see the difference Another colour scheme would be favorable.–negative

TABLE III
NEGATIVE REVIEWS RELATED TO LOOK AND FEEL

C11: Used to be great, but in the newest version the trend lines have all gone, and individual points are no longer plotted on the graphs, making it largely useless.
C12:..., Further issue is related to the graph size.
C13: Very hard to see weight trends and you have to zoom weigh in on a finicky scale to see daily weights plotted.
C14: unfortunately now the scale used for the weight graph is so huge that your weight line looks completely flat.

TABLE IV
NEGATIVE REVIEWS RELATED TO DEVICES ADAPTABILITY

C15: Weight graph scale is difficult to read on a smart phone and their website
C16: charts not responding to the touch not able to expand charts
C17: Biggest frustration is there's no landscape mode Not useful looking at graphs in portrait.

to the device functionality limitation and not addressing the features and limitations of the smartphones. Therefore, it is required to reframe building m-health apps by focusing on data visualisation components.

This paper introduces 3 recommendations for research opportunities related to data visualisation in m-health apps. Recommendations 1 and 2 are linked to each other. First, the

TABLE V
NEGATIVE REVIEWS RELATED TO FUNCTIONAL REQUIREMENT

C18: I've used this app for a while and I've liked it but lately the app keeps crashing. It's not saving my weights. Tells me that there's "no chart available".
C19: Carb tracking function works ok, but the weight chart is blank. Also, there is no way to incorporate exercise into this program, other than logging steps.
C20: When I try to see the graph of my weight loss (by turning the phone sideways) it doesn't show.

development and design process of m-health data visualisation should be parallel process. All aspects identified in the discussion need to be considered when developing and designing charts for m-health apps. A further recommendation is related to the app review system, in which the authors highlighted the need to include the data visualisation aspect of the reviewing system.

Developing data visualisation: It is argued that data visualisation development needs special consideration due to the unknown multi-users. For example, it needs to adopt a complete set of functional requirements and data related to users' control and understanding of the graphs. That is, users should control their entries and be able to chart their progress easily. Further reviews associated with the functional needs are related to the device compatibility. For example, the touch, tap and rotating interaction are facilities provided by smartphone manufacturers that enable users to navigate and control their app screen easily.

Designing data visualisation: Data visualisation design has been discussed widely in the academic and industrial sectors. However, still, there are some limitations related to smartphone design. These limitations are chart size, scale, colour adoption, font size, data and interactivity.

Including data visualisation in the app review: Since app review does not include chart evaluation in the app feedback, it was not easy to find a protocol to classify the apps based on data visualisation reviews. So, it is recommended to add data visualisation feedback in the app review as it is a central part of health tracking.

From threats to validity perspective, we have identified the following limitations and threats:

- The apps considered in this paper were collected using an existing Google Play Store search API where it could only provide 250 apps through passing keywords and it returns a random list of apps whose titles match the search keywords. Thus, it is acknowledged that the considered apps in this paper are only samples of mHealth apps, and it does not reflect all of the available apps in the store.
- Some comments have been excluded as they were written in another language rather than English.
- The research team randomly evaluated a sample of these comments and solved the border cases.
- The research team used screenshots to extract the charts and tasks. However, analysing apps' screenshots and descriptions might not be accurate.

Finally, this paper targeted Android health apps that limited Android users' results. iOS platform is acknowledged. So, an extension to this paper have been planned to involve both mobile device operating systems' comments.

VI. Conclusion and Future Work

This paper presented a manual analysis and categorisation of app reviews of data visualisations in 217 health tracking apps. We identified 8,406 comments app reviews related to data visualisations. Overall, the number of the positive reviews was more than the number of negative reviews. However, the negative comments raised concerns regarding the m-health data visualisation aspect. The concerns included missing visualisations, missing visualisation tasks, look and feel and missing or incorrect data. Functional requirements and data aspects were the top concerns reported by mHealth app users. M-health app developers and data visualisation designers need to consider these concerns. Especially the target audiences, as mHealth apps are provided for all individuals who have smartphone access. In the future, the authors plan to dig deeper into user reviews across different mHealth apps, e.g., food vs physical activity and chronic conditions. It would help in identifying the differences between issues across different health domains. We also plan to work on designing mHealth data visualisation guidelines.

References

[1] L. Mamykina et al., "Personal discovery in diabetes self-management: discovering cause and effect using self-monitoring data," Journal of Biomedical infromatics, vol. 76, pp.1–8, 2017, doi.org/10.1016/j.jbi.2017.09.013

[2] S. G. Archambault, J. Helouvry, B. Strohl, and G. Williams, "Data visualization as a communication tool," Library Hi Tech News, vol. 2, pp.1–9, April 2015, doi.org/10.1108/LHTN-10-2014-0098

[3] M. Aparicio and C. J. Costa, "Data visualization," Communication design quarterly review, vol. 3, no. 1, pp. 7–11, November 2014, doi.org/10.1145/2721882.2721883

[4] Choe, E.K., Dachselt, R., Isenberg, P. and Lee, B, "Mobile data visualization (Dagstuhl seminar 19292)." Dagstuhl Reports (2019), doi.org/10.4230/DagRep.9.7.78

[5] B. Lee, E. K. Choe, P. Isenberg, K. Marriott, and J. Stasko, "Reaching broader audiences with data visualization," IEEE Computer Graphics and Applications, vol. 40, no. 2, pp. 82–90, 2020, doi.org/10.1109/MCG.2020.2968244

[6] J. Gu, S. Mackin, and Y. Zheng, "Making sense: An innovative data visualization application utilized via mobile platform," in 2018 IEEE 20th International Conference on High Performance Computing and Communications; IEEE 16th International Conference on Smart City; IEEE 4th International Conference on Data Science and Systems (HPCC/SmartCity/DSS). IEEE, pp. 1105–1109, 2018, doi.org/10.1109/HPCC/SmartCity/DSS.2018.00184

[7] D. Katz, N. Dalton, S. Holland, A. O'kane, and B. A. Price, "Questioning the reflection paradigm for diabetes mobile apps," in eHealth 360°, Springer, pp. 315–326, 2017, https://doi.org/10.1007/978-3-319-49655-9_39

[8] A. Jena et al., "The next billion users of visualization," IEEE Computer Graphics and Applications, vol. 41, no. 2, pp. 8–16, 2021, doi.org/10.1109/MCG.2020.3044071

[9] D. Huang et al., "Personal visualization and personal visual analytics," IEEE Transactions on Visualization and Computer Graphics, vol. 21, no. 3, pp. 420–433, 2014, doi.org/10.1109/TVCG.2014.2359887

[10] V. N. Inukollu, D. D. Keshamoni, T. Kang, and M. Inukollu, "Factors influencing quality of mobile apps: Role of mobile app development life cycle," 2014, arXiv preprint arXiv:1410.4537

[11] D. Pagano and W. Maalej, "User feedback in the app store: An empirical study," in 2013 21st IEEE international requirements engineering conference (RE). IEEE, pp. 125–134, 2013, doi.org/10.1109/RE.2013.6636712

[12] A. Di Sorbo et al., "What would users change in my app? summarizing app reviews for recommending software changes," in Proceedings of the 2016 24th ACM SIGSOFT International Symposium on Foundations of Software Engineering, pp. 499–510, 2016, doi.org/10.1145/2950290.2950299

[13] C. Iacob and R. Harrison, "Retrieving and analyzing mobile apps feature requests from online reviews," in 2013 10th working conference on mining software repositories (MSR). IEEE, pp. 41–44, 2013, doi.org/10.1109/MSR.2013.6624001

[14] E. Guzman and W. Maalej,"How do users like this feature? a fine grained sentiment analysis of app reviews," in IEEE 22nd international requirements engineering conference (RE). IEEE, pp. 153–162, 2014

[15] L. Hoon, R. Vasa, J.-G. Schneider, and J. Grundy, "An analysis of the mobile app review landscape: trends and implications," Faculty of Information and Communication Technologies, Swinburne University of Technology, Tech. Rep, 2013

[16] J. Gebauer, Y. Tang, and C. Baimai, "User requirements of mobile technology: results from a content analysis of user reviews," Information Systems and e-Business Management, vol. 6, pp. 361–384, 2008, doi.org/10.1007/s10257-007-0074-9

[17] C. Caldeira et al., "Mobile apps for mood tracking: an analysis of features and user reviews," in AMIA Annual Symposium Proceedings, vol. 2017. American Medical Informatics Association, p. 495–504, 2017

[18] H. Khalid, "On the link between mobile app quality and user reviews," Master thesis, Queen's University, 2014

[19] B. Saket, A. Endert, and C¸ . Demiralp, "Task-based effectiveness of basic visualizations," IEEE transactions on visualization and computer graphics, vol. 25, no. 7, pp. 2505–2512, 2018, doi/10.1109/TVCG.2018.2829750

[20] "all about your a1c," Available at https://www.cdc.gov/diabetes/managing/ managing-blood-sugar/a1c.html [retrieved: September, 2021]

[21] A. Thudt, D. Baur, S. Huron, and S. Carpendale, "Visual mementos: Reflecting memories with personal data," IEEE transactions on visualization and computer graphics, vol. 22, no. 1, pp. 369–378, 2015, doi.org/10.1109/TVCG.2015.2467831
[22] M. van der Velden and M. M. Sommervold, "The koolo app," International Journal on Advances in Intelligent Systems, vol. 9, no. 3,4, 2016
[23] E. K. Choe, N. B. Lee, B. Lee, W. Pratt, and J. A. Kientz, "Under- standing quantified-selfers' practices in collecting and exploring personal data," in Proceedings of the SIGCHI conference on human factors in computing systems, pp. 1143–1152, 2014, doi.org/10.1145/2556288.2557372
[24] B. Lee et al., "Data visualization on mobile devices," in Extended Abstracts of the 2018 CHI Conference on Human Factors in Computing Systems, pp. 1–8, 2018, doi.org/10.1145/3170427.3170631
[25] T. Broens, A. Van Halteren, M. Van Sinderen, and K. Wac, "Towards an application framework for context-aware m-health applications," International Journal of Internet Protocol Technology, vol. 2, no. 2, pp. 109–116, 2007
[26] R. Schnall et al., "A user-centered model for designing consumer mobile health (mHealth) applications (apps)," Journal of biomedical informatics, vol. 60 , pp. 243–251, 2016, doi.org/10.1016/j.jbi.2016.02.002